Democracy and the
Status of Women
in East Asia

Democracy and the Status of Women in East Asia

edited by
Rose J. Lee
Cal Clark

LYNNE
RIENNER
PUBLISHERS

BOULDER
LONDON

Published in the United States of America in 2000 by
Lynne Rienner Publishers, Inc.
1800 30th Street, Boulder, Colorado 80301
www.rienner.com

and in the United Kingdom by
Lynne Rienner Publishers, Inc.
3 Henrietta Street, Covent Garden, London WC2E 8LU

Library of Congress Cataloging-in-Publication Data
Democracy and the status of women in East Asia / edited by Rose J. Lee, Cal Clark.
    p. cm.
    Includes bibliographical references and index.
    ISBN 1-55587-888-1 (hc. : alk. paper)
    1. Women and democracy—East Asia. 2. Women in politics—East Asia.
3. Women—Government policy—East Asia. 4. Women's rights—East Asia.
5. Patriarchy—East Asia. I. Lee, Rose J., 1936– II. Clark, Cal, 1945–
HQ1236.5.E25 D45 2000
305.42'095—dc21

                                                                99-048191
                                                                CIP

British Cataloguing in Publication Data
A Cataloguing in Publication record for this book
is available from the British Library.

Printed and bound in the United States of America

The paper used in this publication meets the requirements
of the American National Standard for Permanence of
Paper for Printed Library Materials Z39.48-1984.

5 4 3 2 1

Contents

PART 3   CONCLUSION

Illustrations

Preface

This book began when Rose J. Lee organized the panel "Women and Democratization in East Asia" for the Seventeenth World Congress of the International Political Science Association, held in Seoul, Korea, in August 1997. Because the panel evoked a lively discussion, we decided to recruit more papers with this theme and create a book. As the project evolved, its intellectual scope broadened. Initially, we focused on the question of whether democratization in East Asia had allowed women enough access to political processes (i.e., empowerment) to shape public policies that would improve their status in society (i.e., emancipation). However, as the book took shape and the individual chapters were reworked, we came to the conclusion that the expansion of civil society that accompanies democratization in East Asia (and elsewhere) is extremely important because it allows grassroots activism that goes beyond the conventional definition of politics. What appears central, thus, is that autonomous groups of women are gaining the power to help themselves in both the political and nonpolitical spheres.

We would like to express our appreciation for all the help we received from Dan Eades and Leanne Anderson of Lynne Rienner Publishers. Without their support and confidence, this project might not have reached fruition; without their keen editorial insights, the book would be less coherent and, presumably, less interesting and insightful. Nancy Borland and Phillis Hodge of Auburn University's Department of Political Science provided invaluable assistance in preparing the manuscript, especially the illustrations. We also want to thank our families for their support while we struggled longer than we had planned with the question of whether democratization in East Asia has made any contribution to the empowerment and emancipation of women there.

—*R.J.L.*
C.C.

1

Women's Status in East Asia

CAL CLARK & ROSE J. LEE

In almost all societies, women as a whole are forced into subordinate roles and statuses that are embedded in and reinforced by a wide array of patriarchal cultures. Several decades ago the dominant paradigm in development studies optimistically predicted that patriarchal restraints on women would fade away with the increasing modernization of societies (i.e., the far-reaching cultural, social, and economic changes that accompany industrialization). Unfortunately, the many barriers to full equality for women in both the developing and the developed worlds appear to be far more formidable than the optimistic modernization model predicted.

If industrialization and social change have proved to be far from panaceas for improving the status of women, might there not be some other means for empowering and emancipating women? One possibility is that political change might open new avenues for women to pursue their goals in society. From this perspective, more space could be opened for women to pursue their autonomous objectives by political liberalization and the transition to democracy, defined broadly for our purposes as a system where public officials are chosen in open elections and where fundamental political rights, such as freedom of speech and the right to organize voluntary organizations, are guaranteed for all citizens. From this perspective, democratization opens the way for women to exert political influence resulting in policy and legal reforms that can be used to prohibit discriminatory patriarchal practices and to create opportunities for women to pursue more fulfilling and rewarding life horizons. The logic here is that public policy can be used to change and soften the patriarchal features of a society more directly than waiting for the long-term implications of economic and social change to play out.

Because democracy provides broader avenues for influencing

1

public policy, previously excluded and marginalized groups such as women might gain some impact on governmental activities through two distinct mechanisms, as presented in Figure 1.1. First, women could become public officials themselves with the power to enact reforms lessening discrimination against their sex. Second, greater political and civic freedom could provide a conducive context for the emergence of independent women's groups pushing a government to enact desirable reforms. In either case, the end result is that government policy can be used to loosen and remove the restrictions on women erected by patriarchal cultures. However, as also suggested by Figure 1.1, the strength of the existing patriarchal culture will inevitably influence both the extent of women's autonomous participation in the public sector and the efficacy of government policy. This model assumes that state-enforced reforms can be used to soften the restrictions on and discrimination against women in patriarchal cultures, but also that women can become fully empowered only after significant cultural change. In sum, the central question we examine in this book is whether democratization promotes women's rights, specifically whether the recent democratization that has occurred in East Asia shows any evidence of promoting positive changes in the status of women.

Democracy's impact (or the absence thereof) on the status of women in East Asia should be especially interesting for two reasons. First, the emancipation and empowerment of women have long presented a vexing challenge throughout the region. East Asia is viewed, at least in stereotype, as composed of highly patriarchal cultures, such as Confucianism, that have historically relegated women to an extremely subordinate position—symbolized, for example, by such horrors as foot-binding. In fact, Western revulsion against the treatment of women in Asia served in the late nineteenth and early twentieth centuries as the basis for strong international support for social change in the region or, more cynically, as a hypocritical rationale for imperial domination over the nations of East Asia. From many perspectives, though, East Asia is a leading candidate for change in the status of women.

Second, East Asia has what appears to be a very distinctive set of relationships among its traditional cultures, patterns of industrialization, and progress in political development. During the 1980s and 1990s (at least before the Asian Financial Crisis of 1997–1998), East Asia has had the most dynamic economies in the world. Yet, for the most part, regimes in the region remained quite authoritarian until very recently, with only Japan having a long-term stable democracy. Furthermore, the indigenous cultures of these nations have generally

Figure 1.1   How Democratization Can Promote the Status of Women

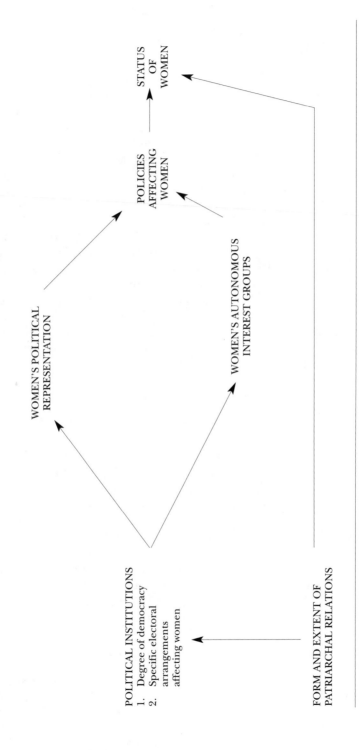

been seen as making important contributions to their economic dynamism, in direct contrast to most Western theories that traditional values and norms are incompatible with rapid industrialization (Chan, 1993; Fallows, 1994; Hofheinz and Calder, 1982; Pye, 1985). One might therefore expect on the basis of this social and cultural situation that political reforms and democratization should have particularly weak effects in Asia. Thus, any progress that women have made in the region would be particularly significant.

The first part of this introductory chapter briefly describes two general disappointments for advocates of women's empowerment: (1) the limited success of industrialization and modernization in emancipating Third World women during the postwar period; and (2) the failure of democratization in two other developing regions (Latin America and the former Soviet bloc) to improve the position of women. Taken together, these two historical phenomena have doleful implications for the hope that democratization could stimulate much improvement in women's status in East Asia. With this as background, we then provide an overview of the nine substantive chapters, summarizing their central arguments. As will be seen, the findings in these chapters are generally more positive than might have been expected, raising the question of what might explain this progress in East Asia.

DISAPPOINTMENTS IN THE SEARCH
FOR DYNAMICS THAT EMPOWER WOMEN

Scholars in the past identified two sets of trends, one socioeconomic and one political, that might well have been expected to promote the emancipation of women. But both have produced rather disappointing results thus far. This section provides a brief overview of these trends as a background for assessing the relationship between democratization and changes in women's status in East Asia. The first part discusses how economic modernization failed to improve the status of women to anywhere near the expected extent in many parts of the Third World, and the second considers a similar failure of the "third wave" of democratization during the 1980s and early 1990s to bring anticipated benefits to women in several important regions.

Modernization and the Reproduction of Patriarchy

During the 1950s and 1960s, there was widespread optimism that socioeconomic and political development would lead to equality for women who had long been suppressed in patriarchal societies nearly everywhere in the world. According to this perspective, industrialization should bring much greater affluence, thus permitting and indeed requiring mass education, and should rearrange production relationships and lifestyles. Moreover, development was expected to encourage democratic politics through which women could push for legal and policy reforms. Taken together, these complex social, economic, and political changes create "modernization," which erodes traditional patriarchal norms and gives women a variety of resources with which they can pursue their own goals autonomously (see Black, 1966, and Eisenstadt, 1973, for the modernization model).

In theory, the social and economic changes associated with modernization should help women overcome many of the barriers to more equitable treatment in East Asia and in other developing societies. Figure 1.2 suggests how these processes might be expected to work. Cultural change and modernization should directly undermine traditional patriarchal norms and, by stimulating industrialization, should indirectly set off a series of socioeconomic changes favorable to women: (1) women's greater participation in the formal labor market; (2) growing prosperity and opportunities for education; and (3) a more urbanized society in which the repressive power of extended kinship systems is diminished. Together, these changes should give women more autonomy, resources, and a sense of self-sufficiency, thereby promoting women's liberation and resulting in a marked improvement in the status of women.

Historical reality, unfortunately, did not live up to the theoretical potential. Instead, the much more perverse scenario diagrammed in Figure 1.3 unfolded. The processes by which modernization actually worked, to the detriment of women in many cases, had both concrete economic and more abstract ideological components. At the more concrete level represented by the top part of Figure 1.3, the economic changes accompanying industrialization proved to be far less favorable for women than anticipated by early modernization theory, as argued fairly early in the pathbreaking work of Ester Boserup (1970). Thus, many women face marginalization, rather than liberation, from such disparate facets of modernization as the mechanization of agriculture, the breakdown of strong kinship ties and the extended family, and the evolving division of labor in industrial urban centers. For example, new agricultural techniques (e.g., the Green Revolution in South Asia) were dominated by men, thereby marginalizing women in agricultural production (Boserup, 1970; Roy, 1994); and women's contribution to the industrial workforce was largely limited to the least skilled and most tenuous positions (Charlton, 1984; Scott, 1995;

Figure 1.2   Modernization's Supposed Attack on Patriarchal Social Systems

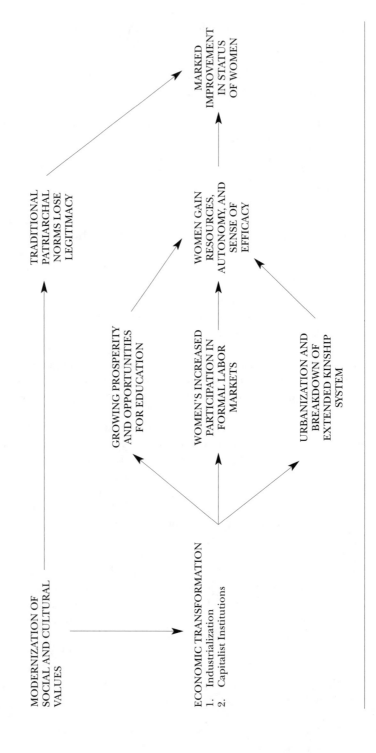

Figure 1.3   How Modernization Undercuts the Status of Women

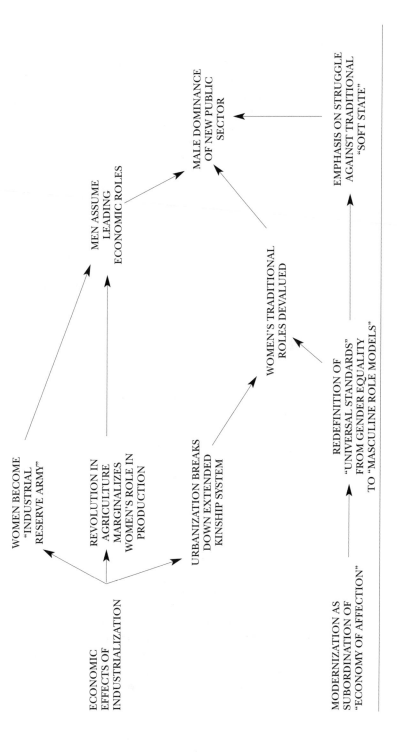

Tinker, 1990; Truong, 1999; Wellesley Editorial Committee, 1977). Even in the most advanced industrial societies, the "feminization of poverty" is becoming a central social problem (Goldberg and Kremen, 1990; Kemp, 1994). Consequently, though women in some social groups and classes have clearly benefited from industrialization, the accompanying economic and social transformations have reproduced and reinforced patriarchy in myriad ways.

The failure of industrialization and modernization to revolutionize the status of women was exacerbated by a change in scholarly and political perspectives on the relationship between modernization and the status of women. At the philosophical or theoretical level, the prime target of modernization came to be regarded as subordinating traditional economies and social relations—what Goran Hyden (1987) has called an "economy of affection"—to the supposedly much more efficient and transformative norms of the market or national planning (Scott, 1995). This philosophical stance, although certainly consistent with the central thrust of modernization theory, turned modernization theory on its head regarding the role and status of women. In the initial formulation, women were expected to benefit from "the passing of traditional society" (Lerner, 1958) with its highly patriarchal norms. In direct contrast, the "economy of affection" came to be seen as embodying the world of "irrational backward-looking women."

So, rather than liberating women, modernization came to represent the domination of masculinist role definitions in both the economy and the new, emerging public sector. Those concerned with government leadership blamed underdevelopment in the Third World on "soft states" (with traditional, feminized characteristics), which are neither able to stand up to imperialist powers nor to lead local development projects. A successful developmental state, hence, must become "hard" by taking on modern and masculine values and characteristics, thereby justifying the marginalization of women in the all-important public sphere. Likewise, those with more faith in neoclassical economics emphasized the magic of the "hard" market, which worked much more to marginalize than to liberate women (Scott, 1995). Thus, the initial positive implications that modernization theory had for women's emancipation were offset by unexpected dynamics of industrialization and by a redefinition of the "modern," which turned to masculinized definitions of the economic or political structures necessary to promote industrialization and economic transformation. Together, these two factors combined perversely to (re)produce patriarchy in the social, economic, and political institutions that evolved as a result of industrialization.

The Disappointments of Democratization

If the slow socioeconomic processes set off by industrialization have had an unexpectedly limited ability to emancipate and empower women, could women use democratic freedoms to exercise political power that could, in turn, jump-start changes that would reduce patriarchal domination? Unfortunately, recent history outside Asia has not been particularly kind to this scenario of using democratic means to improve women's status in society. Just as industrialization turned out to be far from an automatic mechanism for improving the status of women, the hope that gaining the vote would allow women to use democratic politics to achieve social gains has yet to be fulfilled. For example, women remain woefully underrepresented among political officials in all but a very few polities, even in the developed world (Darcy, Welch, and Clark, 1994; Rule, 1987, 1994). In particular, the third wave of democratization that occurred during the 1980s and early 1990s (Huntington, 1991) proved disappointing to women in two major regions. Women made few gains from democratization in Latin America, at least in the short term, despite the leading role of women in the movements that pushed aside the existing authoritarian regimes; and democratization in the former communist nations of Europe has brought to women increased problems and pressures (Waylen, 1994).

The ideological stances of the authoritarian regimes in Latin America and the former Soviet bloc were, of course, at opposite ends of the spectrum. Correspondingly, the position of women differed considerably in these two systems. The communist governments of the Soviet Union and the East European nations had a formal or symbolic commitment to gender equality that resulted in their selecting a comparatively high number of women for legislative positions (though this was generally not extended into executive positions or leadership roles in the ruling communist parties) and sponsoring official women's groups with ostensibly high political status. In contrast, the primarily right-wing and in many instances military regimes in Latin America actively excluded women and reinforced the patriarchal norms that existed in those societies (Chou, Clark, and Clark, 1990; Waylen, 1994). Furthermore, the socioeconomic transformations the communist regimes implemented, such as universal education and widespread industrialization, also enhanced the status of women and undercut traditional patriarchal norms, but there was much less progress along these lines in Latin America, where educational levels were lower and gender inequality much more broadly entrenched.

On one level, the democratic transitions in Latin America and the former Soviet bloc can be described in simple and fairly analogous terms. A combination of economic stagnation and middle-class resentment produced growing alienation from the ruling regime. When the regime fell into the hands of more soft-line leaders, an opening was created in which the strategic goals of reformers from above and pressures from below ultimately interacted to produce relatively free elections that led to power being assumed by new parties or coalitions of parties. A crucial difference does exist, however, between the transitions in these two regions. In Latin America, the process was almost completely autonomous, in the sense that internal political and socioeconomic forces played out over a significant amount of time (O'Donnell, Schmitter, and Whitehead, 1986). In sharp contrast, in Eastern Europe in 1989, Gorbachev's implicit renunciation of the Brezhnev Doctrine (i.e., that the USSR would act as a guarantor of communist rule throughout the bloc) unleashed pent-up forces that produced rapid democratic transitions (Przeworski, 1991; Stokes, 1993); and the failed military coup against Gorbachev produced a similar phenomenon two years later.

The role of women in these two transitions was quite different, although the results for women turned out to be similar. In Latin America, women were almost completely excluded from the authoritarian regimes that dominated most countries. However, their low status in the patriarchal Latin culture actually gave them one advantage. Because opposition activities by women were not seen as being as dangerous for the authorities as those by men, they were tolerated to a much greater extent. Consequently, women (especially the mothers and wives of jailed or "disappeared" dissidents) took the lead in many of the early human rights demonstrations. Their traditional domestic role also pushed them to the forefront of consumer protests against harsh economic conditions; and, of course, feminist groups (especially in Latin America) are almost exclusively composed of women. In short, women played a strong leadership role at the beginning of many democratization movements. Success in forcing these authoritarian regimes from power, however, brought traditional political parties to power, which generally pushed women back into subordinate political roles. Moreover, the enforced austerity programs for the indebted Latin American economies precluded any attempt to pursue the social goals that women's groups and women leaders had advocated (Alvarez, 1990; Jaquette, 1994; Saint-Germain, 1997; Waylen, 1994).

In the Soviet bloc, official women's groups and women's holding of a considerable number of not particularly influential positions in the regimes linked women to the discredited establishment in the eyes of many. In addition, although women participated in the anti-regime demonstrations in large numbers, they did not assume major leadership roles in the political opposition in the USSR and Eastern Europe. Consequently, just as in Latin America, the success of these opposition movements did not create a major role for women in the new governments and parties in the successor states; and, in fact, the proportion of women legislators and lower-level officials fell drastically throughout the Soviet bloc. In addition, women were the victims both of the rising popular appeal of traditional (i.e., precommunist) values and of the massive unemployment brought on by economic restructuring (Waylen, 1994).

Women and the social interests associated with them can thus be considered losers in the democratic transitions in both regions. Democratization in Eastern Europe and the USSR undercut women's previous political and socioeconomic gains. In Latin America, the situation was slightly more complex. There before democratization, the position of women was much worse than in Eastern Europe, so they had little to lose in absolute terms. However, given the prominent role of women in many of the democratization movements, their failure to benefit materially must be considered disappointing (Chowdhury and Nelson, 1994; Waylen, 1994). A priori, there is considerable reason to believe that increasing democratization should open the political sphere to women, permitting them to influence public policy that can force social practices to become less repressive and more egalitarian. Yet, the recent experience of democratization in both Latin America and the former Soviet bloc casts considerable doubt on an optimistic viewing of the impact of democratic reforms on women's emancipation.

These cases raise questions about what the effects of democratization will be in East Asia, where the third wave arrived even later than in Latin America and the former Soviet bloc. Do the disappointments that women experienced in those nations suggest that little change can be expected in East Asia as well? Or, are there characteristics of the East Asian political economies that provide a more hospitable context for improving the status of women? Given East Asia's long and strong history of patriarchy, any progress there should be considered significant. The next section explores whether democratization in East Asia has had any discernible impact on the status of women in that region.

WOMEN IN EAST ASIA:
DOES DEMOCRATIZATION MAKE A DIFFERENCE?

Despite the theoretical potential for political liberalization to empower women, democratization in both Latin America and the former Soviet bloc, at least initially, led to surprisingly little progress. This incongruity calls for empirically evaluating what democratization in East Asia has brought for women, rather than assuming that a particular outcome, either positive or negative, has occurred. Our discussion of the impact of democratization on the status of women in East Asia therefore explores two central sets of questions:

1. Has democratization opened up space for women to pursue their own goals and interests?
   - Has democratization led to better representation for women in specific Asian countries? What factors seem to create more equitable representation for this grossly underrepresented group?
   - Have opportunities for other types of political participation increased? Have autonomous women's associations been formed? Have they been effective in getting women's issues on the political agenda and developing relevant policy reforms? What types or social groups of women do these associations represent?
2. If women have become more politically active, have they been able to improve their status in society?
   - Does better representation lead to more favorable policies? What policies to improve women's status and conditions have been enacted? Have they been effective or merely symbolic? Do similar policy patterns emerge in most of these nations?
   - Is there evidence that policy outcomes affecting women are influenced by women's autonomous values? What are women's goals in a particular setting—that is, what do they seek to achieve with emancipation? Do changing work patterns and social structures provide greater opportunities for women, reproduce patriarchal dominance, or create a more complex pattern?

Part 1 of this book explores the question of whether democratization promotes the empowerment of women. Two political mechanisms for improving the status of women that might be set off by democratization are: (1) the increased representation of women in policymaking elites; and (2) the increased political activities by autonomous women's groups. Both offer the potential for women to use public policy to limit and control the patriarchal components of East Asian cultures. Yet, these very cultures would certainly be expected to place sharp constraints on women's participation in politics. For example, most East Asian nations have comparatively few women serving in their parliaments; and East Asian cultures would certainly not be expected to provide a supportive context for feminist groups. The first three chapters of Part 1 examine the question of women's representation, and the last two discuss the political activities of women's groups.

The section begins with a demonstration that women's representation in East Asian legislatures is determined by more than just the widely cited patriarchal constraints. Japan's legislature is often viewed as a prime example of how the patriarchal nature of Confucian culture severely limits opportunities for women to pursue political careers and, consequently, to use public policy to limit the repression and discrimination of patriarchal relations in East Asian societies. Despite having had an election system that should favor the election of women, Japan has the lowest percentage among the developed democracies of women parliamentarians who serve in the powerful lower house (House of Representatives) of the Japanese Diet (never reaching even 5 percent since 1950). However, Ray Christensen's analysis in Chapter 2 presents two challenges to the simple stereotype that Confucian patriarchy by itself limits women's access to the public sector. First, women have done much better in the elections for the upper house (House of Councillors), where they won approximately 25 percent of the seats in two of the last three elections. Second, other minorities, who should face similar discrimination to that against women in Japan, have done much better than women in gaining positions in the House of Representatives.

These discordant facts lead Christensen to search for an institutional explanation—that is, one that is based on how specific rules and procedures (i.e., institutions) produce political outcomes (in this case, the low numbers of women in the House of Representatives). Christensen argues that the key institutional factor in House elections has been the severe restrictions that exist on campaign activities. This, in turn, has led to heavy reliance on personal political support groups called *kōenkai*. Cohesive minorities can easily establish such groups, but for a variety of social and political reasons women have been at a tremendous disadvantage in creating and leading such organizations. In addition to this explanation for women's low representation in the House of Representatives, women's relative success

rates under Japan's complex and changing electoral laws also provide
support for the more commonly cited institutional factors that promote women's candidacies: (1) proportional representation; (2) multimember districts; and (3) less powerful legislatures (Darcy, Welch,
and Clark, 1994; Rule, 1987, 1994).

The other two chapters on representation also confirm the
important impact that institutional factors have on promoting or
inhibiting women's representation in Asian democracies. In Chapter
3, Rose J. Lee presents a comparative study of South Korea and
Taiwan. The two countries share many key characteristics: (1) a patriarchal Confucian culture; (2) a long postwar period of authoritarian
rule during which at least some elections occurred; (3) rapid economic growth and industrialization since the 1960s; and (4) a recent
transition to democracy starting in the late 1980s. Yet, their records in
terms of women's representation are polar opposites. Women's representation in South Korea has been very low throughout the postwar
era (generally in the 1 to 3 percent range at both the national and
local levels); and democratization has had only a marginal impact on
this disappointing trend. In Taiwan, in sharp contrast, women's representation in legislative bodies at both the national and local levels has
increased over time and now seems fairly stable in the 15 to 20 percent range. In addition, although the upward trend preceded democratization, women have made appreciable gains since the democratic
transition began in 1986.

In Chapter 3, Lee explores why Taiwan has been so much more
successful than Korea in promoting women's legislative representation. Unfortunately, South Korea, rather than Taiwan, is now the typical case for East Asia. Yet, as Chapter 2 showed about Japan, we
should not jump to the conclusion that patriarchal Confucian culture
by itself precludes women from entering the political arena.
Certainly, the "Taiwan exception" demonstrates that cultural determinism should not be accepted blindly. In fact, it is easy for Lee to
adduce the reason for women's atypical ability to win elections in
Taiwan. Throughout the postwar period, Taiwan has had an electoral
system that reserves or guarantees about 10 percent of the seats for
women. The use of reserved seats to gain access for women to the
"game of politics," moreover, is gaining popularity in Asia. The
Philippines and India, for example, have adopted such systems for
their local governments with a consequent substantial jump in
women's representation. Thus, Lee advocates such a system for Korea
as the most effective strategy for promoting more equitable representation for women.

Lee's arguments are buttressed by the detailed case study

described by Janet and Cal Clark in Chapter 4. One major problem of a quota or reserved seats system for women is that the women legislators so elected would become simple tokens, with no effective power base of their own. Given Taiwan's strong Confucian culture, this danger would appear particularly strong there. Yet, the Clarks argue, over time in Taiwan women have become political leaders in their own right. This is demonstrated, for example, by the fact that women now generally win half again as many seats as are reserved for them, indicating that a significant number of women legislators must be gaining office on their own merits.

Clark and Clark present two more direct sets of evidence that women have become autonomous actors in Taiwan's politics. First, a survey of Assembly members from the mid-1980s shows that even then women and men legislators were surprisingly similar in their political careers and activities and that there was little evidence of women's expected disadvantages. Second, several case studies of women politicians confirm their ability to emerge as independent and respected political leaders. The Clarks, like Christensen and Lee, offer an institutionalist explanation for why women were able to take advantage of the reserved seats system in Taiwan, in particular how the quota system interacted with the informal political networks or factions that lie at the heart of Taiwan's politics. Yet, they also point out that the way these "institutions" operate within the context of a Confucian Chinese culture almost certainly constrains women's ability to increase their still limited influence in Taiwan's polity.

The next two chapters turn our attention to the ability of autonomous women's groups to articulate women's issues with case studies from the Philippines and South Korea. In Chapter 5, Maria Ela Atienza compares three groups in the Philippines and finds that their effectiveness varies with their own organizational features and with the types of relationships they are able to establish with governmental bodies. The 1991 Local Government Code in the Philippines specifically recognized the need to integrate women into the processes of local governance and provided two avenues for pursuing this goal: one was mandating that a women's representative be included on every local government council; the second encouraged the inclusion of women's groups (and other nongovernmental organizations) in local governance.

Atienza analyzes the successes and problems of a city Women's Council that is a member of the National Council of the Women of the Philippines; a provincial women's federation that is affiliated with a national organization (the Democratic Socialist Women of the Philippines); and a network of indigenous women's organizations that are also affiliated with national and international women's organizations. Clearly, a complex and vibrant structure of autonomous women's groups has emerged, although their success has been quite varied. Women have seemingly been much more able to influence selected policies than to challenge men for the effective control of city and community affairs. The gender bias in the Filipino political culture undoubtedly makes a large contribution to these cultural constraints on women's political activities—constraints that can be seen, for example, in the tendency of most Filipino women themselves to equate women's empowerment with economic well-being and welfare services.

If (as appears likely) the autonomous activity of women's groups pushing for reform has played a key role in the limited success that women have had in improving their status in East Asia, the specific goals and strategies of these groups become extremely important. In Chapter 6, Mikyung Chin presents a history of the feminist movement in South Korea and argues that its current strategic focus may be undercutting its effectiveness.

Chin details how the postwar feminist movement in South Korea became divided into two very distinct coalitions. One was composed primarily of middle-class women and became closely tied to the authoritarian regime. A more radical stream of feminism came from the activation of rural and working class women who became allied with students and intellectuals. Both have national organizations with affiliated component groups and focus on somewhat different sets of issues. Following democratization and the establishment of autonomous local governments in the early 1990s, women in both camps felt that participation in local government would be especially valuable for women, both because local governments have responsibility for many central women's issues, or "life politics," and because women have had a very hard time getting elected to South Korea's National Assembly. But Chin believes that this strategic redirection of the feminist movement toward local politics is misdirected and counterproductive. She argues that the idea that women should be primarily concerned with "life politics" itself represents an unconscious gender bias and that women need to be concerned with the central issues of national politics. Thus, she calls for a reconceptualization of the Korean feminist movement.

Part 2 examines the second question of this book, how political activities have (or have not) led to changes in the status and quality of life enjoyed by women in East Asia. In Chapter 7, Patty Hipsher and R. Darcy provide an excellent overview of policies affecting women in Asia and how they are embedded within broader cultural traditions.

The chapter begins with a review of Asian cultures. Although all have a well-deserved reputation for patriarchy, two important caveats must be noted concerning this stereotype. First, Asia's religious traditions vary significantly in their implications for the treatment of women. Second, and very importantly, strong indigenous movements for promoting women's liberation can be found in the history of many of these nations. Certainly, improving the status of women in Asia is not a project imported from the West.

Hipsher and Darcy then examine the extent to which nineteen Asian nations have adopted eight laws that guarantee or promote equal rights for women in four different areas. In terms of the pattern of adoption, almost all the Asian countries have legislated basic women's rights—political (e.g., voting and running for office) and economic (e.g., property ownership and equal pay)—whereas only a few have ventured into the area of social relations (e.g., spousal rape, domestic violence, and sexual harassment). Abortion occupies a middle position, probably more because of government interest in population control than in promoting women's rights. There is also significant variation among the Asian nations in their support for women's rights. China, Singapore, Malaysia, and South Korea have fully adopted five or more of these policies; in contrast, Burma, North Korea, Pakistan, and Laos extend full protection to women in one or two of the areas.

The data presented by Hipsher and Darcy suggest that although there is some tendency for nations that are more democratic to have stronger legislation in the area of women's rights, this relationship is far from overwhelming. Table 1.1, for instance, shows that 64 percent of the countries that hold fairly competitive elections—which includes a significant number of "semi-democracies" (Case, 1994) like Singapore and Malaysia—have fully adopted four or more of the laws under consideration, in contrast to only 38 percent of the autocracies. This produces a fairly strong correlation coefficient (gamma = .49), but because of the small number of cases (i.e., countries), the association comes nowhere near meeting conventional levels of statistical significance. Thus, the dynamics posited in Figure 1.1 may be operating in Asia, but it is hard to reach a conclusive verdict from the statistical data alone.

The case study presented in Chapter 8 by Rose J. Lee makes a more positive case for democratization's aiding the cause of women's liberation. In South Korea, the authoritarian military government came under growing pressure from an increasingly restive middle class. To try to hold these pressures in check, the regime was willing to respond to the demands of women's groups to institutionalize

Table 1.1   Association Between Democratization and Laws
              Promoting Equal Rights for Women

| Women's Rights | Democratization | | Total |
	Authoritarian	At Least Some Competitive National Elections	
Fully protect less than 4 of rights in Hipsher-Darcy study	5 62%	4 36%	9 47%
Fully protect more than 4 of rights in Hipsher-Darcy study	3 38%	7 64%	10 53%
Total	8 42%	11 58%	19 100%

Gamma = .49
Approximate Significance = .25

their influence through creating a research institute; a ministry primarily concerned with women's issues; and the Council on Women's
Policy, which is associated with this ministry. The first elected government was the fairly conservative Roh regime. However, women's
groups were able to get it to follow up on promises made during the
competitive campaign to enact significant policies in the areas of family law, equal employment, and child care over the strong opposition
of Confucianist traditionalists.

The more liberal Kim administration that followed strengthened
these laws, passed a partial domestic violence law (the most progressive
in Asia), and greatly strengthened the Council on Women's Policy by
creating women's sections reporting to it in each bureau and local government. Lee sees substantial results coming from these policy changes:

> The legislative accomplishments have gone beyond the written laws
> and have begun to affect women's lives and their social, familial sta-
> tus. Decisions handed down by regular or family courts have led to
> the acceptance of an equitable distribution of community property,
> women's initiatives in divorce, and fair rules regarding child custody.
> Similarly, on equal employment, the government has been imple-
> menting a higher quota for women in government and other public
> sectors. The government's supervision has extended to the private
> sector as well, starting with large enterprises. . . . To be sure, gender
> equality has a long way to go in Korea, but giant steps have been
> taken at an accelerating pace.

Autonomous women's groups have been in the forefront of pushing these reforms. Indeed, the reforms are all the more striking because very little progress has been made in increasing women's woefully low representation in the legislature and executive decisionmaking positions (see Chapters 3 and 6). Democratization, therefore, evidently opened space in which these groups can operate.

In Chapter 9, Catherine Farris compares postwar China and Taiwan and reaches three major conclusions. First, China's socialist system initially promoted very beneficial changes (e.g., the Marriage Reform Law and support for women's entering the labor force) in line with Mao's dictum that "women hold up half of heaven." However, the communist emphasis on women's participation in the labor force as the centerpiece of women's rights left other important areas untreated. Second, Deng Xiaoping's market reforms in the 1980s and 1990s have been associated with, if anything, a reassertion of patriarchal norms in China. This is probably most marked in the countryside, but urban women also seem to be falling under the thrall of a "feminine mystique" of domesticity. These first two conclusions, then, might be taken to support the logic of a third, "socialist feminism"—that socialism, and only socialism, promotes women's liberation. Yet, Farris's third conclusion is much different: that some combination of a more prosperous and advanced industrial society than exists in China (which reflects a type of "modernity" that is somewhat different from the Western model) and democratic politics has now created substantial genuine progress for women in Taiwan.

Based on this analysis, Farris makes a much broader argument about the need to reexamine universal definitions of women's liberation, such as those advocated by socialist or liberal feminists. Rather, the position of women should be evaluated within specific societies and cultural contexts. Chinese culture, for example, is much more concerned with the complementarity, rather than the equivalence, of gender roles. Women derive power from their places in long-standing social networks. Thus, unlike Western societies, where women's liberation is generally perceived as involving liberation from the family, women's liberation in China can involve strengthening women's position within such networks by ending male abuses. Consequently, she argues, women's liberation can be understood only in cultural context:

> The process of women's liberation from Chinese patriarchy is taking different forms in the PRC and in Taiwan and cannot be expected to have the same outcomes in both places. To the extent that the battle is waged against a similar set of values, beliefs, and customs, we can expect the solutions to look similar. To the extent that these Chinese

societies have distinct modern histories, we might see divergent outcomes. In either case, we should not make the assumption that the evolution of women's liberation in either Chinese society will resemble that of our own.

In Chapter 10, L. H. M. Ling provides a more pessimistic perspective on the importance of East Asian culture. She argues that Western theories of democratization have been misapplied to East Asia, where the cultural context within which politicians and governments operate is radically different from that of the Western world. Consequently, the empowering implications that democratization could have for women, such as those suggested in Figure 1.1, are gravely weakened and distorted. Her model, then, can be used to explain the continued widespread subjection of women to patriarchal repression throughout East Asia despite the legal commitment to economic and political rights that the Hipsher-Darcy analysis found.

Ling argues that the patriarchal family has historically served as the model for government and for state-society relations in East Asian cultures. More recently, state-led economic development in postcolonial East Asia has been justified philosophically as necessary to preserve the national masculinity of the former victims of imperialism. The resulting "hypermasculine development," therefore, represents a perverse combination of patriarchal East Asian culture with the logic of the market to justify limiting women to traditional family roles and to being a source of cheap, repressed labor (including prostitution). This has led, moreover, to what Ling terms "sage man politics," in which male politicians use pursuit of the national interest to cloak self-aggrandizing political games:

> In politics as in economics, hypermasculinity protects the patriarchal elite. It allows individual (male) leaders to maneuver contending ideologies and institutions for personal gain, as long as they conform to the traditional moral rhetoric about public life.

Consequently, democratization offers very limited opportunities for women to fight back against patriarchal domination in most parts of East Asia.

The concluding chapter, by Cal Clark and Rose J. Lee, seeks to find a balance in the somewhat disparate pictures painted by the various essays. Clearly, some contributors are much more optimistic or pessimistic than others on whether democracy holds out much hope for improving the status of women in East Asia. Legal reforms have only slightly softened many aspects of patriarchy. Women's groups have become active in most of these nations, but their success has been quite varied and dependent on political factors outside their control. Moreover, gaining legislative representation for women has been difficult and, unfortunately, not particularly efficacious when it has been achieved. More broadly, as Ling argues, the overarching culture and political economy of East Asia have many hidden (and not so hidden) biases against women. These are no small obstacles, given the importance of culture and institutional arrangements discussed here. Still, we argue, democratization has given women new tools to improve their position. How effective these tools can be and how well they are used differ radically among the individual East Asian nations. Still, we believe that a long journey toward women's emancipation and empowerment in East Asia has begun.

PART 1

Representation and Issue Advocacy: Can They Be Effective?

2

The Impact of
Electoral Rules in Japan

RAY CHRISTENSEN

Among the advanced industrial democracies, Japan is widely seen as a hostile environment for women in politics. Its business and bureaucratic elites are extremely male dominated. This characterization carries over into the electoral realm, where Japan is notorious for the low representation of women in the Diet (Japan's national legislature), perhaps the lowest in the developed world (see Figure 2.1). Many would take this to indicate a "cultural determinism" explicable by the highly patriarchal nature of Japan's culture and society. Yet, a closer look at how women candidates have fared at the polls in postwar Japan destroys this simplistic stereotype, for two important reasons. First, women have done quite well in certain types of elections. Second, other minority groups, who are subject to the same cultural disdain faced by women, have managed to gain proportionate representation in the same elections in which women have fared abysmally. Thus, something besides cultural determinism must certainly be at work.

This chapter examines the puzzle of women's representation in Japan by applying an "institutionalist" perspective. This is that certain types of electoral systems advantage or disadvantage nonestablishment groups such as women. The Japanese case provides some support for this perspective. As we shall see, however, the key factor in Japan is not the type of electoral system per se. Rather, it is the way in which election laws have structured campaign activities that disadvantage women while advantaging more cohesive and organized minority groups.

ELECTION SYSTEMS AND WOMEN'S
REPRESENTATION: A JAPANESE EXCEPTION?

The low numbers of women in Japan's House of Representatives (the powerful lower house of the Diet) is an anomaly because the electoral

Figure 2.1 Percentage of Women in National Parliaments, 1987–1991

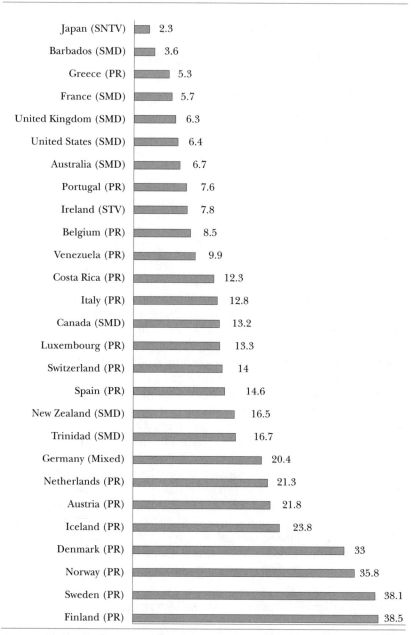

Japan (SNTV) 2.3
Barbados (SMD) 3.6
Greece (PR) 5.3
France (SMD) 5.7
United Kingdom (SMD) 6.3
United States (SMD) 6.4
Australia (SMD) 6.7
Portugal (PR) 7.6
Ireland (STV) 7.8
Belgium (PR) 8.5
Venezuela (PR) 9.9
Costa Rica (PR) 12.3
Italy (PR) 12.8
Canada (SMD) 13.2
Luxembourg (PR) 13.3
Switzerland (PR) 14
Spain (PR) 14.6
New Zealand (SMD) 16.5
Trinidad (SMD) 16.7
Germany (Mixed) 20.4
Netherlands (PR) 21.3
Austria (PR) 21.8
Iceland (PR) 23.8
Denmark (PR) 33
Norway (PR) 35.8
Sweden (PR) 38.1
Finland (PR) 38.5

Source: Rule, 1994, p. 17.
Notes: PR = proportional representation; SMD = single-member districts; SNTV = single nontransferable vote; STV = single transferable vote.

systems used in Japan should facilitate the representation of women and minority groups. Most of Japan's elections have been held under proportional representation systems or in multimember districts that use a single nontransferable vote for a candidate (Grofman and Lijphart, 1986; Lijphart, 1994; Taagepera and Shugart, 1989).

Such systems should, in theory, create opportunities for women and minority groups. The proportionality of both systems should allow smaller parties to gain representation, thus opening a pathway to greater diversity. In addition, larger parties run multiple candidates in multimember districts, and all parties run multiple candidates on party lists. When parties run multiple candidates, there is a greater tendency for a woman or a minority group member to be one of the multiple candidates. In fact, recent research suggests that the type of electoral system may be the most important factor in determining how well or poorly women are represented (Darcy, Welch, and Clark, 1994; Rule, 1987, 1994). Furthermore, Shugart (1994) also theorizes that high expectations of constituency service, such as exist for Japanese legislators, should facilitate the election of women and minorities.

Despite all these advantages, women are woefully underrepresented in Japan's multimember districts for the House of Representatives, as demonstrated by the comparative data in Figure 2.1. Japan had the dubious distinction of having the lowest percentage of women parliamentarians during the late 1980s and early 1990s among the nations included in this figure. Moreover, its low position was also an exception to the general pattern that countries with proportional representation systems had higher levels of representation for women than did those with single-member districts.

The data in Figure 2.1, unfortunately, are not unrepresentative of women's representation in Japan's lower house during the postwar era, as indicated by Figure 2.2, which presents the percentage of women elected to the lower and upper houses between 1946 and 1996. Women constitute 51 to 52 percent of the electorate, yet they have won only 1 to 8 percent of the seats in the House of Representatives. If the 1946 and 1996 elections are excluded, the maximum value becomes 3 percent. In the House of Councillors, in contrast, women have fared much better, winning 6 to 26 percent of national constituency seats and 1 to 13 percent of district seats.

The Japanese case depicted in Figures 2.1 and 2.2 supports the argument that the type of electoral system influences women's representation and demonstrates that other factors besides the electoral system are evidently operating to limit women's victories at the polls. In the upper house (the House of Councillors), more women are

Figure 2.2 Representation of Women in Japanese Diet

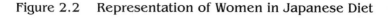

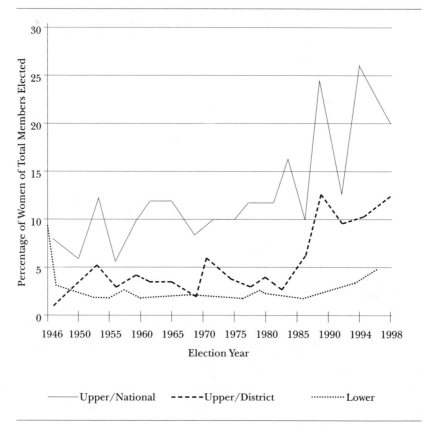

Sources: Asahi Shimbun, 1992–1995; Asahi Shimbun Senkyo Hombu, 1990; Darcy and Nixon, 1996, p. 6; Ogai, 1995, pp. 42–45; Senkyo, 1983–1995; Sanshū Ryōin Meikan, 1990.

consistently elected from the national proportional representation district (close to 25 percent in several recent elections) than are elected from prefectural (provincial) districts. This pattern suggests an institutional explanation: a large-magnitude proportional representation district elects a greater proportion of women than do smaller multi- and single-member districts. Similarly, the one-time use of large magnitude districts in the first postwar elections for the lower house created the highest number of women ever elected to the House of Representatives. On the other hand, Japan's multimember districts in the House of Councillors and (especially) the House of

Representatives elect very few women compared to other countries. In these districts, the representation of women lags behind not only countries that use proportional representation, but also single-member district nations.

Another anomaly comes from the fact that several minority groups, who should face discrimination similar to that against women in Japanese culture, do much better in terms of gaining parliamentary representation. For example, the Sōka gakkai, a lay Buddhist organization, has constituted between 6 and 10 percent of the electorate since the early 1960s. Beginning in 1962, it organized its own political party, the Clean Government Party (which merged into the newly formed New Frontier Party in 1993). For the thirty years during which it campaigned as a distinct entity, the Clean Government Party parlayed 6 to 10 percent of the electorate into 5 to 11 percent of the House of Representatives, 12 to 18 percent of the House of Councillors national constituency, and 3 to 8 percent of that House's district seats. Labor unions have also done well in gaining representation. Union members were 16 percent of the electorate in the late 1970s; and in the two elections of that period, 17 and 18 percent of the members of the House of Representatives had union backgrounds. In the 1990 election, this share was still above 17 percent. In the 1977 and 1980 House of Councillors elections, trade unionists constituted 24 percent of those elected to the national constituency and from 13 to 17 percent of those elected from districts. Thus, both trade unions and the religious Sōka gakkai come close to or exceed their proportion of the electorate in electing members to the Diet.

In addition, even smaller groups have been successful in electing their members. These groups are most successful in the national constituency of the House of Councillors. For example, Rishō kōseikai, with a membership that approximates 6 percent of the electorate, elected 4 and 6 percent of the national constituency in 1977 and 1980; and Seichō no Ie, with nearly 4 percent of the electorate, also elected 2 percent of the national constituency in the same elections (Hori, 1985: 121). The Buraku Liberation League, an organization of 150,000–200,000 descendants of the "outcastes" in Japan's feudal system, elected one member of the national constituency and, in the House of Representatives, typically elected two members on the Socialist Party ticket. In addition to these League members, several conservative legislators are also Burakumin.

Several explanations have been adduced for this anomaly. Taagepera (1994) suggests that interparty competition in SNTV systems makes parties reluctant to put up a "weaker" female candidate. He speculates that recent advances in women's representation are helping to change this attitude. Shugart (1994: 38–39) examines the low numbers of women in both Japan and Italy and cites the strong personal support networks that candidates have in these countries as an explanation for women's low representation. The incumbents, who are mostly male, have "nearly captive supporters"; women are unable to break into the system. Darcy and Nixon (1996) find that women's representation is low in Japan because of the advantage of incumbency, the domination of politics by the conservative Liberal Democratic Party (LDP), and the dearth of women in the pool of prospective candidates. They also show that women are not weaker candidates in the Japanese context and, with Shugart, suggest that local support organizations are extremely important in Japan. Few women are elected in Japan, because they neither inherit these important support organizations nor are they well positioned to build them.

These findings turn our attention to another institutional feature of Japan's electoral environment besides the electoral system itself. In Japan, an important and unstudied institution that influences representation is the strict regime of campaign regulations (Darcy and Nixon, 1996; Shugart, 1994). These regulations make organizations extremely important in Japanese elections. Because organizations are so important, minority groups that are organized send many representatives to the Diet, but groups that lack such organization do not have such representation. Women are in the latter category, whereas unions, religions, and other organized minorities enjoy quite high levels of representation under the same electoral system.

ELECTORAL RULES AND THE IMPORTANCE OF CANDIDATE SUPPORT ORGANIZATIONS IN JAPAN

In any country, the cohesion and the organizational strength of a minority group help determine its political relevance. A group that lacks an organization that helps direct its members' political participation or lacks the cohesion to vote largely as a group even without organizational direction usually becomes politically irrelevant. In Japan, a group's organizational strength and cohesion are similarly important. However, this generic importance of organizational strength is further heightened by legislation governing election campaigns. These rules make organizations the only means by which a candidate can reach out effectively to prospective voters. Door-to-door campaigning is prohibited, and media advertising is strictly limited and regulated. The number of pamphlets that may be distributed in an election campaign is controlled. Similar restrictions apply to the number of posters, mailings, campaign offices, campaign vehicles, and the like. There are also tight limits on fund-raising activities and the spending of campaign funds.

Campaign legislation in Japan is strict, but most observers would agree that these laws are honored only in their breach. It is a mistake, however, to assume that these laws are irrelevant or do not influence campaign practices, campaign structures, or the types of candidates that run for office in Japan. For example, though candidates typically evade campaign spending laws by maintaining two sets of books, no candidate evades the restrictions on purchasing media advertising. Similarly, campaign workers may evade restrictions on door-to-door campaigning by stuffing mailboxes with campaign literature, but because of the ease of being caught, no candidate in Japan ever canvases door-to-door.

Organizations are crucial in Japanese elections because they are the only vehicle through which candidates can get their message out to the electorate. Just as soft money creates a loophole for candidates in the United States to evade spending limitations, organizations in Japan provide a way for candidates to evade the myriad of restrictions on their activities. A candidate or election worker may not canvas door-to-door in Japan, but the same worker may go door-to-door visiting members of an organization. The number of campaign mailings is strictly limited, but an organization may provide information on its endorsements to all of its members without state oversight or regulation. Organizations are not a supplement to media campaigns as they might be in other countries; they *are* the campaign in Japan. The importance of organizations in Japan is illustrated by the enormous amount of time and money spent by candidates to create personal support organizations or *kōenkai* (Curtis, 1971). Candidates go to this trouble and expense because without the existence of such an organization, with its all-important membership list, it becomes impossible to effectively reach the electorate.

The importance of an existing organization is exemplified by one of the few politically active female-dominated organizations in Japan, the Seikatsu Club. The Seikatsu Club is a cooperative purchasing organization that is concerned about issues of food safety, quality, and economy. Largely female and urban, the club takes a progressive stance on environmental issues. It has established autonomous political organizations called networks in each area. The network organizations operate in campaigns much like any other politically involved organization. First, the organization is used as a vehicle by which the members can be mobilized and have a campaign message sent to them. Campaign information and appeals for campaign help are simply included with the other information in foodstuff deliveries. At network meetings, endorsed candidates appear and make an appeal directly to the members.

The club fulfills a second function in reaching out to voters who are not organization members. Members are asked to provide lists of friends, relatives, colleagues, and neighbors to whom an electoral appeal can be made. Typically the persons providing the names will call or visit the nonorganization people to ask for their support of a specific candidate on election day. These friends of members are put on a list and are contacted again and again in subsequent campaigns. They are deleted from the list if they repeatedly respond negatively to electoral appeals; if they cooperate, they are asked to introduce other people, contribute time or money to the campaign, or allow campaign posters to be put up at their house. Through these activities, the organization creates an important list of organizational outsiders that can be mobilized along with the organization members in an election.

The experience of the Seikatsu Club is common to other organizations in Japan. Sōka gakkai members not only canvas their local friends, relatives, neighbors, and colleagues, but they routinely take family vacations that coincide with tight races for Sōka gakkai candidates in other areas of Japan. On these vacations they visit friends and relatives to encourage their support of the endorsed candidate personally (Kitagawa and Gogatsukai, 1995). It is also common for individual union members to contact not only local people but also friends in other election districts in which a union candidate is running (Sugai, 1996). An organization with strong links to the electorate is correspondingly important in elections. One campaign supervisor stated that the electrical utility union is very important in elections despite its small number of members. These union members visit homes daily on repair calls, and in some rural areas they still make the rounds collecting electric utility payments. Because of these contacts, members of this union can introduce many nonunion members to the campaign (Sakata, 1995).

The personal support organizations built up by conservative candidates vary in structure and composition. Nevertheless, most kōenkai combine the support of existing organizations with a candidate's personal contacts that are based on school, professional, or neighborhood friendships and relationships. The existing organizations usually retain their autonomy and maintain their own separate list of members and contacts. Such existing organizations take many forms. In addition to business or agricultural organizations, some candidates rely heavily on the kōenkai of local politicians who are elected to city, town, or prefectural assemblies in their district. Just as Mayor Daley could turn out the vote in Chicago for national or statewide Democratic candidates, city councillors or prefectural representatives will mobilize their kōenkai to turn out the vote for allies running in a Diet election.

The support of these existing organizations is important not only for the organization's membership but also for the friends and neighbors of those members. For example, a business organization will augment its small membership by appeals to employees, business contacts, friends, relatives, and neighbors. These additional people will be mobilized without the business organization turning over its list of contacts directly to the campaign. The organization will keep the list to preserve its importance in election campaigns. Similarly, a local politician will mobilize his or her kōenkai on behalf of a candidate for national office but not turn over the membership and contact list to the other campaign.

The personal element of the kōenkai operates differently. In this part of the organization, personal contacts of the candidate introduce friends, relatives, business associates, and others; and these new people are added directly to the kōenkai lists. In this manner, through repeated introductions, people who have no connection whatsoever with the candidate become members of her or his kōenkai. The personal connection between these members and the candidate is maintained by city or neighborhood subunits of the kōenkai. The leaders of these units work closely with a full-time member of the politician's staff assigned to work with the kōenkai units in a specific area. These local kōenkai leaders provide the crucial link between the candidate's organization and the rank-and-file kōenkai members in a neighborhood. The local organization handles mobilization and recruiting efforts, with occasional visits from the politician. Kōenkai membership lists, therefore, can grow enormously. An estimate suggests that three kōenkai memberships are necessary to produce one vote. The costs of these organizations are enormous too. A strong kōenkai with the requisite offices and full-time staff costs around 100 million yen a year ($1 million a year at a 100-to-1 exchange rate).

This level of organizational activity is quite remarkable. Its importance, however, is not in the level of activity but in the fact that these activities are the core of Japanese campaigns. Most of the other allowed campaign activities are quite ineffective. Candidates travel around the district in sound trucks repeating their name over and over; they give speeches in front of train stations; they may attempt to get some free press by staging novel campaign activities. Each of these activities increases name recognition and is marginally effective, but it is the activities of organizations that decides an election. Only through the loophole of organizational activities can a direct appeal be made to a prospective voter. In Japan, organizational activities are the cornerstone of the campaign, with the other more visible activities of candidates considered to be of little significance.

Though some might argue that this form of campaign organization is culturally determined, the more convincing explanation lies in the campaign rules in Japan. The supposed links between a candidate and the kōenkai members are so attenuated that it is difficult to imagine that the Japanese penchant for face-to-face relationships is driving this form of campaign organization. In addition, this type of campaigning is time consuming, costly, and inefficient. Enormous resources are spent creating and maintaining such organizations (Curtis, 1971). Cultural attitudes no doubt play a role in the specific form that campaign organizations have taken in Japan, but it is unlikely that this inefficient method of campaigning would remain the dominant form if candidates were allowed to advertise or use direct mailings.

Having established the importance of organization-based campaigns, I now turn my analysis to how this feature of Japanese campaigns affects the electoral prospects of women in Japan, and how this feature operates differently in Japan's different election systems.

ORGANIZATIONAL POLITICS AND THE REPRESENTATION OF WOMEN IN THE LOWER HOUSE

Until the party realignment of 1993 and electoral reform of 1994, the two paths to a seat in the House of Representatives were through the Liberal Democratic Party (LDP), which has held power during most of the postwar era, or through one of the opposition parties (e.g., the Socialists, Clean Government Party, Communists, or Democratic Socialists). Organizational affiliations were crucial to recruitment in either path, but because of differences in the types of organizations, the paths were widely divergent, especially with regard to the opportunities they presented for women and minorities.

The LDP path to office required a personal support organization. The first and easiest way to obtain such an organization was to inherit it from a relative. Professor Takeshi Sasaki quips that passing on such organizations to an heir is about the only way to pass something of value on to the next generation without paying an inheritance tax. In theory, inheritance should be a method of increasing both occupational and gender diversity. Not every politician will have a son to whom he can pass on his seat. Many second-generation politicians will not necessarily be the best and brightest but will have had a variety of prepolitical careers. However, in practice, the inheritance system works against diversity. Adoption for business or inheritance reasons is quite common in Japan. A couple unable to have children will adopt from a relation or other close family connection. A father without a son, for example, will legally adopt his son-in-law. Therefore, in practice, Japanese politicians have passed on their support organizations exclusively to their male relatives, a practice best explained by cultural attitudes. These second-generation politicians are also not significantly diverse in terms of backgrounds. Even those unable to enter the elite public universities can enter the expensive elite private schools with lower standards. After graduation they can work in a company affiliated with their father, as a journalist or as a political secretary. Their work experiences are typically elite-connected and not very diverse.

A second method of obtaining a kōenkai is to build it gradually while working up through the ranks of local politicians. This method should and does create diversity in the ranks of LDP politicians. Many local politicians have not gone to elite schools or had an illustrious prepolitical career. The most prominent example is former prime minister Tanaka Kakuei, who never attended high school. These politicians, called "party" politicians, are the greatest source of occupational diversity in the LDP. A third method is related to the second. An aspiring young man will get a job as a political secretary to a politician. After several years of learning the ropes, he might run for a local high office as described above. He might also run directly for the Diet at his boss's retirement or in a neighboring district, building his kōenkai from the ground up.

A fourth method is to retire from a job in the highly esteemed bureaucracy and either step into a support organization that is looking for a candidate or work with the support of others in building a support organization. Early-retiring bureaucrats are actively pursued as potential candidates, and they have an easier time creating kōenkai because they are already tied into the educational and occupational elite that controls much of Japan. As high-level bureaucrats, they are guaranteed the best that Japan has to offer, having graduated from the best educational institutions. Though less common, lawyers and business leaders also have a similarly respectable pedigree, and they will sometimes be recruited for or decide to stand for such races. Despite the variety of methods of building or obtaining a kōenkai, doors are more generally open only to the economic or educational elite and those who are politically connected. This bias in favor of the politically connected can be explained in part by cultural attitudes, but certainly the enormous expense of building and maintaining an effective kōenkai also constrains who will be successful at this effort.

Do women and minorities play a role in LDP House of Representatives elections? Women are typically organized within the kōenkai structure, and often a candidate will have a separate women's group as part of the structure. Certain LDP-affiliated religions also play a crucial role in supporting conservative candidates. However, in the House of Representatives, these religions do not put up their members as candidates, because they cannot defeat the more organizationally connected elites who can build larger and more effective kōenkai.

The former (prereformulation) opposition parties recruited candidates in an altogether different manner. The dominant support organization of each party largely determined the composition of the candidate slate. Similar to the Labour Party in Britain, organizational affiliation matters more than the familial, educational, or occupational connections so important in LDP recruitment. The Socialists and the Democratic Socialists recruited primarily from their affiliated labor unions. The Buraku Liberation League was also an important Socialist support group, running some of its members on the Socialist ticket. The Clean Government Party ran candidates who were members of or had close ties to the lay Buddhist organization Sōka gakkai. The Communists put up party members; and because of their strength in many labor unions, many of their candidates also were union members. Because these groups largely recruited internally, the organizational elite from which these candidates were drawn differed greatly from the national elite from which most conservative candidates were drawn. As a result, there have been many trade unionists, religious believers, and other minorities winning seats in Japan's House of Representatives.

This system allowed for greater representation of minorities, but it also had some pitfalls. Each of the former opposition parties suffered from the perception of being captive to its respective supporting organizations. These parties found it difficult to attract supporters beyond their specific sector of the electorate. One such example can be seen in the "Madonna" boom of the Socialist Party in 1989, under the leadership of Doi Takako. As the first woman leader of a major political party in Japan, she made a sincere effort to increase the appeal of the Socialist Party beyond its shrinking union core. A large number of nonunion candidates were recruited, especially women candidates. Unfortunately, in many districts these candidates were competing against established union-based incumbents or incumbents of affiliated opposition parties with which the unions had longstanding reciprocal cooperative arrangements. These new women candidates lacked strong connections to these organizations, and in some cases they were unable to gain effective union support. In some instances the unions continued their cooperative arrangements with another party's incumbent rather than switching to back a new and relatively unknown candidate from their own Socialist Party. At best, these difficulties were inherent problems of an organizational-based election. At worst, these problems represented union efforts to prevent any diminishing of their exclusive control of the Socialist Party (Kunihiro, 1996).

ORGANIZATIONAL POLITICS AND THE REPRESENTATION OF WOMEN IN THE UPPER HOUSE

The first of the three different election systems used in the House of Councillors is the district or prefectural constituencies. Three-fifths of the seats are elected from each of Japan's forty-seven prefectures. Each prefecture elects from one to four councillors. This system should on balance be less friendly to women and minority groups because one-third of the seats are elected from single-seat districts; and until 1992 there were only two four-seat districts and four three-seat districts. In fact, union and religious groups do worse in these districts than they do in the larger-magnitude multimember districts of the lower house. However, as a percentage, more women are elected from these lower-magnitude districts than are elected from the House of Representatives districts (see Figure 2.2). Why do women do better in lower-magnitude districts but other minority groups do worse?

The performance of minority groups is easy to explain. Because of the lower magnitude of these districts, the LDP wins a greater percentage of the seats. Because the former opposition parties win fewer seats, there are fewer seats for union members, religious groups, and other minorities. The greater success of women candidates requires a more complex analysis. Part of the explanation lies in the different nature of House of Councillors districts. Because these districts are coterminous with Japan's prefectures, some of the districts can be quite large. In populous urban prefectures, an upper house district will cover up to eleven lower house electoral districts. Similar to senatorial candidates in California or New York appealing to a huge electorate, some upper house district candidates must also appeal to all of the voters of Tokyo or Osaka. The top ten district winners in 1995 each received an average of more than 700,000 votes. For candidates trying to garner such large numbers of votes, name recognition and personal popularity become crucial campaign attributes in addition to organization support. Because of the heightened importance of name recognition, some candidates are recruited from a different pool. What the Japanese call "talent" candidates (sports figures, TV personalities, authors, etc.) become credible candidates in some of these upper house districts. Talent candidates are usually derided in Japan. However, they are a great improvement over the typical conservative lower house candidate in terms of the diversity they bring to the Diet. These talent candidates may not include more union or religious minorities, but they do include more women in their ranks. Talent candidates, though, do not entirely explain the relative success of women in the district races of the House of Councillors. This house also has different and lesser powers than the House of Representatives. This probably makes the seats less competitive and more open to women candidates, in line with a pattern that has been found in a variety of other nations (Darcy, Welch, and Clark, 1994).

The second voting system used in the House of Councillors was a single national constituency in which fifty seats were at stake and each voter had one ballot to cast for the candidate of his or her choice. This system was used up to and including the 1980 election. In 1983, this system was replaced by the third system, a proportional representation system with the same fifty seats in a national constituency. The major change was that, beginning in 1983, ballots were cast for parties rather than candidates. The party lists for this PR system were closed lists, and seats were apportioned by the D'hondt method.

Both systems should have been friendly to women and minority groups. The national constituency allows smaller groups to win a proportion of seats equal to their votes. Religions, unions, and other minorities can elect candidates in the national constituency if they can mobilize sufficient support. Because not all voters in the national electorate are organizationally affiliated, room was also created for candidates with high name recognition. In fact, as Figure 2.2 shows, women did significantly better in the national constituency (where they won, on average, about 10 percent of the seats) than in the electoral districts (where they averaged less than 5 percent of the seats) before the PR voting system was introduced in 1983.

In 1983, the system of voting in the national constituency changed from "open" voting for individual candidates to voting for a party list. Under the former system, the party could deny the nomination to an individual, but it could not dictate the order of victors.

Under the new system of true proportional representation, the party gained the power to designate sure victors, marginal candidates, and sure losers on their lists. Simultaneously with this electoral change, a significant increase in women's representation occurred, as Figure 2.2 clearly shows. In the mid-1980s, explicit party slating was only slightly more favorable to women than their own previous individual campaigning in the "open" national constituency had been. However, their share of seats in the national constituency ultimately doubled from just over 10 percent in the early 1980s to almost 25 percent by the mid-1990s.

The various parties in Japan would not normally be expected to be equally enthusiastic about slating women candidates. Table 2.1, therefore, presents a breakdown by party of the percentage of successful candidates in each election who were women. Though the

Table 2.1 Women's Percentage of Winners/Candidates in National Constituency by Party

	LDP	Socialists	Commu-nists	Clean Govern-ment	Demo-cratic Socialist	Other	Total
1947[a]	21/16[b]	6/3	0/0	—	—	5/4	7/5
1950	0/5	20/16	0/0	—	—	0/4	5/5
1953	5/2	9/5	0/0	—	—	17/10	11/7
1956	0/6	14/10	0/0	—	—	0/5	6/6
1959	9/8	12/8	0/0	—	—	8/8	10/8
1962	14/8	13/11	0/0	0/0	0/0	33/11	12/8
1965	8/6	17/13	0/0	11/11	0/0	50/10	12/8
1968	5/9	17/13	33/33	0/0	0/0	0/7	8/9
1971	10/12	18/15	0/0	13/13	0/0	0/5	10/8
1974	11/11	10/17	13/13	0/0	0/0	25/5	9/8
1977	17/14	10/25	33/14	11/11	0/0	0/21	12/18
1980	10/13	11/10	33/17	0/0	0/0	40/7	12/9
1983	16/17	11/11	40/36	25/18	0/12	0/11	16/16
1986	9/12	11/17	20/32	14/12	0/12	0/25	10/22
1989	13/20	30/28	50/28	33/18	0/18	0/26	24/25
1992	5/15	20/20	0/28	25/24	0/18	17/19	12/20
1995	20/21	33/28	40/24	22/23	—	33/32	26/25
1998	18/10	50/41	25/36	14/28	25/24	0/19	20/24

Sources: Asahi Shimbun, 1992–1995; *Asahi Shimbun Senkyo Hombu,* 1990; Darcy and Nixon, 1996. p. 6; Ogai, 1995, pp. 42–45; *Senkyo,* 1983–1995; *Sanshū Ryōin Meikan,* 1990.

Notes: a. For elections before 1955, the antecedents of the LDP are counted as LDP. Similarly, in 1995, the numbers for the New Frontier Party are listed under the Clean Government Party; and in 1998, the numbers for the Democratic Party are listed under the Democratic Socialist Party.

  b. All numbers are percentages.

Socialists have a well-earned reputation of being favorable to women candidates, the LDP has run a substantial number of women candidates, at least in this national constituency. The findings concerning the Communist Party are somewhat surprising. Despite the high number of women candidates that the Communists run now, until 1968 they had never run a woman candidate in the national constituency. Similarly, the Democratic Socialists began running women candidates only in 1983 and have never placed a woman in a high enough position to win a seat. New parties, such as the New Frontier and Democratic Parties, run a greater percentage of successful women candidates than does the LDP. Perhaps women candidates help these parties in their efforts to create images as new, reform-minded alternatives to the LDP.

There is little direct evidence of a strong contagion or copying effect (Darcy, Welch, and Clark, 1994: 153). For example, the number of LDP women winners did not rise appreciably during the 1989 election when the Socialists ran so many more women, despite newspaper reports that both the LDP and the Democratic Socialists were moving women up on their PR lists in response to the Socialist strategy. These moves caused consternation within the LDP by representatives of organized groups that were displaced by the higher placement of nonorganizationally affiliated women (*Nihon Keizai Shimbun,* 1989). At other times, parties have dramatically increased the representation of women on their lists, but these changes also seem to have been made independently without reference to other political parties. The Communists began running women in 1968; and the Clean Government Party increased its representation of women in 1983 from one slot every other election to one or two slots every election.

Though there is no evidence of a significant contagion effect in the short term, Japanese parties have been increasing the number of safe slots given to women candidates. This trend is perhaps best shown by the newer parties and their solicitude toward women candidates. In this manner, the actions of one party may affect the actions of other parties in the long term. Gradual advances by women on proportional representation lists may have created a stronger and stronger imperative of first including women on such lists and then increasing the number of women on them.

THE NEW HOUSE OF REPRESENTATIVES ELECTORAL SYSTEM

In 1994, the Diet changed the House of Representatives electoral system to a mixed system. Two hundred seats are elected by D'hondt-style proportional representation with a strict party list from eleven regional constituencies. The remaining 300 seats are elected from single-member districts. There are two separate ballots, one for a party and one for a candidate; and the two apportionment schemes are not linked. Therefore, the 500 total seats are not apportioned proportionately to the parties; only 200 seats are apportioned proportionately. The proportional representation constituencies and single-member districts are linked, though, in that candidates may run both in a single-member district and on the party list for their region. The first election under this system was held in November 1996.

Because the system is a mixed system, the effects of the new system on women's representation will probably also be mixed. In theory, the new single-member districts should reduce opportunities for women candidates. Conversely, party lists for proportional representation should present favorable opportunities for women. However, other significant changes have occurred in campaign practices, campaign funding, and party structures. Cultural attitudes also seem to be changing. Each of these changes also affects women's electoral chances for the new House of Representatives.

The performance of woman candidates under this new system more closely mirrors that of the other minority group candidates than it did under the former system. More women are being elected to the lower house because of the proportional representation lists. In 1996, twenty-three of 500 representatives elected were women. This represents 4.6 percent, the highest percentage of women elected to the lower house since the first postwar election, with seven of 300 women elected in the single-member districts (2.3 percent) and sixteen of 200 women elected in the proportional representation districts (8 percent). The single-member districts are electing approximately the same percentage of women as the former multimember districts did, even with conservatives (who typically run fewer female candidates) winning a larger share of seats than they did under the multimember district system. The 8 percent of the proportional representation seats won by women is a definite increase over the former electoral system, but it still lags far behind the 10 to 25 percent elected on the proportional representation lists for the House of Councillors.

Table 2.2 presents the data on women representatives and candidates broken down by political party. The data show a continuity with trends manifested in the House of Councillors data. The much shrunken Socialist Party and the growing Communist Party continue their strong support of women candidates. The brand-new Democratic Party and the New Frontier Party continue the trend of newer parties, sponsoring a larger share of women candidates than

Table 2.2   Women's Performance in the 1996 Election for
House of Representatives

Party	Total Winners	Winners on PR Lists	Winners from Districts	All Candidates
LDP	4 women, 1.7%	2 women, 2.9%	2 women, 1.2%	2.8% women
New Frontier	8 women, 5.1%	5 women, 8.3%	3 women, 3.1%	4.4% women
Democrats	3 women, 5.8%	3 women, 8.6%	None	6.1% women
Communists	4 women, 15.4%	4 women, 16.7%	None	20.6% women
Socialists	3 women, 20.0%	2 women, 18.2%	1 woman, 25.0%	16.7% women
Minor and Independents	1 women, 8.3%	None	1 woman, 8.3%	7.5% women

Sources: Asahi Shimbun, 1992–1995; *Asahi Shimbun Senkyo Hombu,* 1990; Darcy and Nixon, 1996, p. 6; Ogai, 1995, pp. 42–45; *Senkyo,* 1983–1995; *Sanshū Ryōin Meikan,* 1990.

Note: All percentage figures represent percentage of total winners or candidates in a specific category.

does the LDP. The New Frontier Party inherited the stronger support of women candidates that was characteristic of the Clean Government Party, one of its founding parties. The Democrats, similarly, partially inherited the Socialist tradition of supporting women candidates.

These data underscore again (1) the influence of electoral systems on the representation of women and (2) stable party differences in the sponsorship of women candidates. However, the data also raise additional questions that a further inquiry into the electoral institutions can help answer. First, why is proportional representation in the House of Representatives less effective at electing women than its equivalent in the House of Councillors? A partial answer lies in the practice of double-listing candidates in House of Representatives races, a practice that does not occur in the House of Councillors. Many of the people elected on the proportional representation list for the 1996 election were also running in the single-member districts. Although they lost their single-member district races, they were still elected to the House of Representatives because of their placement on a party proportional representation list. The more of these double-listed candidates, the more the party list becomes a simple copy of the party's slate of candidates running in the single-member districts. Eighty-four of the 200 winners from party lists simultaneously ran in the districts. Of these 84, 5 (5.9 percent) were women. In contrast, 11 of the 116 (9.5 percent) non-double-listed party list winners were women. The contrast is not as stark as perhaps expected, but of the 5 double-listed women victors, 4 of them were from the Communist Party; and 3 of these 4 were incumbents or past incumbents. If the Communist Party is excluded from the totals, only 1 of 69 (1.5 percent) double-listed victors was a woman.

A second question arises concerning whether parties differ in their support of women candidates and, if so, what factors might influence these differences. In particular, based on cross-national patterns, it might be expected that the conservative LDP would have fewer women parliamentarians than parties of the left. Given the importance of double listing for explaining the total number of women elected, this factor should also be helpful in explaining differences in the representation of women between parties; and, indeed, this appears to be the case. If a party has more double listing, there will be fewer opportunities for women candidates on party lists. The New Frontier Party double-listed only 3.3 percent of the winners from its party list. In contrast, 45.7 percent of the LDP and 71.4 percent of the Democratic victors were double-listed. The New Frontier Party eschewed double listing out of a fear that double-listed candidates would work less hard in their district campaigns. Party strategists also feared that supporters of rival candidates in the same district would collude if one candidate were double-listed in a safe party list position. If one candidate were guaranteed election, it was feared that her or his marginal supporters would switch and support the opponent in order to also ensure their candidate's election. In effect, the district could send two representatives to the Diet instead of one. To prevent such collusive deals and to encourage energetic campaign races, the New Frontier Party generally did not double-list candidates on its party list. This policy helps explain the higher number of successful women candidates on the New Frontier Party list, but this explanation fails to explain the high numbers of women victors on the Democratic Party list.

The number of women incumbents coming into an election and the number of slots available for new candidates should also affect the chances for electing more women (Darcy, Welch, and Clark, 1994). What do the party-specific data in Table 2.3 tell us about these factors? The data on slots available for new candidates suggest a partial explanation for the lower percentage of successful women candidates from the LDP. The LDP recruited a smaller percentage of new candidates for the 1996 election than did either of the two other major parties, and women fared better overall in the cohort of new candidates. In 1996, 115 of the 500 elected were "new" candidates. Of this 115, twelve (10.4 percent) were women. Of the 385 incumbents or former incumbents, eleven (2.9 percent) were women. By percentage, the LDP had fewer new candidates. Consequently, this accounts

Table 2.3   New Member Victories in House of Representatives
              by Party

Party	Percentage of "New" Victors in Total House	Percentage of "New" Victors in Single-Member Districts	Percentage of "New" Victors on Party Lists
LDP	20.5	18.9	24.3
New Frontier	23.1	20.1	26.7
Democrats	32.7	23.5	37.1

Sources: Asahi Shimbun, 1992–1995; *Asahi Shimbun Senkyo Hombu,* 1990; Darcy and Nixon. 1996, p. 6; Ogai, 1995, pp. 42–45; *Senkyo,* 1983–1995; *Sanshū Ryōin Meikan,* 1990.

for some of the LDP deficit in the number of successful women candidates. However, the difference between the three major parties is not so substantial. The influence of other factors seems likely.

Another explanatory factor is the party affiliation of the women incumbents (and former incumbents) who were reelected in 1996. The New Frontier Party had five of the eleven incumbents, and the Communists had three. Two were from the LDP, and the Socialists had one. Given that the New Frontier Party elected a total of eight women in 1996 and the LDP elected four, the fact that the New Frontier Party had three more women incumbents than the LDP is quite significant.

Analyzing all these factors together leads to the intriguing and tentative conclusion that the LDP is perhaps as amenable and supportive of women candidacies as any of Japan's other parties. The prime opportunity for women candidates should have been on party lists for slots that were not double listed and were not occupied by incumbents or former incumbents. The LDP had only four victors who met all these criteria, and two of them were women. The New Frontier Party had fifteen victors who met these criteria, and three of them were women. The record of the Democrats is identical to that of the LDP. The Socialists had two such victors, and both of them were women.

A trend is neither created nor described by only two successful women candidates out of the 239 elected by the LDP. However, these numbers suggest that the relative deficiency of LDP women representatives is better explained by incumbency rates, patterns of double listing, and numbers of female incumbents than it is by an alleged conservative bias against women candidates. This bias certainly seems to have existed in the past; whether it has ended or is continuing can only be seen in subsequent Japanese elections.

INSTITUTIONS AND THE
REPRESENTATION OF WOMEN IN JAPAN

Japan provides an exciting test case of several propositions with regard to the representation of women and minority groups. In the two houses of the Japanese Diet, no less than seven different electoral systems have been used since 1945. This variety of electoral systems provides a fertile testing ground for theories of representation and electoral systems developed elsewhere. For example, the impact of open or closed party lists (in proportional representation races) on the representation of women can be assessed. In Japan, neither option produces an inherent advantage for women. However, there are significant differences among parties in how strongly they promote women's representation. It also appears, at least in the short term, that one party's action in increasing the number of women candidates does not lead to other parties following suit in subsequent elections. In concordance with findings in other countries, incumbency rates and candidate pools greatly influence the advancement of women into the ranks of politicians. Similarly, the parties of the left in Japan tend to be more supportive of women candidates; however, in the 1996 elections, there were some indications that the conservative LDP had become more amenable to sponsoring women candidates.

In more theoretical terms, the Japanese example provides convincing evidence of the importance of institutional factors in explaining variations in women or minority group representation rates. The best explanation of the low numbers of women in Japan's House of Representatives is not the low status of women in the Japanese culture, nor is it simply the electoral institution. This anomalous low representation is better explained by considering campaign regulations in Japan. These regulations make organizational support crucial for a successful election campaign. As a result, women, who generally lack such organizational support, win few seats. In contrast, organized minorities, such as religious groups or labor unions, are able to elect their proportional share of seats. If bias or the electoral system alone explained this anomaly, these factors should similarly depress the representation of disliked minority or religious groups. These groups, however, have ample representation, suggesting the importance of organizations in these elections.

Questions remain about long-term trends in the representation of women under this new electoral system. I have shown that Japan's multimember districts were hostile to women candidates because of the heightened importance of organizational strength under the new system. However, this system has not only changed district magni-

tudes but has also changed some of the electoral rules that will perhaps make organizations less important in future elections. The
results of the first election cannot adequately illustrate this more
gradual change in campaign practices; thus, the following discussion
is somewhat speculative.

Under the new election system, political parties are now able to
run relatively unfettered media campaigns for the proportional representation races. Campaign regulations and internal norms of equality have at least for now precluded the possibility that party media
campaigns will be exploited by running candidate-centered media
campaigns under party sponsorship. However, the influence of an
effective party media campaign on district races is significant, and
many campaign operatives expect it to grow in significance over time.
Especially in urban areas where there are more voters who are not
linked to any politically relevant organization, the party media campaign might be the deciding variable in a district election. If this
occurs, there will be less need to select district candidates based on
the strength of their personal support organizations or other organizational support. If such nonorganizationally affiliated candidates
come to be viable, at least in urban areas, candidates will be drawn
more from other pools of potential candidates. These other pools,
such as talent candidates, are likely to have a greater proportion of
women.

Finally, recent elections give some anecdotal evidence that attitudes toward women candidates are changing. It is becoming more
acceptable, for instance, for women to follow their father into a
career in politics. In 1993, Tanaka Kakuei's daughter Makiko was
elected as an independent in her father's old district of Niigata 3. She
easily won reelection in 1996 on the LDP slate, winning the new
Niigata 5 district. She is joined by the daughter of the sitting governor
of Saitama prefecture. Governor Tsuchiya's daughter ran as an independent, and she also won her race with ease. These two examples
are not the first time that women relatives of powerful male politicians have won elections in Japan, but the context is now different in
that the women seem to be running on their own merits. The recent
cases are noteworthy because they evidence a possible shift in attitudes toward acceptance of women heirs of political organizations. It
is, however, too early to tell, because even in these two instances the
women are not inheriting an organization but rather capitalizing on
name recognition alone. It remains to be seen whether the next step
of actually passing on kōenkai to women heirs will occur, but if it
does, it will represent a crucial breakthrough of women into an
important pool from which candidates are drawn.

3

Electoral Reform and Women's Empowerment: Taiwan and South Korea

ROSE J. LEE

Democratization has the potential to promote women's empowerment in highly patriarchal societies. Thus, the "third wave of democratization" that swept over much of the Third World during the 1980s and 1990s should be of major interest to those concerned with advancing the status of women. Yet, for a variety of reasons, the recent literature on democratization has been remarkably silent on women's issues (Waylen, 1994). In fact, Latin American feminists have become quite disillusioned with the consequences of democratization in that region. Despite the leading role that women and feminist groups played in the movements to oust the previous authoritarian regimes, politics in most Latin American countries quickly returned to the male-dominated status quo following the democratic transitions (Alvarez, 1990; Jaquette, 1994; Molyneux, 1985; Waylen, 1994).

The new wave of democratization that swept Latin America equally affected East Asia. Unfortunately, the literature on democratization in East Asian countries also overlooks the role of women in democratic transitions and remains uninterested in the consequences of democratic consolidations for women's political empowerment. Asian feminists are yet to follow Latin American feminists in analyzing how democratization has affected the political power of women. This gap in the literature is rather surprising, because women in Asian countries not only participated in the democratic transitions there but are also demanding their increased participation in the political arena, which they regard as their democratic right (Lee, 1995a). This chapter examines the degree of women's empowerment in two East Asian countries (South Korea and Taiwan) following their democratic transitions by considering the degree of women's representation in the national and local legislative bodies of the two countries.

RESEARCH EXPECTATIONS

South Korea and Taiwan are quite similar in many important ways. Both have strongly patriarchal Confucian cultures, postwar histories of authoritarian rule by conservative U.S. client states, extremely dynamic economies, and democratic transitions in the late 1980s (Amsden, 1989; Clark, 1989; Gold, 1986; Hahm and Plein, 1997; Pye, 1985; Woo, 1991). Yet, they differ dramatically in the key area of women's representation. One has the very low representation of women in the national and local legislative assemblies that is unfortunately typical of much of Confucian East Asia. The other has made dramatic progress in increasing women's share of seats to a level of 15 to 20 percent, which is quite impressive by the standards of developing nations—and, until recently, even developed countries.

Given the cultural similarity between the two countries, one might assume that patriarchal biases against women entering politics would also be roughly the same. Two other factors would appear relevant for explaining the large differences in women's representation between them. One is the nature of the electoral system, and the other is the level of democratization at any particular time.

Comparative research on electoral systems has yielded consistent findings that the type of electoral system is the most powerful determinant of the level of women's representation in democratic polities (Darcy, Welch, and Clark, 1994; Matland, 1994; Norris, 1985; Norris and Lovenduski, 1990; Rule, 1981, 1987, 1994). In particular, three types of electoral systems have been found to help women overcome the barriers they face as political candidates. Proportional representation (PR), which has been widely adopted in Europe, emerges as the leading electoral system promoting the election of women. PR's favorable disposition toward the election of women is due to the electoral system's tendency to lower the direct and indirect barriers to women's running for office. Under the system, the power of slating candidates is concentrated in the national party leadership, which enables women to overcome their low political resources and voter discrimination. Likewise, women fare better in large multimember districts. Finally, quota systems that ensure women a minimum level of representation guarantee women some access to participation in the decisionmaking elites.

The second explanatory factor of democratization might also be expected to promote better representation for women. Democratization should enhance women's political participation by activating civil society—that is, by strengthening the activities and demands of voluntary associations. Women's groups, in particular, can use the freedom to organize to create strong associations that are well positioned to demand their place in the political system. The new democratic government is likely to respond to the demands of women's groups, including greater political representation of women, because of the need to court women voters during elections.

SOUTH KOREA: A BLEAK HISTORY OF NEAR EXCLUSION

Korean women have run for and won election to South Korea's legislature, the National Assembly, throughout the postwar era. However, as Table 3.1 shows, their success has been limited, and neither democratization nor supposedly favorable electoral changes have been effective in increasing their representation much past the 2 to 3 percent level. Thus, South Korea's record on women's representation appears to be just as doleful as that of Japan's House of Representatives (see Chapter 2).

The elections for the first five National Assemblies (1948 to 1960) occurred in a fairly democratic polity under the presidency of Syngman Rhee. The elections themselves were conducted on a

Table 3.1   Korea: Women in the National Assembly

National Assembly	Number of Women Candidates		Percentage of Women Candidates		Number of Women Winners		Percentage of Women Winners	
1 (1948)	22		2.3		1		0.5	
2 (1950)	11		0.5		2		1.0	
3 (1954)	10		0.8		1		0.5	
4 (1958)	5		0.6		3		1.0	
5 (1960)	8		0.5		1		0.4	
6 (1963)	7	(4)	0.7	(0.5)	2	(1)	1.1	(0.8)
7 (1967)	8	(4)	1.0	(0.6)	3	(1)	1.7	(0.8)
8 (1971)	8	(2)	1.1	(0.3)	5	(0)	2.5	(0)
9 (1973)	10	(2)	2.4	(0.6)	10	(2)	4.6	(1.4)
10 (1978)	11	(4)	2.0	(0.8)	8	(1)	3.5	(0.6)
11 (1981)	25	(10)	2.9	(1.6)	8	(1)	2.9	(0.5)
12 (1985)	16	(7)	2.6	(1.6)	8	(2)	2.9	(1.1)
13 (1988)	27	(14)	2.2	(1.3)	6	(0)	2.0	(0)
14 (1992)	35	(19)	2.9	(1.8)	3	(0)	1.0	(0)
15 (1996)	37	(22)	1.2	(1.5)	9	(2)	3.0	(0.9)
Total	240	(88)	1.6	(1.0)	70	(10)	1.9	(0.5)

Sources: National Assembly, 1997; Shin, 1990, p. 26; Song, 1986, p. 240.
Note: Figures in parentheses indicate the number of women who ran or were elected from single-member districts.

winner-take-all basis from single-member districts, which—especially in a developing country with a strongly patriarchal culture—would be expected to create a disadvantageous context for women candidates. Unfortunately, these expectations turned out to be well founded. In the first national legislative election of 1948, for example, there were twenty-two women out of a total of 948 candidates (2.3 percent) running for the National Assembly; and one woman was elected to the 200 seats, creating a pitiful representation ratio of 0.5 percent. The next four elections were hardly any better for women. In these four elections, women never again constituted even 1 percent of the candidates, whereas their high points of representation were 1 percent of the seats in 1950 and 1958.

Following a coup in 1961, more than two decades of military rule ensued, although an elective National Assembly was permitted. Its electoral system changed, however, to an exotic scheme that combined proportional representation with district elections (in a manner that was presumed to work to the advantage of the ruling party). Because of the PR aspects of the system, party leaders' discretionary power, particularly that of the ruling party leader, could be used to recruit additional women for party slates. The military-turned-civilian regime, which lasted from the sixth through the twelfth National Assembly elections (1963 to 1985), in fact saw a noticeable increase in women's representation—from 1.1 percent in 1963 to 1.7 percent in 1967 to 2.5 percent in 1971 to an average of 3.5 percent for the 1973 to 1985 elections. The data in Table 3.1 also indicate that all of this increase in the number of women legislators resulted from their being included in the party slates subject to PR apportionment. In terms of district elections, women candidates increased marginally from less than 1 percent to about 1.5 percent of the total, but women's share of the elected winners remained at the very low share of the earlier period (slightly over 0.5 percent).

There have been three National Assembly elections (1988, 1992, 1996) since South Korea's return to democracy. The electoral system itself was modified somewhat but continued to contain a combination of district and PR voting. The results of these elections for women have been disappointing in a number of ways. First, democratization certainly did not bring the increase in women's candidacies that might have been expected. In fact, just the reverse occurred. Women's share of the total candidates fell by more than a half, from 2.6 percent in 1985 (the last election under the military regime) to 1.2 percent in 1996. Moreover, almost all of this decline occurred in the party slates, because the percentage of district candidates stayed constant. Here then, there seems to be a parallel to the Latin

American case, in which democratization brought a return to male-dominated party politics.

Second, democratization did not bring increased representation of women in the National Assembly, although the latest elections in 1996 were at least a little promising. Given the much greater success of women on the PR slates than in districts, the drop in the number of women candidates being slated could have resulted in a decimation of the already very low representation of women in the Korean legislature. Indeed, this seemed to be occurring when women's representation dropped by nearly two-thirds, from 2.9 percent to 1.0 percent between 1985 and 1992. In 1996, however, women's representation recovered to 3 percent. Although no women had been elected from districts in the first two elections under democracy, there were two winners in 1996 (0.9 percent of the total). Moreover, while women's share of the names on the PR slates went down, their positions obviously went up significantly, as the number of women winning in the PR part of the election tripled from 3 to 9.

Democratization also brought a reinstitutionalization of elected local government bodies at the county and provincial levels (the military government had abolished "home rule" to augment its centralized powers). This return to local self-government made women's groups hopeful about making substantial inroads into politics, as they felt that local governments were closer to them and their experiences (see Chapter 6 for a critical review of these feelings). Moreover, women felt that they might be more competitive in these nonpartisan elections, and the poor showing of women candidates in the 1988 National Assembly elections provided an added motivation to work harder. As the first elections for local government approached in 1991, therefore, women's groups and research organizations trained women candidates to run electoral campaigns.

As Table 3.2 demonstrates, however, the electoral results at both county and province levels in 1991 disappointed women and their sympathizers. At the county level, 40 of the 122 women who ran were elected; women constituted 1.2 percent of all candidates and 0.9 percent of all elected. At the provincial level, 8 of 63 women who ran were elected, amounting to 2.2 percent of all candidates and 0.9 percent of all elected. Four years later, the data for women were slightly (but only slightly) better. The number of women running for county-level seats almost doubled to 206, although the number of women running in provincial elections dropped by a third. In both sets of elections, women fared slightly better, winning about 1.5 percent of the seats, compared to just under 1 percent in the first set of local elections. Still, women's representation at the provincial and county

Table 3.2   Korea: Women in the Local Legislatures

		Number of Women Candidates	Percentage of Women Candidates	Number of Women Winners	Percentage of Women Winners
1991	County	122	1.2	40	0.9
	Province	63	2.2	8	0.9
1995	County	206	NA	71	1.6
	Province	40	NA	13	1.4
	Total	431	—	132	1.2

Sources: Chosun Daily, 1991, p. 26; *Kyung Hyang Daily,* 1991, p. 23; Korean Women and Politics Institute, 1995; *Women,* 1991, p. 43.
Note: NA indicates that figures were not available.

levels remains, if anything, slightly behind their success rate in the National Assembly, exactly the reverse of what most feminists and women's groups had expected.

Overall, therefore, if a pattern exists for women's legislative participation in Korea, it is an unimpressive sideways, not forward, movement. A range exists: the proportion of women candidates and members varies from one election to another, from less than 1 percent to between 3 percent and 4 percent. Throughout the postwar period, women in the national legislature has remained below 5 percent and on average at less than 2 percent, placing Korean women's representation among one of the lowest in the world (Sivard, 1985: 35–37).

TAIWAN: QUOTAS DRIVE
UP WOMEN'S REPRESENTATION

The situation concerning women's representation in Taiwan is quite different from that in Korea, and much more positive. Women's representation is much more advanced, now falling in the 15 to 20 percent range. Throughout the postwar era, women have held approximately 10 percent or more of the seats in all of Taiwan's legislative bodies, and this percentage has grown gradually and cumulatively over time. Thus, Taiwan stands in stark contrast to Korea in the sense that women have received significant legislative representation for a considerable length of time and, if anything, appear to be expanding it.

There are two reasons for this comparatively good performance. First, although its impact was undoubtedly marginal until recently,

Taiwan has multimember districts, some fairly large; and voters can vote for only one candidate, using a single, nontransferable vote, or SNTV (Chou, Clark, and Clark, 1990). Such a system allows candidates to win with a fairly small number of total votes, which should help women and minority groups (Darcy, Welch, and Clark, 1994). By far the most important reason for the level of women's representation, though, is the provision in the 1946 Constitution that "reserves" about 10 percent of legislative seats for women. For example, if one seat is reserved for women in a multimember district with eight positions, the woman candidate receiving the most votes wins a seat even if she finishes ninth or lower. This quota system, hence, forced women to be included in parliamentary bodies (Chou, Clark, and Clark, 1990).

Table 3.3 contains the electoral data for Taiwan's two national-level bodies: the Legislative Yuan (which serves as the parliament) and the National Assembly (which has to approve constitutional changes and which, before 1996, served as the electoral college in presidential elections). For both these bodies, elections were not held until 1969 because of the government's claim to represent all China

Table 3.3   Taiwan: Women in the National Legislatures

Year	Number of Women Candidates	Percentage of Women Candidates	Number of Seats in Women's Quota	Number of Women Winners	Percentage of Women Winners
		National Assembly			
1969	2	6.9	2	2	13.3
1972	10	12.8	5	8	15.1
1980	17	9.2	7	12	15.8
1986	25	14.8	8	16	19.0
1996	103	17.0	NA	61	18.0
		Legislative Yuan			
1969	4	16.0	0	1	9.1
1972	6	10.9	3	4	11.1
1975	4	6.6	3	4	10.8
1980	17	7.8	5	7	10.0
1983	22	12.9	5	8	11.3
1986	12	8.8	6	8	8.0
1989	26	8.7	7	13	12.9
1992	36	10.0	NA	17	11.0
1995	39	12.0	NA	13	14.0

Sources: Chou, Clark, and Clark, 1990, pp. 90–92; Women's Department, 1995.
Note: NA indicates that figures were not available.

(so that the members elected in the mainland in the late 1940s kept their seats). Beginning in 1969, "supplemental elections" for the National Assembly and Legislative Yuan were held regularly to increase the Taiwanese representation, but the full bodies were not reelected until the early 1990s (Clark, 1989). Tables 3.4 and 3.5 present similar data for the various local government assemblies in Taiwan: the Provincial Assembly, the Assemblies of Taipei and Kaohsiung after they were given "provincial" status, and the aggregate of all county and city assemblies and of all township and village councils.

The pattern for all these legislative bodies is quite similar and

Table 3.4   Taiwan: Women in Province-Level Legislatures

Year	Number of Women Candidates	Percentage of Women Candidates	Number of Seats in Women's Quota	Number of Women Winners	Percentage of Women Winners
		Provincial Assembly			
1951	12	8.6	5	5	9.0
1954	18	16.4	6	6	10.5
1957	22	18.6	9	9	13.6
1960	18	14.3	9	10	13.7
1963	14	10.2	9	10	13.5
1968	19	14.7	10	11	15.5
1972	21	17.4	10	12	16.4
1977	23	18.4	10	13	16.9
1981	34	17.1	9	10	13.0
1985	28	17.7	9	13	16.9
1989	30	19.1	9	14	18.2
1994	32	18.0	NA	16	20.0
		Taipei City Council			
1969	8	10.4	4	7	14.6
1973	8	12.7	4	7	14.3
1977	8	13.1	5	8	15.7
1981	11	13.3	5	7	13.7
1985	10	13.5	5	9	17.6
1989	24	24.0	6	10	19.6
1994	29	20.0	NA	12	23.0
		Kaohsiung City Council			
1981	15	18.5	5	6	14.3
1985	13	18.3	5	6	14.3
1989	14	14.9	5	6	14.0
1994	16	12.0	NA	6	14.0

Sources: Chou, Clark, and Clark, 1990, pp. 90–92; Women's Department, 1995.
Note: NA indicates that figures were not available.

Table 3.5   Taiwan: Women in Local Legislatures

Year	Number of Women Candidates	Percentage of Women Candidates	Number of Seats in Women's Quota	Number of Women Winners	Percentage of Women Winners
		City/County Assemblies			
1950	116	6.3	70	69	8.5
1952	224	12.1	74	74	8.6
1954	142	9.0	94	94	10.1
1958	168	10.4	102	101	9.9
1961	162	9.9	91	95	10.2
1964	230	14.7	108	123	13.6
1968	208	16.5	100	123	14.5
1973	206	13.9	99	119	14.0
1977	190	14.9	93	121	14.1
1982	226	13.4	89	115	14.4
1986	209	14.2	97	127	15.2
1990	265	15.2	NA	128	15.2
1994	NA	NA	NA	128	15.0
		Township/Village Councils			
1952	NA	NA	None	11	0.2
1954	NA	NA	NA	550	8.6
1958	NA	NA	NA	629	9.2
1961	1068	12.0	NA	660	12.5
1964	668	7.8	NA	385	8.1
1968	736	9.5	NA	495	10.6
1973	516	9.3	NA	378	10.1
1977	878	13.5	NA	488	12.9
1982	878	13.1	397	490	13.2
1986	901	14.9	417	560	14.9

Sources: Chou, Clark, and Clark, 1990, pp. 90–92; Women's Department, 1995.
Note: NA indicates that figures were not available.

supports three conclusions. First, the impact of the reserved seats system appears quite marked. This can be seen when one looks at how women fared in the one set of elections held without a minimum number of seats being reserved for women candidates. These were the 1952 elections for township and village councils, in which women won just eleven seats or 0.2 percent of the total, lower than even the women's success rate for Korea's national legislature at the same time (see Table 3.1). However, a mere two years later, after the electoral reform had been brought down to this lowest level of elected office in Taiwan, women won 8.6 percent of the seats—a forty-three-fold increase in the representation ratio! This was surely no coincidence.

Second, because the quota system was clearly enforced, it provid-

ed an effective means for women to gain at least a modicum of representation in Taiwan's elected bodies. Dating from the early 1950s,
women won approximately 10 percent of the seats for the elective
bodies at that time (Provincial Assembly, city and county assemblies,
and village and township councils). A similar pattern emerged when
elections began for the Legislative Yuan and National Assembly in the
late 1960s and the Kaohsiung City Assembly in the early 1980s.
Moreover, when "provincial-level" elections were instituted in the late
1960s for Taipei City, the more urbane and liberal capital of Taiwan,
women actually came close to doubling their quota, winning seven
seats in comparison to a "reservation" of four.

The efficacy of the reserved seats system for ensuring women's
legislative representation might be something of a double-edged
sword, though. On the one hand, women constituted about a tenth of
these bodies. On the other hand, this is not a high level of representation; and, especially since independent legislative politics did not
really develop in Taiwan until the 1980s, the effectiveness of women
as representatives certainly might be questioned. In particular, given
that most won because of the special electoral arrangements, they
may well have been viewed much more as tokens than as political figures with their own clout.

It is this danger of women legislators being regarded as politically
irrelevant tokens that makes the third trend so important. This is that
women have come to win substantially more seats than their reserved
minimums in all but one of these assemblies (the Kaohsiung City
Council). This trend began in the early 1960s for city and county
assemblies and, probably, for township and village councils (although
data on the number of reserved seats in these elections have not been
available until recently). By the early 1970s, the trend toward increasing women's representation could also be seen in the National
Assembly, Provincial Assembly, and Taipei City Council; and women
began winning more than their reserved minimums in the Legislative
Yuan in the 1980s. If anything, this temporal pattern suggests something of a grassroots phenomenon that started at the lower levels of
government and now appears well entrenched in Taiwan's political
culture. By the mid-1990s, then, women held about 20 percent of the
seats in the National Assembly, Provincial Legislature, and Taipei City
Council; and they won 15 percent of the positions in the other four
bodies. Thus, women were clearly becoming independent political
actors in their own right, since at least some of the victors were beating out men in competitive elections (Chapter 4 discusses this topic
in much more detail).

QUOTAS AND THE LEGISLATIVE
REPRESENTATION OF WOMEN IN DEVELOPING NATIONS

The contrast between Taiwan and South Korea in terms of women's representation in legislative bodies is certainly striking. In Taiwan, women's representation is five times greater (and for some legislative bodies even more) than in Korea. But the differences are less stark in terms of democratization's effects; democratization seems to have had a noticeable, if far from overwhelming, positive impact on women's representation in Taiwan but has not yet produced any gains for women in South Korea. As was seen in the first section, women's representation at neither the national nor local level in South Korea has yet been able to surpass the 3 percent representation that existed in the last National Assembly (1985) elected under the authoritarian system. If the founding of the opposition Democratic Progressive Party (DPP) in 1986 is taken to mark the start of Taiwan's democratic transition, women's representation has improved in many of the island's legislative bodies since then: the National Assembly, 16 to 18 percent; the Legislative Yuan, 11 to 14 percent; the Provincial Assembly, 17 to 20 percent; and the Taipei City Council, 18 to 23 percent.

These strong differences in the level of women's representation between South Korea and Taiwan defy common expectations that similarities in culture, economic development, and certain political experiences, such as an authoritarian regime followed by democratization, might lay a foundation for a similar pattern of political empowerment for women. In seeking an answer to these unexpected participatory differences, we must turn to the electoral system to which feminist scholars have repeatedly called attention as a mechanism for ensuring more equitable representation for women. The data from races for Korea's National Assembly are consistent with previous findings that proportional representation (PR) systems should promote women's legislative candidacies. However, the overall level of women's representation in Korea remains so low that this effect, by itself, must be rated as marginal. This PR effect, incidentally, explains the paradoxical finding that women in Korea fared somewhat better under the authoritarian regime than after the democratic transition (unless the 1996 elections herald a new trend of expanding women's representation). This was the period when the PR system gave party leaderships, especially in the ruling party, considerable discretion over party nominations. An unprecedented number of women were placed on the at-large candidate list by the ruling party and were consequently elected. But because such practice was carried out on an ad hoc basis under the leader's "paternalism," it disappeared when the democratic transition occurred. Only a more institutionalized approach could have weathered the change in government and could have built on previous gains.

Therefore, the central factor underlying the findings presented here is the effectiveness of Taiwan's reserved seats system in promoting more equitable representation for women, even in a developing country with a highly patriarchal culture. Furthermore, the fact that women now win at least half again as many seats as are reserved for them in almost all of Taiwan's assemblies demonstrates that women can build upon the opportunities opened up by such a set of quotas to become legitimate and independent political actors in their own right. In contrast, the Korean government has yet to provide a permanent solution to deal with women's representation. In a male-dominated political system, a laissez-faire policy in fact condones existing barriers against women's political entry. The absence of such intervention explains Korean women's political predicament, because only through political intervention can these barriers be demolished.

These results should possess some broader implications about strategies for promoting women's empowerment in developing nations. One such strategy is to use "women-friendly" systems, such as proportional representation. Comparativists often view the proportional representation system as the solution to the underrepresentation of minority groups, including women's groups (Darcy, Welch, and Clark, 1994; Matland, 1994; Norris, 1985; Norris and Lovenduski, 1990; Rule, 1987, 1994). However, examples proffered in support of the proportional representation system tend to be drawn from Western democracies. Certainly, such countries under a proportional representation system send more women to the parliament than countries under single-member district and plurality voting. In Scandinavia, for example, women's parliamentary representation exceeds 30 percent, the highest of all nations.

However, the nations where PR has proved so successful are long-term democracies with highly industrialized societies. When social foundations for gender equality have been laid, removing political barriers by altering the electoral system becomes a nation's last act to give women fair representation. On the other hand, the proportional representation system may not be able to tear down the gender barriers as easily in a new democracy where the social change wrought by the industrial revolution is just beginning, as the very limited effects of PR in South Korea imply. Instead of a PR system, quotas such as those in Taiwan's reserved seats system seem more likely to be effective in developing democracies. Women in developing nations should not have to wait for long-term social and political change to occur before receiving more than the most marginal representation. Instead, a legislated minimum level of representation for women will provide support for aspiring political women and inspiration for initially unmotivated women to move into the political arena. In fact, several other countries (e.g., India and the Philippines) have recently enacted such quota systems for women in local government (Aguilar, 1997; Shrivastava, 1997), suggesting that this approach may be gaining in salience and popularity.

4

The Reserved Seats System
in Taiwan

JANET CLARK & CAL CLARK

As outlined in Chapter 1, the "third wave of democratization" (Huntington, 1991) did not prove especially auspicious for women in either Latin America or the former Soviet bloc. In the former, women took a leading role in the prodemocracy movements, but they were marginalized when party politics returned to its male-dominated normalcy following democratization. Moreover, the economic crisis facing the region pushed feminists' concerns with far-reaching social reform off the political agenda. In the former Soviet bloc following democratization, women's fairly high level of legislative representation plummeted; and the social welfare nets of the previous regimes were grievously cut. Moreover, democratization seemingly stimulated a resurgence of patriarchal norms and behaviors in civil society throughout both regions (Waylen, 1994).

This chapter presents a contrasting case study from East Asia, where democratization's consequences for women turned out somewhat better. Taiwan shared both similarities and differences with Latin America and the former Soviet bloc. This combination of factors resulted in neither the absolute loss of women's status that occurred in the former Soviet bloc nor the disappointment of "rising expectations" that occurred in Latin America. Rather, the number of women holding political office continued its gradual upward trend (see Chapter 3); and, more important, women officeholders have over time moved from being tokens essentially beholden to some other leader to being independent political actors in their own right. The first section compares Taiwan to Latin America and the former Soviet bloc in terms of how the country's democratic transition affected the political position of women. The other two sections then discuss women in the political opposition during democratization and women with more establishment positions.

WOMEN AND DEMOCRATIZATION
IN TAIWAN IN COMPARATIVE PERSPECTIVE

The authoritarian regime and the transition to a more democratic polity in Taiwan combined some elements of both the Latin American and former Soviet bloc experiences. As might be expected, this resulted in the position of women in Taiwan evolving somewhat differently from those in either of the other two regions. While they may not have gained appreciably from Taiwan's political reforms, neither have they suffered the "losses" that occurred in Latin America and the former Soviet bloc.

The authoritarian regime that ruled Taiwan during the postwar era was a strange amalgam of the Latin American and Soviet bloc types. On the one hand, like most of the authoritarian governments in Latin America, the government led by Chiang Kai-shek and, later, his son Chiang Ching-kuo was clearly right-wing and procapitalist; and Chinese culture is marked by strong patriarchal traditions. On the other hand, reflecting its revolutionary origins in the early twentieth century, the ruling Nationalist or Kuomintang Party (KMT) was organized (by Russian advisers to the original leader, Sun Yat-sen) along Leninist lines and, at least in theory, supported an egalitarian ideology, the Three Principles of the People (Clark, 1989).

The results for women in Taiwan politically were in between those for women in Eastern Europe/Soviet Union and Latin America (see Chapter 1 for a brief overview of how women fared in those democratic transitions). The 1946 constitution guaranteed women approximately 10 percent of the legislative seats at all levels of government, and from the late 1960s they generally won a somewhat higher share (12 percent to 20 percent). Thus, women's representation in Taiwan's assemblies fell about halfway between the high level of the Soviet bloc countries and the low one of Latin America (Chou, Clark, and Clark, 1990). Like the Soviet bloc, though, women were almost completely excluded from top-level executive positions in the government and the ruling party. In socioeconomic terms, women in Taiwan received universal education, like those in communist countries; and Taiwan's much more dynamic economy undoubtedly offered them more opportunities for social and economic advancement than existed in Eastern Europe and the Soviet Union.

Political reforms in Taiwan were much more gradual than in either Latin America or the Soviet bloc. In fact, democratization there can be seen as a three-stage process that was drawn out over a forty-year period (although the government remained fairly dictatorial until the final stage). During the first stage in the 1950s and 1960s when political power was concentrated in the hands of Mainlanders (i.e., the 15 percent of the population who had come to Taiwan with Chiang Kai-shek in 1949), local elections were permitted that involved strong competition among local factions and political groups, mostly within the framework of the ruling KMT. Political repression kept direct opposition to the regime at a minimum, but local elections created a valuable base for future reform: (1) electoral competition became legitimized and regularized; and (2) Islander (i.e., Chinese whose families had lived on Taiwan for at least several generations) political factions and groups were integrated into the lower levels of the regime (Clark, 1989).

The second stage might be termed the Chiang Ching-kuo reforms because they dated from his assumption of the premiership in 1971 and reflected a policy of gradual liberalization that included expanding the role of electoral politics, bringing more Islanders and educated technocrats into high-level positions, and (albeit with periodic crackdowns, such as the one after the Kaohsiung Incident in 1979) tolerating a more open opposition. This last was especially important because it permitted the formation of the human rights groups and social movements that began to exert significant pressure on the regime (Copper, 1988; Tien, 1989).

Finally, the regime entered the third stage of real democratization reforms with its acceptance in 1986 of the formation of a major opposition party, the Democratic Progressive Party, or DPP (before then the formation of new parties was illegal under the martial law that had been imposed at the time of the Chinese Civil War in the late 1940s, although non-KMT candidates could run as Independents). Subsequently, martial law was abolished; the "senior legislators" elected from mainland constituencies in the late 1940s, who had given the KMT a guaranteed majority in the Legislative Yuan and National Assembly, were forced to retire; and direct elections were instituted for the top executive positions, including the governor of Taiwan Province, the mayors of Taipei and Kaohsiung, and finally, in March 1996, the powerful president (Chu, 1992; Moody, 1992; Tien, 1989, 1996; Wu, 1995). Thus, Taiwan now qualifies as a democracy in the formal institutional sense that a majority of the population can select whatever government it chooses.

Taiwan, therefore, was something of a hybrid of the Latin American and Soviet bloc situations. While the regime type and its treatment of women was much closer to Eastern Europe than to Latin America (ironically so from an ideological perspective), the drawn-out nature of the transition and its primarily indigenous dynamics followed the Latin American pattern. In one respect, though, Taiwan was very different. Democratization occurred at a time of economic affluence rather than collapse. This undoubtedly contributed to a second fundamental difference. Unlike the Soviet bloc and Latin America, where democratization brought a fundamental change in regime, the Kuomintang was able to retain power in Taiwan, albeit in the face of increasingly stiff electoral competition.

Democratization in Taiwan, as noted above, combined elements of both the East European and Latin American patterns. Not surprisingly, therefore, both types of women's participation in politics appeared as well. As in the Soviet bloc, women held a significant number of positions in the government but did not assume top leadership roles among the reformists in the regime in promoting political liberalization. As in Latin America, they took much more visible leadership positions in several human rights groups and social movements, which generally were weakened once the democratization reforms succeeded. These combined effects, however, produced a much more salutary outcome than in either of the other two cases. Although women did not make dramatic gains during democratization and may have slipped a bit in their power within the opposition, political reform did not cost them their previous progress, as it did in Eastern Europe. Thus, a much better base exists for pursuing women's political and socioeconomic agendas in Taiwan than in either Latin America or the Soviet bloc.

WOMEN IN THE OPPOSITION

The role of women in the political opposition in Taiwan parallels the two key circumstances in the Latin American case. First, historical circumstances pushed women to the forefront of the opposition movement at a key moment when confrontation with the regime set off a process of profound political liberalization; and, second, the growth of normal party politics was seemingly associated with the reassertion of male leadership in the opposition. However, drawing this analogy is perhaps a little too pessimistic for Taiwan, because many of the women who entered politics by this route remained active as the reform period progressed.

Chiashu Campaigns:
From Powerlessness to Officeholding

To understand how this came about, it is necessary to trace the historical evolution of political opposition to the Kuomintang regime.

When the Chiang Kai-shek government arrived in Taiwan in 1949, it strongly repressed anyone suspected of supporting either the Chinese communists or Taiwanese nationalism, but it did tolerate a "democratic" opposition composed primarily of Mainlander intellectuals. When this democratic opposition tried to forge links with Islander politicians and form an opposition party in 1960, it too was repressed, and little open opposition was allowed throughout the 1960s. With the beginnings of political liberalization during the 1970s, though, a semiopposition (called the *tangwei,* or literally those outside the party) gradually emerged advocating greater democratization and, in a much more muted fashion, Taiwanese nationalism. Throughout most of the 1970s, the space for political dissent gradually opened. However, after violence erupted (for reasons that are still unclear) at a large demonstration in Kaohsiung in December 1979, the regime responded with the arrest and jailing of major opposition leaders, thus creating the opportunity for women to become symbolic leaders of the *tangwei* in the typical Latin American pattern (Clough, 1978; Cohen, 1988; Teng, 1991; Tien, 1989).

One important role played by women in the opposition culture was as *Shounan Chiashu,* or relatives of political prisoners (Teng, 1991). Women made this role famous as political activists and as candidates for public office. Motivated by first-hand experience of KMT suppression, the imprisonment of their husbands, and the confiscation of their property, they felt that they had nothing to lose by becoming candidates. The absence of men in the opposition leadership, following their arrests, gave these women a greater sense of responsibility for the movement. They viewed elections as symbolic and used electoral platforms as political forums to promote anger against the political persecution of the opposition by the KMT. Votes were solicited as an expression of sympathy for the jailed leaders and of solidarity against injustice. Chiashu campaigns, therefore, became channels for the expression of dissent. The 1980 election was a watershed event in the history of the opposition movement when two wives of Kaohsiung defendants (Chou Ch'ing-yu and Hsu Rung-shu) ran surprisingly successful campaigns (Teng, 1991). Initially, the first Chiashu campaigns were run more for moral or symbolic reasons than for gaining political power. According to Chou:

> We didn't have money, we didn't have power, the chance of winning was about 1 percent. . . . It was just for the meaning. I thought, as long as it is right I will do it. I don't care whether I'm elected, because in reality I don't know anything about elections. I didn't try to think of winning or not, just whether it had meaning or not, so I decided to run. . . . Farmers came up to me and said, "This is unfair,

this is injustice, just stand up and let people know the real situation." I thought, this is right, I should let the facts be known. I wasn't
saying that I had great ability to do anything. It was just that I want-
ed to make some affairs clear, not let the people be fooled. This was
just a simple hope, that's how it started. (Teng, 1991: 31)

Despite her limited ambitions, Chou was easily elected, winning
the highest number of votes in her multimember district for the
National Assembly. Consequently, other wives of political prisoners
began to run Chiashu campaigns, in many cases winning office. This
election success of the wives of the arrested leaders was generally
viewed as reflecting a broad social reaction against political repression. Thus, these women used their public office to champion the
opposition "cause." The elected wives of the Kaohsiung defendants
maintained the push toward democracy through September 28, 1986,
when they helped establish the Democratic Progressive Party (Arrigo,
1994; Teng, 1991). Liberalization in the regime continued with the
government declaration of the end of martial law in July 1987. Thus,
male leaders of the opposition were released from jail and gained
control of the various factions that now make up the DPP. Although
women did not assume top leadership positions in the DPP or benefit
from their husbands' charisma, some of the Chiashu remained active
in politics, using their past accomplishments as springboards to
demonstrate their abilities. According to one of Chou's campaign
workers in the late 1980s,

The new *Chiashu* will not emphasize their pitiful aspect; they will
also emphasize that they are very strong even though they are
Chiashu. They also emphasize that they have ability in politics. . . .
Other than those few voters who will vote for you because of the
political battle, you must let other voters think you have the ability
to take on the role of a public official. (Teng, 1991: 38–39)

The Growing Role of
Social Movements and Feminist Groups

Another role played by women in the democratization of Taiwan was
as activists in "social movements," which have been seen as playing a
key role in Taiwan's democratization; because they focused on narrow
issues, the authoritarian regime was much more tolerant of them in
the 1970s and early 1980s than it was of the "political" opposition
(Hsiao, 1991). During the 1980s, various women's organizations were
formed. In 1986, for instance, Chen Hsiu-hui established the Home-
makers Union, which was concerned with the protection of the environment and a wide range of social issues. The growth in the number
and kind of women's organizations demonstrated concern not only

for the traditional women's issues of child care and hospital services but also for broader social goals. Women displayed an increased willingness to focus on shared substantive issues such as prostitution, pornography, and discrimination in the workplace. They also participated in protests related to nuclear development, pollution, police-protected prostitution, and aborigines' land struggles (Arrigo, 1994; D.W. Chen, 1994; Chiang and Ku, 1985; Farris, 1994).

In contrast to the numerous women's social organizations that existed on Taiwan, only one association, the Women's New Awakenings Foundation, openly promoted feminism and women's rights before the end of martial law in the late 1980s, even though women continued to suffer substantial handicaps. For example, despite the fact that the constitution proclaimed equality of the sexes, many laws discriminated against women—especially the marital property law, which prevented married women from developing economic independence. The feminist movement actually began fourteen years before the formation of the DPP. In 1972, Lu Hsiu-lien (Annette Lu), who had been exposed to American feminism during her studies in the United States, launched the Taiwan movement with a talk on International Women's Day. In the face of repression from the KMT, which viewed feminism as contrary to its women's policy aimed at preserving the patriarchal tradition, the foundation's journal, *New Awakenings,* had to struggle in its work to raise female consciousness, encourage self-development, and voice feminist opinion. The magazine was considered radical by many and failed to win a wide readership (Farris, 1994; Lu, 1994).

Fortunately, the 1990s proved to be more supportive of the feminist movement in Taiwan. As discussed in more detail in Chapter 9, democratization opened up space for more feminist groups and advocates, such as Josephine Ho. In particular, the diversity (as well as the number) of feminist groups increased to meet the needs of particular groups of women. For example, the Feminist Studies Association became quite active in academic life, the Warm Life association was formed by divorced women, and the Taipei Association for the Promotion of Women's Rights and a group called Pink Collar Solidarity support working women against the still prevalent patriarchal norms in Taiwan's economy and society (Farris, 1994; Ku, 1998).

WOMEN IN ESTABLISHMENT POLITICS

Superficially, the participation of Taiwan women in what might be termed "establishment" politics followed the Soviet bloc pattern. A progressive ideology stimulated the regime to guarantee women a significant share of legislative seats and medium-level government positions without really ceding them much effective power. Consequently, there were no women among the major reformist KMT leaders, who at one point or another were seen as pushing liberalization (including Chiang Ching-kuo, Lee Huan, Sun Yun-suan, Lee Teng-hui, and James Soong). Yet, in reality, the political positions of a significant number of women were much more autonomous and powerful than such a stereotype would imply.

A Surprising Success in Legislative Activities

One area of establishment politics women have entered into in significant numbers is Taiwan's elected assemblies, where the constitution guarantees them about 10 percent of the positions. This reserved seats system clearly helped women win office. For example, in the 1952 elections for township and village councils, which were held before the reserved seats requirement was instituted, women could win only eleven of 5,685 council seats, for a pathetic representation ratio of 0.2 percent. Only two years later, however, after the quota system was introduced, women won almost 9 percent of the seats on the township and village councils. It seems reasonable to assume that most of these victories were for reserved seats. At the county/city level, for instance, women never won more than their assigned minimum quota throughout the 1950s. At the national and provincial levels, moreover, the number of seats won by women did not exceed their minimum reservation significantly until the 1980s, except for the Taipei City Council and the National Assembly (Chou, Clark, and Clark, 1990).

However, as detailed in Chapter 3, women clearly became competitive in their own right over time, as evidenced by their winning significantly more than their minimum number of reserved seats. During the 1970s and 1980s, they consistently won between a fifth and a third more local council positions than they had been guaranteed. Women's ability to win more than their minimum quota was much slower to develop at the provincial and national levels, except for the Taipei City Assembly and National Assembly, where they have generally won a third or more than their minimum reserved seats. Finally, women were able to exceed their minimum quota by a significant extent by the mid- and late 1980s in Taiwan's other elective legislatures (particularly the Provincial Assembly and Legislative Yuan) as well (Chou, Clark, and Clark, 1990). Thus, women have clearly become independent actors in the sense that they win enough legislative races beyond their reserved minimums to demonstrate that they are viable candidates in their own right. However, since the late 1980s, their share of the seats in most assemblies has grown only marginally, and proposed constitutional changes that would create primarily single-seat districts might well result in a significant setback.

The reserved seat system, therefore, has clearly been beneficial for promoting women's political representation in the Republic of China. Because of the quota for women, the proportion of women serving in Taiwan's assemblies is quite high in comparative terms, especially in light of the island's patriarchal society and development level. Furthermore, women politicians have evidently built upon their ensured representation to increasingly transform themselves from mere tokens, elected because of the quota, to competitive candidates who win significantly more than their reserved minimum. While assemblywomen fall far short of providing equal representation for their gender, it cannot be denied that they have made more than modest progress.

Gaining entrance to a legislature, of course, does not necessarily mean that women will be effective in participating in legislative affairs or in pursuing their policy objectives. This is especially true for Taiwan, where the patriarchal Confucian culture and the way in which the reserved seats system has served to recruit women parliamentarians might well result in women officeholders acting and being treated as second-class tokens. Surprisingly perhaps, this was not the case by even the mid-1980s. Table 4.1 compares matched samples of approximately forty women and men in Taiwan's major assemblies in 1985 (Chou, Clark, and Clark, 1990).

In many ways this table demonstrates a very surprising equality between male and female legislators in Taiwan. On a psychological basis, women differed little from men in terms of their self-confidence. This psychological equality, furthermore, carried over into involvement in nonpolitical groups, which can be helpful to a politician's career. The data are more ambiguous concerning whether assemblymen held an advantage over women parliamentarians in terms of political experience. On the one hand, there was no difference at all between the sexes in terms of elective legislative experience, indicating that Taiwan's assemblywomen must have electoral career patterns surprisingly similar to those of their male competitors. On the other hand, men ranked moderately but significantly above women on the other three dimensions concerning appointive and party experience. This suggests that cumulatively assemblymen could have a considerable advantage in political contacts and resources and might confirm that party leaders may well be biased against women.

Table 4.1   Political Activities by Gender, 1985

	Assemblywomen (%)	Assemblymen (%)
Self-confidence		
Own qualifications are above average	67	72
Women are as qualified officials as men	95	74
Women make important political contribution	97	63
Group member		
Political	77	42
Religious	44	49
Civic	54	56
Professional	28	35
Leisure	23	30
Two or more types	72	63
Political experience		
Substantial electoral officeholding	77	77
Substantial appointive officeholding	10	16
Substantial party officeholding	33	42
Party training for Assembly	15	28
Assembly activeness		
Work 50+ hours per week	59	49
Held two committee chairs	41	44
Sponsored 15 resolutions/session	34	52
Success in Assembly		
Above average influence	54	51
Over 60% resolutions passed	46	35
Enjoy public office	85	56
No sense of accomplishment	56	40

Source: Chou, Clark, and Clark, 1990, pp. 127, 140, 150, 161, 173.

The potential disadvantage for women legislators implied by the political experience items does not appear to have materialized, however, because assemblywomen and assemblymen seem very similar in their approach to their legislative duties. In particular, with one notable exception, women parliamentarians did not differ significantly from their male colleagues in how active they were in performing their official duties and in how successful they seem to have been within their assemblies. The expectation that women would be less active and successful than men generally does not hold except for the much greater propensity of men to sponsor resolutions. There was almost no difference between women and men in having held two or more committee chairs, and women were somewhat more likely to devote more than fifty hours a week to their legislative work. Moreover, women even claimed to be slightly more successful within the assemblies than men in terms of possessing above-average influence and in terms of having a high success rate for their resolutions. For the results concerning the more indirect psychological indicators of success, the evidence is mixed. Assemblywomen were far more likely than their male colleagues to enjoy holding public office, but they were also considerably more apt to say that they did not gain any sense of accomplishment from their political careers. On most dimensions of legislative activity and success, therefore, there clearly was a surprising similarity between assemblymen and assemblywomen.

Furthermore, there is some evidence that women in Taiwan's legislatures pursued issues and agendas related to what have traditionally been considered women's issues. This can be seen in the data on legislative role orientations contained in Table 4.2. For example, women were almost twice as likely as men to have served on education and culture committees. They also pursued a distinctive style of representation. Assemblywomen were much more interested than their male colleagues in performing constituent service and, probably as a result, introduced many more resolutions concerning local development to help the citizens in their districts (Chou, Clark, and Clark, 1990, discuss this in much more detail). This is consistent with cross-national findings that women legislators emphasize personal service more than men, presumably because of their greater socialization into concern with human relations (Richardson and Freeman, 1995; Thomas, 1994).

Women's Limited Entrance into Executive Positions

Democratization has greatly expanded the role of legislatures in Taiwan's politics. Yet, many executive positions continue to hold more power and prestige than Assembly seats. In this area, women's entrance into "establishment politics" has been much slower. In fact, it was not until 1988 that a woman, Shirley W. Y. Kuo (an Islander), gained a cabinet position in the government (minister of finance) and membership on the KMT's Central Standing Committee, which includes the approximately thirty top party leaders. Kuo holds a Ph.D. in economics and followed a typical technocratic career, serving for a decade as vice-chair of the Council for Economic Planning and Development and as deputy governor of the Central Bank before becoming minister of finance. She also was politically well connected in that she married a higher-ranking KMT official, Nieh Wen-ya (a

Table 4.2   Legislative Role Orientations by Gender, 1985

	Assemblywomen (%)	Assemblymen (%)
Important roles for legislator		
Administrative oversight	69	65
Decisionmaking	64	49
Constituent service	92	70
Subordination to others	28	16
Resolutions introduced		
Many areas	23	37
Economic affairs	15	37
Public works	5	19
Local development	54	33
Education and culture	18	14
Elections, civil and human rights	13	15
Foreign affairs and defense	3	0
Committee assignments		
Economic affairs	62	61
Interior and civil affairs	44	26
Budget and local government	33	35
Education and culture	49	26
Legal and judicial	13	16
Foreign affairs and defense	15	9
Ethnic and overseas Chinese	5	5

Source: Chou, Clark, and Clark, 1990, p. 161.

Mainlander), who was the longtime president of the Legislative Yuan until his retirement in 1989. In 1989, Kuo became famous when, as minister of finance, she led the Taiwan delegation to an Asian Development Bank meeting in Beijing, thus becoming the first high-ranking Taiwan official to cross the Taiwan Strait (although neither Beijing nor Taipei considered this an official visit). Since then the number of women in the cabinet has gradually increased. Now there are six, including the minister of the interior; a minister without portfolio (Shirley Kuo); and the directors of the Council on Cultural Affairs, the Fair Trade Commission, the National Youth Commission, and the National Council on Physical Education and Sports ("Siew Cabinet Shuffle," 1999).

Similarly, women did not hold any executive positions at the county and city level until the mid-1980s. The first victories by two women in the twenty-one races for county magistrate (chief execu-

tive) and city mayor in 1985, though, showed their growing acceptance as local political leaders. Although women have generally not
had much success in winning elections for local executive positions,
Yu Chen Yueh-ying provides an interesting exception. Originally
recruited by her father-in-law, Yu Teng-fa (a powerful factional leader
in Kaohsiung), to run for a legislative seat, she became a valuable
resource in her own right. Her daughter subsequently pursued a
political career following exactly the same route. Well educated and
from a prominent local family, Yu Chen served two terms as magistrate of Kaohsiung County (the area surrounding Taiwan's second
largest city) and compiled an excellent record for providing social
services and responding to the public. Her record of diligent voter
service and efficient administration made her one of the most popular politicians in Taiwan. Thus, Yu Chen represents a good example of
a woman succeeding in establishment politics, ironically so since the
Yu political machine has always been in opposition to the KMT
regime; and Yu Chen came close to being elected chair of the DPP
(Teng, 1991).

THE SOCIAL AND POLITICAL INSTITUTIONAL
BASES OF WOMEN'S POLITICAL STATUS IN TAIWAN

Despite the similarities that Taiwan has to both Latin America and the
former Soviet bloc, the impact of democratization on the status of
women in Taiwan was considerably less doleful than in either of the
other cases. In terms of opposition politics, women in Taiwan fared
somewhat better than their counterparts in Latin America. Although
the creation of "normal" democratic and party politics in the late
1980s in Taiwan was associated with a diminution of the role of
women as top leaders in the opposition (i.e., the new Democratic
Progressive Party), several women who had established their political
careers during the "heroic days" of the human rights movement continued to be significant political figures. In terms of establishment
politics, women came out much better than in the former communist
countries because they did not suffer the devastating political losses
that occurred there. In combination, then, women fared far better
under democratization in Taiwan than did women in either of the
other two regions. Consequently, women in Taiwan retain a significant presence among policymakers that hopefully will help them put
women's issues on the crowded agenda for government's response to
the complex problems facing the nation today. Still, women remain

almost entirely excluded from the top levels of power (within the opposition as well as within the establishment) and are quite under-represented in absolute terms in the island's legislative assemblies.

To explain both why women fared comparatively well in Taiwan's politics during democratization and why considerable limits on their political opportunities remain, we need to examine the interaction between Taiwan's Confucian culture and the strategic goals of the ruling Kuomintang Party. As we will see, certain policies and political institutions that were implemented by the KMT modified the normal functioning of the patriarchal culture in such a way as to help improve the political status of women. However, this same set of evolving processes also creates limits or barriers to women's moving beyond their current niche in the polity.

Three aspects of Chinese Confucian culture appear vital for understanding the evolving political status of women in Taiwan. First, the culture is quite patriarchal in the sense that women hold a subordinate and devalued status, in large part because they leave their natal families upon marriage (see Chapter 9). Second, education is highly valued and viewed as the central basis for political and social mobility. Third, social, economic, and political life is organized around informal networks based on kinship and other types of personal relations or *guanxi* (Pye, 1985). Such networks have been and still are extremely important in Taiwan. For example, they are credited with undergirding the complex networks of small firms that have contributed so much to the nation's economic success (Greenhalgh, 1988; Kuo, 1995; Lam and Clark, 1994; Lam and Lee, 1992; Skoggard, 1996; Winn, 1994) and are viewed, often in a far less positive light, as being a key element in Taiwan's electoral and patronage politics (Bosco, 1994; Wang, 1994).

When the Kuomintang evacuated to Taiwan in 1949, the regime it established had several similarities to the Leninist states under communism: (1) an authoritarian one-party regime, (2) the repression of competing political parties and visions, and (3) a "modernizing" ideology (Sun Yat-sen's Three Principles of the People, or *San Min Chu I*), which committed it (in principle at least) to promoting rapid development and industrialization and to eradicating class and gender biases in society through such means as legal reform and universal education. However, the KMT in Taiwan departed from the classic Leninist strategy in one vital respect. Rather than destroying the pre-existing social and political groups, the regime attempted to coopt and manipulate them when possible (Clark, 1989; Tien, 1989).

In the political realm (government bodies, farmers associations, etc.), this resulted in the Mainlander "national" elite playing "local" Islander factions off against each other and retaining power by acting as an arbitrator among them. Whether intended or not, the introduction of local elections based on the Japanese system of one nontransferable vote in a multimember district proved perfect for this strategy, because it forces factions of the dominant party to compete against each other directly (Calder, 1988).

Normally, such informal *guanxi* networks would probably discriminate against women because of their linkage to the traditional patriarchal culture. However, the special provision of the Republic of China's 1946 constitution, which "reserved" a minimum proportion of Assembly seats for women, turned this normal patriarchal bias on its head! Some women had to be recruited to run, or else a seat would go by default to a woman from an opposing faction or party. Moreover, unlike the communist systems in which the ruling party exercised control by preventing electoral competition, the KMT's more indirect strategy of divide-and-rule was based on maintaining real competition at the lower levels in order to prevent Islander challenges to the Mainlander top elite. Real competition, in turn, meant that gradually women who were first elected as tokens would almost be forced to develop their own political skills and become viable political leaders in their own right (e.g., the very different career patterns of Yu Chen Yueh-ying, Annette Lu, and the Chiashu candidates). Thus, the growing success of women over time noted in the previous section can be explained by this unintended interaction of electoral institutions and traditional Chinese networks.

Taiwan's development strategy also helped, more indirectly, to enhance women's political status. Rapid industrialization brought women outside the household to new jobs, first in industry, then in services, and finally in professional occupations; and universal primary and then secondary education, coupled with merit-based access to higher education, created an ever expanding group of well-educated women (Chiang and Ku, 1985; Chou, Clark, and Clark, 1990). These socioeconomic processes, in turn, had several important consequences for the political status of women. First, the eligibility pool from which women political leaders could emerge expanded exponentially; second, large numbers of women assumed positions in society that changed their political and social consciousness; and, third, social modernization itself inevitably undercut many aspects of inegalitarian gender roles.

Unfortunately, not all these changes were positive nor did they necessarily imply that women would make steady progress toward equal representation. The very kinship nature of Taiwan's political factions generated several important constraints on women politicians. First, there was an understandable tendency for leaders to recruit relatives or other extremely loyal women to run for "women's seats," which undoubtedly undercut their subsequent ability to gain true independence and political stature. Second, the patronage orientation of most local networks and factions (as well as limited revenue capabilities) gravely limited their ability to attack the social problems of special interest to women. Yu Chen's career in Kaohsiung demonstrates that such obstacles can be overcome in individual cases, but clearly the general constraints remain.

Similar, if not greater, constraints or problems can be seen in opposition politics. The DPP, and the tangwei before it, generally rejected traditional Chinese culture and explicitly promoted more egalitarian norms. In theory, this should benefit women participants in the movement. However, it has in practice been associated with a suspicion of several members from the same family running for office or holding leadership positions because of the image that this is how traditional factions operate. Since the Chiashu had become some of the opposition's leading symbols in the early 1980s, this "cultural modernism" probably on balance hurt the position of women in the DPP. Moreover, the emphasis of the opposition on the politics of national identity (Wachman, 1994) probably contributed to the low saliency of feminism in Taiwan, because many feminists in the DPP subordinate their feelings on this issue to pushing the party's principal "cause." For example, Annette Lu, the first major feminist leader in Taiwan in the early 1970s, became a legislator in the mid-1990s and devoted her primary efforts to pushing for Taiwan's admission to the United Nations; and, most recently, she won election as magistrate (chief executive) in Taoyuan County. In contrast, feminist organizations now draw most of their leaders and members from the Mainlander community—which unfortunately limits their political appeal (Lu, 1994; Teng, 1991).

More broadly, these advances by and constraints on women politicians in Taiwan are consistent with three of the general themes in many of the essays in this book. First, indigenous culture remains extremely important in shaping women's lives. Second, these cultural influences do not necessarily conform to the stereotype of patriarchal subjugation. Rather, they hold somewhat countervailing implications for the status of women in Taiwan and East Asia. Third, Taiwan's experience certainly underlines the importance of autonomous activities by women politicians and women's groups in the pursuit of goals they define themselves. In conjunction, these three conclusions suggest at least a little optimism about the ability of women to use Taiwan's new democracy to promote their empowerment and emancipation.

5

Gender and Local Governance in the Philippines

MARIA ELA L. ATIENZA

The 1986 "revolution" that overthrew the Marcos dictatorship ushered in a number of democratizing trends in the Philippines. A new constitution not only reestablished pre–martial law formal democratic institutions but also strengthened these institutions to avoid the rise of another dictator. But more than the legal framework, democratization in the country became evident in the unprecedented growth of civil society through the formation of nongovernmental organizations (NGOs), people's organizations (POs), and other grassroots organizations.

The rise of the NGOs was also enshrined in the 1987 constitution. It is now the policy of the state to "encourage non-governmental, community-based, or sectoral organizations that promote the welfare of the nation" (Constitution of the Philippines, 1987: Art. II, sec. 23). Moreover, the state recognizes these initiatives and organizations as enabling "the people to pursue and protect, within the democratic framework, their legitimate and collective interests and aspirations through peaceful and lawful means" (Constitution of the Philippines, 1987: Art. XIII, sec. 15).

A further boost to democratization was the enactment of the 1991 Local Government Code. The code radically transformed the nature of the relationship between the national government and the local government units (LGUs) by transferring fundamental responsibilities and accountabilities to the LGUs. In addition, it made the unprecedented move to encourage active participation by the private sector, NGOs, and POs, leading to a Philippine contribution in redefining the notion of "governance"—one that went beyond the parameters of the formal structures and processes of government (Brillantes, 1997).

This chapter attempts to assess the extent to which women's

empowerment has been achieved in the context of one major aspect of the democratization processes in the Philippines: the devolution of powers to local governments. The primary focus will be some of the initiatives taken by women's organizations to achieve substantial participation in local governance and affairs. However, the cases presented here do not claim to be representative of all women's groups in the Philippines. They were merely chosen to make a tentative and very modest attempt at assessing women's empowerment at the local level.

WOMEN'S EMPOWERMENT AND THE 1991 LOCAL GOVERNMENT CODE

Women constitute more than half (50.3 percent) of the more than 60 million Filipinos (National Statistics Office, 1990). The 1987 constitution recognizes the role women play in the task of nation-building and at the same time gives to the state the task to "ensure the fundamental equality before the law of women and men" (Constitution of the Philippines, 1987: Art. II, sec. 14). Based on this constitutional mandate, a number of laws have already been passed to stress the important role of women in their communities and to give them the necessary opportunities as well as protection in all spheres of society.

In particular, the 1991 Local Government Code places importance on the role of women in the process of decentralization and the empowerment of people. It allows, among other things, the explicit entry and membership of NGOs and POs—women's groups included—in the structure and processes of local governance through local legislative councils and special bodies. Local government units can enter into partnerships with women's organizations in the pursuit of common goals. In addition, a women's representative is among the three sectoral representatives that must be included in every municipal, city, and provincial *sanggunian,* or legislative council.

However, though it has been generally recognized by several important laws that women have an equal role in nation-building and must therefore be empowered, conditions in Philippine communities point to the fact that women's empowerment is easier said than done. This being the case, growing numbers of women's groups are working toward gaining equal access to opportunities laid down by the law. Three of these are the Lipa City Women's Council in Lipa City; the Bukidnon Women's Organization, Inc., in the province of Bukidnon; and the indigenous women of the Cordilleras in Northern Luzon.

THE WOMEN'S EMPOWERMENT FRAMEWORK

In order to assess the empowerment levels of the different groups, I utilize Sara Longwe's framework for analyzing women's empowerment (UNICEF, 1993), which gives us a conceptualization of the empowerment process. She argues that women's development can be viewed in terms of five levels or stages of equality, of which empowerment is an essential element at each level. The five levels are (1) welfare, (2) access, (3) conscientization, (4) participation, and (5) control.

Welfare, the first level, addresses only the basic needs of women without recognizing or attempting to solve the underlying structural causes that necessitate the provision of welfare services. Here, women are passive beneficiaries of welfare benefits. Access, the second level, involves equality of access to resources such as educational opportunities, land, and credit. Women must recognize the lack of resources as a barrier to their growth and overall well-being and take action to redress this problem. Only with this recognition and ensuing actions can the moves toward empowerment be initiated.

Conscientization, the third level, is crucial in this framework. For women to take the appropriate action to address gender gaps and inequalities, they should recognize that their problems stem from inherent structural and institutional discrimination. They should also recognize the role that they themselves can (and often do) play in reinforcing the system that restricts their growth. Participation, the fourth level, requires that women take decisions alongside men equally. Mobilization (organization and collective action) is necessary to attain this level. Finally, control is the ultimate level of equality and empowerment. Neither male nor female has dominance over the other at this level. Women play substantial and active roles in decisionmaking and in developing the process. Furthermore, their contributions are fully recognized and rewarded.

THE LIPA CITY WOMEN'S COUNCIL

Lipa City is one of the most dynamic and rapidly growing cities in the Southern Tagalog region. It is also where an organization was developed that initially addressed and focused on the economic problems of women. It realized later, though, that in order for the women's sector to make substantial contributions to the development of the entire city, the organization must also address the problems of social stereotypes and the lack of substantial political participation in the community.

In February 1992, women leaders in Lipa founded the Lipa City Women's Council, or LCWC (Atienza, 1995, 1996). Although it was born out of the initiatives of women, it had the support of an innovative and dynamic local chief executive from the very beginning. Lipa's mayor had encouraged the organization of the women's sector because he believed not only that disadvantaged women need to be helped but also that women have the capacity to help in the development of the city. The LCWC's objective is to promote women's welfare and development with particular concern for, but not limited to, health, education, livelihood, self-enhancement, and community participation. Its eventual goal is to awaken women to their important role in society. However, the LCWC's thrust initially was not in the area of high-level gender awareness but in improving women's economic status through livelihood programs—in particular, the creation of women's cooperatives. Women in the *barangays* (the lowest units of local government) were not yet primed for high-level gender awareness.

The LCWC grew fast. In 1993, it already boasted a total membership of 3,000 women. In 1995, it had sixty-seven chapters, only five chapters short of having one in each barangay in Lipa. An affiliate member of the National Council of Women of the Philippines (NCWP), whose president is a member of the Board of Directors and convenor of NCWP's Cooperative Fund for Women, the LCWC also participated in the Fourth World Conference on Women in Beijing and included the principles of the Platform for Action and the Beijing Declaration in the formulation and implementation of its current program and projects in Lipa.

Most of the programs and projects in which the local government and the women's sector join hands are in the area of livelihood and economic welfare. In the case of Lipa, the city government allotted P 2,256,000 in 1995 for the City Social Welfare and Development Office (CSWDO) to serve as a livelihood fund. One of the target beneficiaries is the women's sector. The role of the LCWC is to assist the CSWDO in the selection of individual women recipients of sewing machines, soft loans, and other assistance to start their own businesses. Livelihood projects are also carried out in cooperation with other NGOs and the city government. In the area of education, the LCWC, in coordination with the CSWDO, conducts modular seminars on health and nutrition, childhood development, self-awareness, and community participation. In the area of public service, the LCWC provides assistance to women through the Women's Center located at the City Hall main building. The center coordinates with various national and local government agencies and NGOs to provide the necessary assistance.

The Local Government Code of 1991 boosted women's empowerment with its provisions on sectoral representation in local legislative councils and local special bodies. However, these do not ensure that women's troubles are over. In the case of the LCWC, it is accredited by the city council and represents women in several local special bodies. The LCWC is also one of the most active sectors in the comprehensive network involving both government and nongovernment sectors initiated by the local government to address the city's problems. The LCWC chapters have been credited for the success of the Class A or model barangays. The women initiated cleanliness and beautification projects as well as infrastructure improvements. However, no sectoral representative for women has been chosen to date to sit on the city council.

Looking at the participation of women in formal positions in the city government, Lipa women have yet to gain a strong foothold in high positions, either elected and appointed. To elaborate, in 1995, only two out of the fourteen elected officials were women. One was a councillor and the other was the Sangguniang Kabataan (Youth Council) president. Of the twelve local department heads, only the city social welfare officer, the city planning and development officer, the cooperative officer, and the city librarian were women. Except for the planning and development officer, these jobs are usually considered women's work. At the barangay level, there were sixty-nine women councillors, representing 13.7 percent of the total 504 barangay councillors who won in the 1994 elections. There were no women barangay captains.

Believing that participation in policymaking is an important step in the advancement of the interests of women, the LCWC is now consciously training and encouraging its members to run for elective positions. The members take pride in the fact that most of the sixty-nine women barangay councillors elected in 1994 were LCWC chapter heads before they ran for office. The council was also instrumental in putting into office the lone woman candidate for city councillor during the May 1995 elections, despite the candidate's not being on the incumbent mayor's ticket and despite the fact that negotiations with the incumbent party failed to produce the inclusion of any women candidates on the party slate.

The LCWC still has to contend with a number of problems, including (1) the perception by some that it is antimale; (2) a continuing gender bias, even from well-meaning government officials who have different notions of "gender equality" and "women's participation" that relegate women to traditional activities such as record keeping, cleanliness drives, and social welfare work; (3) the lukewarm attitude of some women about pursuing more active roles; (4) financial constraints; and (5) the perception by some that it is a mere political arm of the administration.

In Lipa City, therefore, women have reached a certain level of empowerment. The LCWC has been able to address welfare and access issues with some success. However, the pursuit of substantial participation has not yet produced far-reaching results. Conscientization, although crucial, is currently being addressed only to a limited extent. Nevertheless, the LCWC has made some important strides toward more independence and more substantial participation by women in the city's development. While it continues to forge a partnership with the city government in livelihood and other development projects, it is beginning to assert increasing independence by pursuing its own activities. Members of the LCWC are also beginning to realize that although most of their efforts are concentrated on local struggles, they are intimately linked with broader national and international movements working for more comprehensive security and development that will benefit not only women but men as well.

BUKIDNON WOMEN'S ORGANIZATION, INC., AND DEMOCRATIC SOCIALIST WOMEN OF THE PHILIPPINES

The largest women's federation in the province of Bukidnon in Mindanao is the Bukidnon Women's Organization, Inc. (BWOI). Although the BWOI is a provincial federation of 153 women's organizations scattered throughout the province, it is not accredited by the provincial government. Hence, it is not part of the Local Development Council or any other local special body and has no part in formal planning and decisionmaking processes. It does, however, assist in the implementation of various government development projects, even if the local government does not consider its role very important. Unfortunately, instances when a local government considers women representatives to be necessary are rare.

The BWOI deals actively with cases of wife beating, especially in the rural areas. Although many barangay officials think that this is a private family issue and do not act on the matter, BWOI members report wife-beating incidents to the police and refer them to the Department of Social Welfare and Development (DSWD). Rather than concentrating on funding, BWOI focuses more on culture, education, and value orientation through training and seminars. What it cannot do right now at the provincial level is to give financial livelihood assistance to member groups (Agbayani, 1996).

Despite the difficulties encountered at the local level, BWOI continues to encourage and fight for genuine participation for women. It is sustained and supported by a national federation of women's groups of which it is a member. This national federation is the Democratic Socialist Women of the Philippines (DSWP), which guides the different organizations under its wing in the pursuit of women's empowerment in all spheres of society but at the same time gives its member organizations sufficient autonomy to address local issues and concerns. Overall, in terms of Longwe's women's empowerment framework, the BWOI is less successful than LCWC and other member organizations in the DSWP in the area of welfare and access. Nevertheless, with the help of the federation, the BWOI continues the pursuit of women's empowerment in all its stages.

A socialist feminist organization, DSWP considers all issues that concern women and recognizes the importance of addressing both the practical and strategic needs of women. Founded in 1987, it is a national federation of grassroots women's organizations with chapters scattered in eight of the sixteen regions of the country. At present, it has about eighty accredited chapters nationwide, some of which are themselves provincial federations of smaller women's groups, like the BWOI. As of 1997, DSWP has officially 35,000 women members from all over the country. Members come from different sectors of Philippine society, but they are mostly grassroots women representing, for example, the peasantry, trade unions, the informal sector, the urban poor, youth and students, and Muslim and indigenous communities.

The DSWP believes that (1) there exists essential equality between women and men so that women possess the same measure of dignity and capacity to achieve personhood; (2) structural and cultural realities, including the economic system, patriarchy, and the socialization process, bring about gender oppression; (3) women and men can develop more fully in a society characterized by peace, democracy, and social justice; (4) human development must touch both the personal and the social, the abstract and the concrete; (5) Philippine culture is not neutral but reflective of the power relations in society; (6) equality between the sexes must be reflected in equal opportunities throughout society; and (7) solidarity between and among organizations is desirable and necessary to bring about the liberation of women and other oppressed groups.

The DSWP pursues four broad goals. The first is to advance and promote the praxis of feminism to seek concrete expressions of gender equality by combating all forms of discrimination against women. Second, it seeks to promote a *concept of development* that recognizes the coequal and coresponsible role of women and men in the development process, while at the same time striving to develop alternative programs to raise women's level of consciousness and to enhance self-awareness, self-confidence, and economic independence. Third, it encourages women to seek venues for substantive and effective participation at all levels of decisionmaking. Finally, DSWP tries to forge solidarity and linkages with democratic women's sectoral and political organizations in order to promote common goals and objectives.

In terms of programs, DSWP has an educational and training program that uses popularized methodologies geared toward addressing issues of gender sensitivity, consciousness-raising, and orientation on social issues, as well as capability building. When providing technical assistance, DSWP goes to local communities and asks women, based on their situation, in what kind of activities they wish to participate. Most often, poverty and economic needs are cited as the central problem, which explains why a relevant area of the DSWP's work concentrates on livelihood activities. But the training is not solely for livelihood reasons. An accompanying strong educational component in these activities ensures a change in perspective of these women to encourage them to challenge the power structure of the family. Otherwise, the livelihood project would benefit the family as a whole but not the woman who would eventually end up doing even more work than before.

The organization also concentrates on the formation and maintenance of autonomous women's groups. Adhering to the concept of decentralization, the DSWP encourages the autonomy of these chapters to allow them to act on certain local issues. The DSWP helps develop women leaders in the communities who are now occupying positions in various community organizations and are actively involved in the special bodies of their localities. It also trained women in different parts of the country in preparation for the recent barangay elections in May 1997. In connection with this, the DSWP arranged a study tour that took eleven grassroots women to Denmark, where they met Danish women in government and gained perspectives on how the welfare, education, and health systems operate there.

The DSWP believes in the importance of forging solidarity with other groups, coalitions, or networks in the advocacy of issues at the local, national, regional, and international levels. Issues can range from "primarily women's issues"—such as passage of the Anti-Rape

Bill, the migration of women workers, and violence against women—
to foreign debt and globalization—national issues that nevertheless
affect the women's sector. Currently, the DSWP is affiliated with the
Sama-samang Inisyatiba ng Kababaihan sa Pagbabago ng Batas
(SUBOL), a coalition of women's organizations working for legal
reforms; Women Overseas Workers NGO Network (WOWNET); and
the Network to Fight Violence Against Filipina Migrants (NOVA). At
the national level, the DSWP is also affiliated with such multisectoral
groups as the Freedom from Debt Coalition (FDC) and the Partido
Demokratiko-Sosyalista ng Pilipinas (PDSP, or the Democratic
Socialist Party of the Philippines). At the international level, the
DSWP is a member of the Socialist International Women (SIW), the
Coalition Against Trafficking of Women–Asia-Pacific (CATW-Asia-
Pacific), and the Free Burma Coalition.

Taking a positive attitude toward political participation, the
DSWP constantly seeks to develop grassroots women who can occupy
positions in their community and later even national positions. The
organization maintains that the current representative democracy in
the Philippines is not actually representative, in the sense that mostly
people from the elite groups occupy the top positions. People from
the grassroots, who are the ones who experience the problems and
logically know the solution to them, must be given the opportunity to
be in government. But, of course, they first need technical assistance,
which NGOs can provide.

The need to participate in politics also explains why the DSWP
encourages its various chapters to get involved in the affairs of government through "critical collaboration" with local governments.
Critical collaboration means that a chapter will not allow itself to be
coopted; the goal is rather to coordinate on the basis of equality. The
various people's organizations and NGOs can then analyze and criticize the performance of their local government units; their policy
viewpoints certainly deserve representation in the decisionmaking
process.

THE INDIGENOUS WOMEN
IN THE CORDILLERAS AND PILIPINA

The Cordillera mountain range of Northern Luzon is home to seven
major ethnolinguistic groups. It is also the home of a growing
women's movement that seeks not only to address women's concerns
but to link them with the political and development threats surrounding the indigenous peoples of the Cordilleras. Although the people

of the Cordilleras are not exempt from the nationally mandated structures of local governance, they have a unique and indigenous way of conducting local affairs. The Cordillerans are culturally plural-istic and take pride in their own version of democracy, which they consider quite different from democratic practices in the lowlands. Cordillera democracy is based on consultations and consensus build-ing, not simply majority rule. The Cordillerans reject the concept of majority rule, especially in national politics, because this means that the voice of the minority, which includes the indigenous cultural communities in the Cordilleras, will not be heard. The Cordillerans also take pride in their indigenous practices of peace building and conflict resolution, the dispensation of justice, and negotiations and amicable settlements.

But although these processes are often labeled "democratic," Cordillera women leaders themselves are beginning to point out cer-tain flaws and discriminatory aspects of the system. An important example of an indigenous practice that is viewed by many outsiders as democratic but that discriminates against women in certain impor-tant aspects is the *bodong* system, the cultural institution that governs, manages, directs, and controls the political, economic, and social affairs of all the members of the tribes that enter into peace treaties or pacts (called *pagta*) for harmonious coexistence and security. The bodong is a public affair, but one Cordillera woman leader, Mary Foy-os, notes that it hardly involves women in a significant way:

> Women's participation in *bodong* affairs is limited to the bringing of food donations to the *bodong* holder, hosting the celebration, food preparation, washing of kitchen utensils, cooking, and entertain-ment with songs and dances. The delivery of speeches, talks and arguments and discussions and the decision making processes in the *pagta* formation are strictly limited to the men and the elders. The women, at this stage, sit down, listen as audience while the men again display their proficiency in public speaking, always aware of the admiration of those around them. (Rikken and Foy-os, 1996: 2)

The situation of Cordillera women in local affairs prompted the creation of various women's groups advocating not only the concerns of the indigenous people as a whole but the concerns of women specifically. The Mandiga, one group in the province of Kalinga Apayao, has greatly boosted the advocacy of women's empowerment and consciousness-raising among the Cordillera women. It is pushing for more women's participation in all aspects of decisionmaking, especially in very crucial issues like peace and the rights of their com-munities, because these issues also significantly affect women's lives.

Together with the Mandiga, other women's groups and other NGOs in the Cordilleras banded together to strengthen their advocacy.

The result of joint efforts among women's groups and NGOs is the Pan-Cordillera Women's Network for Peace and Development (PAN-CORDI), a network of women's organizations representing the provinces and ethnolinguistic groups of the Cordilleras. Founded in 1995, the network formulated the Pan-Cordillera women's vision for sustainable development and listed six priority issues for action, namely (1) the national government's nonrecognition of the ancestral domain of the indigenous communities; (2) the overall situation of women; (3) the lack of participation of women in local governance; (4) the lack of basic services in the Cordilleras; (5) the breakdown of peace and order; and (6) environmental destruction (Rikken and Foy-os, 1996). These issues eventually formed the basis for policy and program recommendations, collectively known as the Cordillera Women's Political/Electoral Agenda, that were advocated at both national and local government levels.

The forty-one founding member organizations of the PAN-CORDI are NGOs and grassroots women's groups, some of which are already known for their activism in various peace and development initiatives in the Cordilleras. The Mandiga (from Kalinga Apayao) and the Concerned Citizens of Abra for Good Government (CCAGG), for instance, have long taken the lead as conveners in their respective provinces in the pursuit of ancestral land rights and peace through people-based initiatives, such as the establishment of peace zones between 1988 and 1990, the organization of the Cordillera People's Forum in 1991, the conduct of five Ancestral Land Congresses in 1991, and the lobbying that resulted in the creation of the national government's Social Reform Agenda in 1994. With the support of such groups as the Mandiga and the CCAGG, PAN-CORDI plays a critical role in the struggle for ancestral lands, the central issue on which authentic peace and development in the Cordilleras are premised.

At present, the PAN-CORDI is involved in a variety of programs, including:

- participatory research on the natural resource management of the indigenous peoples from the point of view of women
- consolidation of ancestral domain laws for organizing advocacy
- delineation and management of the ancestral domain and its natural resources by women in the Cordilleras
- biodynamic farming

- holistic health care programs
- alternative media
- education and training promoting people's active participation in local governance

The initiatives of the Cordillera women, however, are not isolated but are part of a larger initiative and a wider vision. PAN-CORDI is affiliated nationally with PILIPINA (Ang Kilusan ng Kababaihang Pilipino, or Movement of Filipino Women), which in turn is affiliated with the Center for Asia Pacific Women in Politics (CAPWIP). PILIPINA is a mass-based feminist organization working for women's full participation in leadership and governance, both in public office and in social movements (Rikken and Foy-os, 1996). Its strategies and programs include building a women's constituency through organization and mobilization, training women for leadership roles, mainstreaming and institutionalizing the women's agenda through policy proposals and advocacy, and setting up support systems for women both in the communities and in leadership positions.

Since its founding in 1981, PILIPINA has grown into a national organization with chapters nationwide. While actively pursuing gender sensitivity and other support programs for women and carrying out organization-building activities, each chapter operates autonomously and carries out programs to address the specific needs of poor women in local communities. For example, PILIPINA in Cebu operates a crisis center for battered women and at the same time has organized a community watch program to prevent cases of domestic violence against women. PILIPINA in Davao focuses on the reorientation of educators in the province toward a more gender-sensitive educational system. The National Capitol Region chapter supports working mothers in the urban poor areas by providing day-care services.

PILIPINA was also instrumental in helping organize CAPWIP. CAPWIP's goal is to create a critical mass of competent, committed, and effective women politicians in elective and appointive positions in government who will promote and put into practice women's transformative political agenda. It likewise seeks to develop a responsive citizenry that will guarantee equal rights and opportunities for every member of society in charting the course of development and to serve the common good as opposed to private ends (Center for Asia-Pacific Women). CAPWIP envisions governments in the Asia-Pacific region adhering not only to excellence, integrity, and accountability but also to gender equality and participation, sustainable development, and peace.

As an assessment, the Cordillera women still do not have a concrete set of achievements at the various levels of women's empowerment. Perhaps this is because of the dual nature of their cause. They
advocate the empowerment of both women and the indigenous cultural communities to which they belong. However, it is clear from
their programs and visions, as well as their linkages with national and
international organizations, that they are pursuing the empowerment
of women at all levels.

ISSUES AND PROBLEMS

The different women's organizations examined in this study suggest
that many of the initiatives of grassroots women have resulted in some
achievements at the welfare and access levels of empowerment, even
as all of them continue to work hard for the three more difficult but
more substantive levels of empowerment. However, despite certain
areas where the women's sector and the local government units work
together, there are still some problem areas regarding women's
empowerment at the local level. These problems are as follows:

1. *No sectoral representatives for women have been chosen for the local legislative councils,* or sanggunians, because there is no enabling law
passed by the congress for the selection of sectoral representatives
and because some local officials feel that the election of sectoral representatives is a financial burden.

2. *Substantive participation is still lacking, and effective control of city
and community affairs is still in the hands of males.* Few women occupy
top positions in local governments, elected or appointed. Moreover,
most of the positions occupied by women are usually those traditionally considered "women's work" (e.g., social welfare, library work,
record keeping, health care, etc.).

3. *The prevailing gender bias in society usually results in stereotyped roles*
for men and women and the neglect of women's concerns. Local
chief executives and administrations that look down on women will
naturally not be inclined toward a creative partnership with the
women's sector.

4. There is a prevailing notion that *women's empowerment is merely
equated with economic well-being and welfare services,* such as health and
day-care facilities. Even women themselves, especially those in local
areas, are not yet ready for high-level gender awareness. For example,
women in Lipa and in Bukidnon who are victims of wife-battering are
not yet open to the idea of reporting their husbands.

5. There is a *tendency for the women's sector to be used by certain politicians as a mere political arm of their administration.* This is exacerbated by the fact that women's groups may become too dependent on the assistance being provided by local governments and politicians.

For women to address women's issues effectively at the local level and to ensure that their participation becomes more substantial, they should consider two fundamental points about empowerment and partnership. First, empowerment is not measured solely by the number of women in high positions or in individual advancement. It should be viewed in the context of the collective power of women to make relevant contributions in decisionmaking, accompanied by changing views of both women and men regarding their roles in society. Livelihood projects may not necessarily lead to increasing awareness of women's self-worth, rights, and opportunities. Such projects, without accompanying gender awareness, may in fact increase the load on women as wives, mothers, and, now, small entrepreneurs.

Second, partnership does not mean subjugation to the local government. The sustainability and independence of women's groups should be addressed by strengthening women in the grassroots to be active members and potential leaders of the organization and the community. Furthermore, women's groups should look for more sustainable sources of funding and not be coterminous with any politician's or administration's term of office.

Despite the presence of legal foundations for the more effective participation of women, women's groups will have to work hard to build on those foundations. Efforts toward this end are not lacking. Women's groups are training their members for leadership positions in the community, achieving some success in putting some of them into office, and establishing linkages with national and even international women's groups to achieve goals that go beyond their localities.

6

Self-Governance, Political Participation, and the Feminist Movement in South Korea

MIKYUNG CHIN

Like other Asian societies, Korea has traditionally been strongly male dominated. Confucianism, which laid the groundwork for the social ethos, confined women to the kitchen for the benefit and pleasure of their masters (Mill, 1970). The worldwide thrust of modernization and Westernization in the late nineteenth century affected Korean women too; they became exposed to the world outside the home and were mobilized into social activities. Since this first awakening, the status of women in Korea has clearly advanced in a variety of areas. In the legal realm, the formal equality of men and women is articulated in the constitution. Women are allowed to vote; legal reforms and policies, including family reform law and an equal employment law, have been introduced; and very recently a law against domestic violence, which was long regarded as untouchable by the state, was passed in South Korea—the first such law in Asia.

In the women's movement itself, the growth is exponential, encompassing such diverse activities as a cultural movement for the elimination of the patriarchal family system, a popular movement for democratization and local self-governance, a labor movement, a consumer protection movement, an environmental protection movement, a movement to clean up corruption in education, a movement against sexual violence and prostitution, a peace movement against arms competition, and recently a movement to retrieve the rights of Korean women sexually exploited by Japanese soldiers during World War II. Attempts are being made to raise people's consciousness about gender issues and outdated stereotypes. For example, textbooks for young children are moving away from emphasizing sexually fixed roles by eliminating illustrations in which mothers prepare food in the kitchen while fathers read a book in the dining room. In scope and depth, the expansion of women's rights is remarkable consider-

91

ing the long history of well-defined unequal gender roles in traditional Korean society.

Despite this progress, the status of women is far from satisfactory
when considering the ideal of perfect equality with men. The discrepancy between reality and this ideal appears particularly large when
the political space afforded to women after the current democratization is taken into account. In the euphoria of democratization,
democracy was believed to be a Midas touch that would improve
everything. Democratization generated high hopes for women as
well; a new society without gender discrimination was anticipated.
Such heightened expectations were soon dashed, however, when the
political representation of women at the national level did not
increase noticeably. In addition, the top positions in the executive
and judiciary remained totally closed to women. Women then shifted
their strategic focus to local politics, but progress here was limited as
well. Furthermore, an antifeminist backlash advocating women's
return to the family is resuming and gaining wider acceptance
because of the rising rates of divorce and juvenile delinquency.

What went wrong with the feminist movement in Korea after
democratization? The coexistence of countervailing forces provides
an opportunity to reflect critically on the feminist movement. This
chapter seeks to illuminate the pitfalls that have accompanied the
feminist movement following democratization, especially the argument that local autonomy will increase women's political representation. An understanding of the misdirection of postdemocratic feminism requires a preliminary consideration of the development of the
feminist movement prior to democratization, given that the former is
a by-product of the latter. At present, the women's movement in
South Korea is at a critical juncture where it will either move forward
or face significant setbacks, depending on the direction it takes in the
wake of democratization. It is our goal to make a contribution to has-
tening the day when women's liberation is fully achieved and the
term "feminism" is of no use at all.

THE HISTORICAL CONTEXT
OF PATRIARCHAL CONFUCIANISM

In traditional Korean society, it was Confucianism that provided an
overarching framework regulating human behavior. The essence of
Confucianism lies in a strict hierarchical order, which was assumed to
promote peace and harmony in all facets of life. First, international
relations were viewed as an unequal set of relations between a central
power and its tributary states. Second, in domestic relations, society

was ruled by a hierarchical system based on four classes: the literati (occupying the top echelon), farmers, artisans, and merchants. This rigid system rested on a theory of social utility: each class performed a specific role needed for the maintenance of society. The ruling class maintained social order; farmers produced food; artisans produced goods; and merchants carried goods from place to place. Although traditional society seemed to contain seeds of disruption due to its rigid structure, it succeeded in preserving itself without a challenge to the ruling class from below.

Above all, the most entrenched system of order was found in the family, where relations between husband and wife rested on inviolable inequality without exception. Under this patriarchal system, man was the master and woman was the servant required to pay strict homage to her master. Women's absolute subjection to men was typically demonstrated by the "three ways of subjection." When women were young, they were ordered to obey their father. After marrying, subjection was switched to the husband. When old, subjection to her eldest son was substituted. Because a woman was considered to be incapable of thinking reasonably, she was destined to follow commands from a man. Discrimination did not end there. It extended even to the use of residential space. Usually in the daytime, husbands stayed in the outer part of the house reading books and associating with guests. Wives were confined to the inner part of the house taking care of housework and the children. Women were not to show themselves to strangers, and when they went out, they had to wear veils to cover their faces. Additionally, girls were taught to avoid the physical company of boys after the age of seven. A woman's reason for being was to reproduce for the succeeding lineage. If a wife could not produce a boy, she could legitimately be deserted by her husband. Such patriarchal norms exist even in modern times. For example, prior to the mid-1960s, the birth of a son would set off a major celebration publicized by hanging red pepper (in the Korean language, the pronunciations of red pepper and the phallic organ are the same). Even now, when parents take pictures of their child, sons are normally photographed naked to show off the symbol of masculinity. In sum, the Confucian patriarchal family structure does not include women in the category of human beings.

This gross gender inequality within the family extends into economic activities, even in the modern era. For example, one aspect of the controversy surrounding "Asian values" concerns the contribution made by the patriarchal system to economic development in the sense that it is the task of women to offer men a cozy home in which to rest after work and recharge themselves. A woman's success in society is measured by that of her husband. It is the wife's duty to stay at home as helpmate. The old saying "When the hen clucks, the family will be ruined" means that women's involvement in social activities will result in the destruction of the whole family. The division of labor between the two sexes within the family is even praised as the backbone of a strong nation. The net effect of the perpetuation of the patriarchal family is the perpetuation of women's slavery.

When Korea was drawn into the sweeping changes of modernization, the entrenched patriarchal system worked as a major stumbling block to women's liberation. Although laws and policies encouraging gender equality can be introduced within a relatively short span of time, removal of the patriarchal culture will take much longer.

Feminism can be defined in terms of establishing equality between men and women. If men and women are equal, role distinctions according to sex must be eliminated. According to Confucian philosophy, men should be involved in social activities outside the home, while women should be restricted to the home. In this context, the first impetus for women's exposure to the world outside the home was brought on by the worldwide thrust of Westernization and modernization in the late nineteenth century. Encroaching Westernization set off a tremendous transformation in every corner of traditional society. Educational opportunities were given to women in an effort to raise their consciousness, and movements aimed at abolishing the concubinage system and allowing widows to remarry ensued (Choi, 1979).

The subsequent colonization of Korea by Japan created an environment for the women's movement to merge with the Korean nationalist independence movement. This merger exerted significant influence on the subsequent direction of the women's movement in two ways. One was the cooptation of women by the state to fulfill national goals, with purely feminist issues having low saliency. The second was the split of the women's movement following the split within the male-dominated independence movement. One kind of division occurred along pro-Japanese versus anti-Japanese lines, while another involved conflict between democratic and socialist ideologies. These divisions, which emerged at the outset of the feminist movement, left a mark that can be seen even today (Chung, 1991; H. Lee, 1991; O. Lee, 1985; R. J. Lee, 1995b; Park, 1984).

THE WOMEN'S MOVEMENT IN SOUTH KOREA

Korea won independence at the end of World War II. Freed from Japanese domination, the country offered a much more propitious atmosphere for women to pursue their agendas. Fierce ideological conflict erupted domestically to gain control over a newly independent country in parallel with the conflict at the international level. A tug-of-war between opposite ideological camps resulted in the partition of the country into south and north. A new government founded on democracy was installed in the south.

Presumably, women fared best politically under the Syngman Rhee regime from 1948 to 1960. According to democratic principles, sexual equality was secured in the constitution. Article 11, clause 1 of the constitution clearly stated, "Everyone is equal before the law. No one is discriminated against in any sphere of politics, economy, society, or culture on the basis of sex, religion, or social status." Although it amounted to a symbolic statement, women now had legitimate grounds for claiming equal treatment. Liberated from a deep-seated chain imposed by tradition and custom, women became heavily involved in politics.

In August 1945, women founded the Korean Women's National Party, the only party organized by women in Korean history (it was disbanded when all parties and interest groups were banned following the military coup in 1961). The party waged active political campaigns, ranging from the antitrusteeship campaign right after independence to a women's consciousness-raising movement. It nominated a woman for the vice-presidency. Even though she did not win that position, she was twice elected to the national legislature, running in an election district by herself (rather than being nominated on a party list), and she served as minister of commerce and industry. Another visible woman was elected four times at the district level and played a politically significant role. The political success of these two women, which they achieved in their own right and not as the result of the patronage of male party leaders, is striking given the conservative atmosphere in society on the whole. Nevertheless, sharp limitations existed in women's political participation because most women remained in traditional roles hoping to be admired as a model "wise wife and good mother."

The outbreak of the Korean War in 1950 ushered in a new era in the women's movement. Women who lost husbands on the battlefield became heads of the household and family breadwinners. Moreover, widows, women raped by soldiers, unwed mothers, orphans, and other women dislocated by the war began to participate in social activities and the feminist movement as they sought to take advantage of the government's welfare policies. For its part, the government began to show genuine interest in women's issues.

A military coup in 1961 and the onset of an authoritarian regime

marked a turning point in national politics and in the women's movement as well. The weak legitimacy attached to the military government led it to court women in an attempt to broaden its base of support. For their part, women seized on opportunities to expand their
influence. During the 1960s, the burgeoning of the women's movement among middle-class women paralleled the pursuit of economic
development and ensuing economic prosperity. The introduction of
home appliances such as the washing machine reduced the amount
of time women spent on housekeeping chores. Women now were free
to search for their own identity.

The salient feature of the middle-class–oriented feminist movement was its strong commitment to promoting government policies
favorable to women. An example was its strong advocacy of the family
planning program proposed by the government despite opposition in
the National Assembly, which feared a shortage in the workforce, a
birthrate that would compare unfavorably to North Korea's, and the
violation of human rights (M. Lee, 1989). In November 1961, a family
planning program was adopted by the government to prevent the
adverse effects of rapid population increase on economic development (M. Lee, 1989). A central organization that played a leading
role in disseminating the family planning program was the Korean
National Council of Women (KNCW), an umbrella organization
founded in 1959 by middle-class women. KNCW acted primarily as an
agent to promote government policies, including family planning, as
evidenced by the names of the organization's national rallies for
women: "National Development by Women's Power" in 1964,
"Women's Duty in Modernization" in 1966, and "The 1970s and the
Population Problem" in 1970 (Korean National Council of Women,
1998). Supported financially by the government, KNCW championed
the family planning program; it dispatched birth control specialists,
distributed contraceptives, and performed free sterilization opera-
tions throughout the country.

By actively participating in government programs, women's
organizations could raise their status and increase membership.
However, these primarily middle-class women were unwilling to con-
front fundamental feminist issues and urgent problems associated
with sexual inequality that poor women faced in their daily struggle
to exist. In addition, the organization lost autonomy because of its
dependence on the state.

Against this conservative mainstream, a new branch of the feminist movement took shape in the 1970s. The main actors in this new
branch were female workers. Economic development and industrialization had produced a large number of working women. It is no

exaggeration that the foundation of rapid economic development was laid by the young female workforce. However, they suffered from a dual structure of exploitation. Mainly concentrated in labor-intensive industry, these young female workers were exploited as workers—suffering miserable working conditions and low wages—and were also discriminated against as women. The new interests and orientations of these female workers were a departure from the middle-class–centered movement. Working-class women believed that more emphasis should be placed on the roots of social ills, such as wretched working conditions, sexual harassment, and the violation of human rights, than on social intercourse and friendship among leisure-class women.

In addition, the government's own policies helped to create a more broadly based feminist movement. An unintended positive ramification from the government-sponsored women's movement was the mobilization of rural and lower-class women, which continued with the launching of the New Village Movement in the early 1970s. This movement, which aimed to reduce the discrepancy in living conditions between urban and rural areas, resulted in increased contact between the capital and local areas, improved chances of participation in local government, and ultimately led to the emergence of a pool of potential leaders in rural areas. These rural women cooperated with working women in building up a new, more radical branch of the feminist movement.

This radical branch of feminism was reinforced when it forged an alliance with other newly emerging social groups connected with the labor movement, the student movement, and the democratic movement in a struggle against authoritarianism. For example, the first women's studies course was offered in 1977; and the Korean Association of Women's Studies was formed in 1984. This, in turn, put women's oppression into a broader perspective. Concerted efforts were directed more at changing the basic social structure, the patriarchal system, and cultural sexism than at bringing about limited change in sexual relationships (Lee, 1994). The Declaration of Women as Human Beings in 1975 by young intellectual women clearly stated this:

> The goal of women's liberation movement is cultural revolution and human liberation. We reject limited reforms originated from men's political consideration, merely aiming at enhancing women's status. We deny every idea of oppression and hierarchy. In a larger perspective, our aim is to establish a community based on the liberation of whole humanity, including not only women but also men. (Choi, 1979: 258)

The assassination of President Park Chung Hee in October 1979 fostered high hopes for a return to democracy. The so-called Spring of Seoul was quickly ended by a brutal military coup, which resulted in a regime (Chun) that engendered even stronger popular resistance than Park's regime had faced. The government sought to compensate for this lack of legitimacy by wooing women's organizations. Women took advantage of this situation and, by applying hard pressure, succeeded in gaining significant concessions. A government-sponsored research institute and the Council on Women's Policy were established, and the regime enacted an Equal Employment Law in 1987. Chun's government was followed in 1988 by Roh Taewoo, who introduced a host of reforms, including a revision in the family law, the strengthening of the Equal Employment Law, and new child care and mother and child welfare laws. Thus, women's issues began to be treated in their own right and not as subordinate to other national issues.

Despite these successes of the feminist movement before democratization, the status of women in South Korea remained woefully low. First, women have been almost completely excluded from holding national political office. For example, in the fifteen parliamentary elections between 1948 and 1996, only seventy-eight women were elected compared to 3,532 men. In the mid-1990s, Korea's rate of female legislators ranked ninety-fourth among 119 countries (Lee, 1998: 49).

Women also have been poorly represented in the cabinet, having held only fourteen ministerial posts during the postwar era (Ministry of Women, 1995), most of which have been in minor departments such as environment, social welfare, culture, or women's affairs. Male political leaders frequently say that they cannot find capable women for important posts. Thus, the appointment of women to ministerial posts is a purely symbolic, politically expedient gesture, not a thoughtful action that takes into account women's capabilities. Worse, in 1998 the new government abolished the cabinet post Minister of Political Affairs II (Women's Department), which had been given to a woman in the preceding administrations. Moreover, as Table 6.1 shows, women are quite underrepresented even among civil servants. They constitute only 11 percent of government employees at the national level and 22 percent at the local level, and at both levels they are concentrated in the lowest grades of service.

A second problem derives from a backlash against the antipatriarchal movement. Using feminist theory as a basis (Donovan, 1985; Tong, 1989), Korean feminists have attacked the patriarchal system tying women to men, particularly as it relates to traditional family

Table 6.1   General Government Employees by Grade and Sex

	Total	Women	% Women
National Government Employees			
Total	95,950	10,820	11.3
1st Grade	68	0	0.0
2nd Grade	346	2	0.5
3rd Grade	606	10	1.6
4th Grade	3,490	50	1.4
5th Grade	7,624	135	1.7
6th Grade	20,212	972	4.8
7th Grade	19,828	2,282	11.5
8th Grade	20,409	3,587	17.6
9th Grade	12,413	3,398	27.4
Researcher	1,644	89	5.4
Assistant researcher	9,310	295	3.2
Local Government Employees			
Total	185,071	40,750	22.0
1st Grade	6	0	0.0
2nd Grade	22	0	0.0
3rd Grade	133	1	0.7
4th Grade	2,028	34	1.7
5th Grade	11,881	367	3.1
6th Grade	42,736	2,395	5.6
7th Grade	54,780	9,693	17.7
8th Grade	45,935	15,205	33.1
9th Grade	25,944	12,704	48.9
Researcher	290	15	5.2
Assistant researcher	1,316	336	25.5

Source: Ministry of Government, 1996.
Note: 1st grade is highest classification; researchers rank below the other civil service grades.

relationships. Even though feminists do not directly encourage the dismantling of the family itself, they do urge women to divorce rather than persevere in unhappy marriages; relatedly, the divorce rate tripled from 5.8 to 16.8 per 100 marriages between 1980 and 1995 (Korean Women's Development Institute, 1997: 60). Moreover, increasing juvenile delinquency was also blamed on feminism. Consequently, the women's liberation movement came to be denounced as "divorce science" or "family-destroying science." Thus, the misconception that feminism had instigated the breakdown of the family and undermined a healthy society worked to raise antifeminist feelings that gained a wide acceptance.

A third problem arises from the division of the feminist movement along class lines. The women's movement in Korea has diverged into two camps: the establishment one, which represents middle-class women and serves as an agent for the government; and the opposing one, which consists of lower-class working women aligned with rural women. The conservative umbrella organization for women's groups was formed in 1959 and now has forty suborganizations and nine local branches. Its major issues are women's mobilization for national development, birth control, the environment, unification, the development of women's capacities, and local autonomy. A radical umbrella organization was formed in 1987 that had twenty-eight suborganizations by 1998. It focuses its energies upon democratization, the labor movement, sexual violence, local autonomy, unification, and child care (Korean National Council of Women, 1998). This division among feminists reduces the opportunities for concerted effort, thereby lowering the overall effectiveness of the movement.

LOCAL SELF-GOVERNANCE
AND WOMEN'S POLITICAL REPRESENTATION

Women's strong interest in political representation derives from the fact that political empowerment can produce dramatic change in the status of women. There are two ways to remedy sexual inequality. One is to transform male-oriented patriarchal culture and to establish an egalitarian ethic. The other is to introduce legislative actions and laws. Each method has its own advantages and disadvantages. Although the strength of the former is that it produces fundamental and permanent change, its weakness is that it takes too long. In contrast, the weakness of the latter is that the effect is limited. Nevertheless, it has the advantage of producing a visible effect within a short period of time. Consequently, Korean women have long sought to increase political influence by securing seats in the National Assembly.

Korea's democratization therefore created high hopes for women. However, women in South Korea lost out in postdemocratic participation, just as women did in Latin America and Eastern Europe (Alvarez, 1990; Watson, 1993; Waylen, 1994). Since democratization, three parliamentary elections have been held—in 1988, 1992, and 1996. In the first two elections, no women were elected to the national congress from the individual districts; only two women were elected in 1996. The defeat of women even in the postdemocratic period can be attributed to a variety of factors, such as men's consistent reluctance to elect women as district representatives, the shortage of political funds and organizational support, and the lack of prestige of female candidates in local constituencies. In any case, this defeat at the national level was a turning point in the women's movement, and women's organizations shifted their strategy to gaining more representation in local government institutions.

A return to local politics was enabled by the revival of Korea's local self-governance system following democratization. With the demise of authoritarian rule, a host of attempts were made to consolidate democracy. As a bulwark against the resurgence of authoritarianism, civil society demanded local self-governance to curtail the overgrown power of the central state. Actually in Korea, the fate of a local self-governance system has been closely tied to the fate of democracy. The local autonomy system was implemented in 1952 and lasted until 1961. A military coup in 1961 and the onset of the antidemocratic regime brought local self-governance to an end. The Yushin constitution in 1972, which further strengthened Park Chung Hee's autocratic grip, eliminated the very base of local autonomy with the statement that no local governments would be reestablished until reunification was achieved (Cho and Rothlach, 1988). Democratization sounded the call for local autonomy, however. After an extended tug-of-war among the government, opposition parties, and civil society, local self-governance was revived in 1991 (Cho and Rothlach, 1988).

Local autonomy was particularly welcomed by women as a political outlet; several rationales were developed to encourage women to get involved in local politics, some of which were related to better prospects for success. Because competition at the local level is less severe, the entry barriers to local councils are comparatively low, and women can compensate for their limited funds, organization, prestige, and political experience. More theoretically, the argument that women are better suited for local politics began to gain wider acceptance. Because local politics deals with "life politics," such as waste and sewage disposal, water supply, consumer protection, children's education, and child care, it was assumed that "even a housewife" could qualify. With heightened expectations, women's organizations began to train women candidates for local elections.

However, this reorientation of the women's movement appears to be questionable, for three distinct reasons. First, contrary to expectations, women fared little better in local elections than at the national level. In the first local election held in 1991, women won only 0.9 percent of the seats at both the county and provincial levels, and the number of women victors increased to only about 1.5 percent in the 1995 elections. Given the all-out efforts that women made to gain local representation, these results are extremely disappointing.

However, their failure so far in local elections has not discouraged women's groups that still insist on focusing on local representation.

Yet, there are more important reasons than lack of electoral success for believing that the emphasis of Korean women's organizations on local politics is misplaced. One is that the assumed spillover effect from local to national politics appears questionable. It is claimed that women's participation in local legislatures will help them ultimately move to the national legislature by gaining political experience locally in specialized areas (Pateman, 1970). This argument is easy to refute. Theoretically, the issues dealt with in local assemblies are intrinsically different (e.g., trash disposal, clean water and clean air, and education) from the macro issues (e.g., the economy, finance, foreign affairs, and national security) with which the National Assembly deals. Consequently, training obtained from local politics will not contribute much to building up the specializations required in national politics. At the practical level, Table 6.2 demonstrates that only a small percentage of women candidates pursue local office in order to advance to the national political arena. It seems clear that local representation in Korea does not serve as a springboard for national representation.

Table 6.2   Female Candidates' Motives for Running for Local Assemblies

	1991		1995	
	County (%)	Province (%)	County (%)	Province (%)
Community service	62.6	47.1	76.8	81.8
Individual development	1.9	0.0	2.7	4.6
Advance to national politics	3.7	5.9	4.0	4.6
Promote equal society	29.0	41.2	15.2	9.1
Other	2.8	5.9	1.3	0.0
Number of candidates interviewed	107	51	151	21

Source: Sohn, 1998, p. 96.

More fundamentally, a critical reflection on the argument that women should specialize in local politics reveals that this will perpetuate the subordinate status of their gender. The contention that women are suited to dealing with such trivial local matters as life politics is in line with the contention that women are incapable of handling important national matters such as the economy, foreign affairs, and national security. This is nothing more than another form of sexual discrimination that seeks to legitimize women's subjection on the basis of the different nature of men and women. Because the pseudo-feminist rationale favoring local politics is not blatant but adroit, however, women (even ardent feminists) are very easily deceived. Therefore, even though women favoring local representation are not aware of the discriminatory nature hidden in the argument, the strategy should be rejected because it is very likely to perpetuate the subordinate status of women.

In sum, the strategy of women concentrating on local politics will discourage the development of women's capabilities and deprive them of the chance to advance to national politics. Rather than focusing on local representation, the strategy should be changed to focus on national representation. As many scholars concerned with feminism have pointed out, encouraging entry into national politics through a quota system, even if it may start with currying favor with male leaders, is much more constructive. In Taiwan, for example, a reserved seats system helped women overcome entry barriers to national politics. Once women crossed the threshold to advance to national politics, they later attained admission to national politics in their own right, even surpassing the seats assigned by the quota (Chou, Clark, and Clark, 1990). Thus, the goal of the Korean women's movement should be to enhance women's national political representation through institutional reform, such as implementing a quota system.

NEW DIRECTIONS FOR KOREAN FEMINISM

Since their first awakening in the late nineteenth century, Korean women have made much progress in enhancing their status. But postdemocratic feminists are committing some strategic errors in directing the women's movement. We stand at a crossroads; we either move ahead or retreat, depending on the direction of the policies we adopt. Critical reflection on the feminist movement following democratization will put the feminist movement back on the right track to establishing a society in which women are respected as human beings.

First, the postdemocratic emphasis of the feminist movement on local representation is misdirected, for the reasons outlined in the preceding section. Women's representation at the national level can be increased through the implementation of a quota system. Second, the feminist movement must guard against the rise of antifeminism throughout Korean society. In order for feminism to cope with social prejudice, the feminist movement needs to modify its image as being antifamily, especially in a society like Korea where family ties have strong roots. In this respect, feminists should work with men and other social groups on mutually important issues. Prior to democratization, the feminist movement was successful in extracting legal concessions and reforms from the government by merging feminist concerns with other salient social issues. Following democratization, the energy of women's organizations has focused on purely feminist issues like sexual violence. This leads to the alienation of men, without whose help sexual discrimination cannot be eliminated. Thus, the feminist movement needs to devise more subtle strategies to engage men's interest in achieving a gender-equal society.

Finally, the division in the feminist movement along class lines needs to be addressed. Maxine Molyneux (1986) is correct in arguing that not all women have the same interests and that gender issues vary according to class, religion, ethnicity, nationality, and political ideologies. But in Korea, where the cultural resistance is so formidable, a division in the feminist movement is indeed crippling. But a positive sign is that the umbrella organization centered on middle-class women and the umbrella organization centered on working-class women cooperated in the preparation for the Fourth World Conference on Women held in Beijing in 1995. If these two groups working together can correct some of the misdirections the postdemocratic women's movement has taken, the establishment of an equal society in South Korea will not be an impossible dream.

PART 2

Public Policy
and the Status of Women

7

Women Policies in Asia

PATTY HIPSHER & R. DARCY

In the past, North American and European scholars tended to see the development of women's issues as stemming from the Western tradition and setting (Duverger, 1955; Ostrogorski, 1893; Tingsten 1937). More recent work, in contrast, redresses this myopic view by placing the study of women's issues in a more global perspective (Jayawardena, 1986; Nelson and Chowdhury, 1994). Country-by-country analysis shows Asians have had women's issues on their political agenda for some time. What we do not know is if progress on women's issues follows through developmental stages in different nations or if progress is so conditioned by the unique social, cultural, political, and historical circumstances of individual nations that there is no one broad pattern. This chapter, hence, seeks to address this question. We begin with a brief overview of how North Americans placed women's issues on the political agenda and then discuss in much more detail the development of women's political issues in East and South Asia.

WOMEN'S ISSUES IN NORTH AMERICA: 1848

In Europe and North America, women have been pressing to put a variety of issues on the political agenda since the American and French Revolutions, more than 200 years ago (Darcy, Welch, and Clark, 1994). If we take the American Seneca Falls Declaration of 1848 as a rough guide and a checklist of early nineteenth-century women's issues in North America, we find several areas of demands. First and foremost were demands for political equality, the franchise, and the right to be represented in legislative assemblies so as to have a voice in the laws that govern women. Second, there were demands

107

for being treated as a civic person rather than as a dependent on some male (e.g., a father, brother, husband, or male child). A woman's children should be recognized as hers as well as her husband's; and husbands should not have, under the law, the "power to deprive her of her liberty, and to administer chastisement." Third, there were economic demands. Men should not monopolize "all the profitable employments," and the doors to education should not be closed to her. Fourth, women should not be subordinate in religion, and they should be equal with men in participation in church rituals and decisions. Man "has usurped the prerogative of Jehovah himself, claiming it as his right to assign for her a sphere of action, when that belongs to her conscience and to her God." Finally, there were demands that women should have the same social expectations as men and that society should value women as it does men. "He has endeavored, in every way that he could, to destroy her confidence in her own powers, to lessen her self-respect, and to make her willing to lead a dependent and abject life." Women should have the same respect accorded to themselves as men in similar situations.

These demands reflected the largely Quaker and certainly Protestant perception of mid-nineteenth–century North American society. The United States was still predominately Protestant and Anglo-Saxon. It had progressed well into the industrial revolution yet was still locally self-sufficient in its economy and was elite-dominated in politics; and it had a society where ideas circulated among elites, male and female, but the mass media were not to reach everyone for another hundred years or more. To some extent these sentiments would echo similar expressions in other English-speaking areas at the time and, with some modifications, much of Protestant Northern Europe generally. Certainly it cannot be said that North American society has achieved these goals in the 150 years that have passed. The ideas advanced at Seneca Falls were visionary for that society at that time and, to a degree, remain a challenge for contemporary North American society.

WOMEN'S ISSUES IN THE ASIAN CONTEXT

East and South Asia: Culture and Religion

If we turn to South and East Asia in the first part of the nineteenth century we might expect little audience for the Seneca Falls ideas. The Protestant tradition could scarcely be found among the indigenous peoples. Furthermore, democratic forms might possibly exist for managing village affairs here and there, but national governments were either colonial, despotic, feudal, or all three. Japan would not begin its push to industrialization until the Meiji Restoration in 1868, and the rest of South and East Asia would not industrialize for another century. The dominant religions among the indigenous peoples were Confucianism (not strictly a religion), Islam, Hinduism, Buddhism, and local amalgams of traditional and other religions, shamanism in Korea, Taoism in China, and Shinto in Japan. Like Christianity in the West, the religions of the East took many forms; and, like Western Christianity, there was a tendency for religious orthodoxy to reflect the state of society at the time of its founding. Thus, like Western Christianity, there was a conservative trend in the Eastern religions that added religious and quasi-religious sanction to ancient customs and usages.

Hinduism influenced what are today Pakistan, India, Sri Lanka, Bangladesh, Vietnam, Burma, Thailand, Cambodia, Laos, Nepal, Malaysia, and Indonesia, although today it is virtually confined to India, Nepal, and the Tamil parts of Sri Lanka. It is an ancient religion that took something like its present form about 4,000 years ago. In its most rigid traditional practice, an individual's place in life is determined at birth. A wide range of prescriptions and proscriptions govern the minute details of everyday life and dictate the options available. These vary by caste, age, and sex. Life within the system can be wonderful or horrible depending on the individual and the circumstances. Either way, within the system death is the only escape from one's place. For women there was the possibility of child marriage and even child marriage consummation. The marital asymmetry between men and women is most flagrantly reflected in sati, the practice of the widow throwing herself on the husband's funeral pyre, something not expected of the widower; and a prohibition of widow, but not widower, remarriage. The last is particularly difficult for women, given child marriage, the high death rate among young people, and the absence of a Hindu-sanctioned social role for a woman who will never have a husband, children, or grandchildren (Jayawardena, 1986; Ramusack, 1981). Religious rituals are performed only by males. But it should not be forgotten that Hinduism, like other religions, comes in many forms, so that the actual situation of women varies considerably.

Buddhism began as a Hindu reform movement about 2,500 years ago. It has impacted what is today all the East and South Asian nations of interest here except the Philippines. Today it remains an important part of life in Sri Lanka, Taiwan, China, Korea, Japan, Singapore, Cambodia, Laos, Vietnam, Thailand, and Burma. For women, Buddhism was a liberating force. A woman could become a Buddhist nun, thus offering an alternative to women in otherwise choiceless social systems. K. Jayawardena (1986: 111) quotes Sumangalamata, wife of a Sri Lankan rush-weaver, who, in 80 B.C., became a Buddhist nun:

> O woman well set free! How free am I!
> How thoroughly free from kitchen drudgery
> Me stained and squalid among my cooking-pots
> My brutal husband ranked as even less
> Than the sunshades he sits and weaves.

Buddhism itself did not specifically prescribe particular roles for women and generally fostered a greater equality than could otherwise be found. That is not to say that women were in practice the equals of men. The Buddhist equality was relative only to contemporary alternatives. In Vietnam, Japan, and Korea, periods when women's rights were expanded were periods of Buddhist flowering. During the Buddhist Le dynasty in Vietnam (the fifteenth through eighteenth centuries), women could inherit equally with a man, could own property, and had the right to divorce. Likewise, during the Buddhist Koryo dynasty (A.D. 918–1392) in Korea and the Buddhist Kamakura period (A.D. 1185–1333) in Japan, women were offered expanded opportunities. In each case, the succeeding dynasty associated Buddhism and female freedom with national weakness and imposed neo-Confucian restrictions (Jayawardena, 1986; Kim, 1976).

Under the neo-Confucianism prevalent up to the nineteenth century in Vietnam, Korea, Japan, and China, all women were subordinated to some man. She was subordinate to a father when she was young, to a husband in middle life, and to her son when elderly. Her "rights" were obligations enforced both in law and in social practice. Japan's Kaibara Ekken (1631–1714) wrote in *Greater Learning for Women:* "In everything, she must submit to her husband" (Jayawardena, 1986: 229). The Korean *Three Principles of Virtuous Conduct,* published in 1617, specified a rigorous separation of men and women and a severe limit on women's activities (Kim, 1976: 88, 324). The new Nguyen dynasty in Vietnam after 1800 repealed the liberal Hong Duc Code of 1483, which allowed women to inherit, own property, and divorce (Jayawardena, 1986: 198).

Islam came relatively late into the region but has had a lasting effect on major population groups in Pakistan, India, Bangladesh, Sri Lanka, Malaysia, Indonesia, and parts of the Philippines. Like other religions, Islam varies from situation to situation in its application to women. In Pakistan, India, and Bangladesh, for example, purdah, the seclusion of Muslim women, was practiced, whereas in Malaysia and Indonesia it was not (Jayawardena, 1986). The practice of polygamy, likewise, varied considerably. Until relatively recently, Islam was seen by Muslims as the religion of militarily, politically, socially, culturally, and scientifically superior societies. European defeats of the Moguls in India and the Ottomans in Europe and the Middle East seemed to many to challenge the religion itself. Ideas seen as European—freedom for women, for example—were therefore not viewed as inevitable cultural change but as threats to religion that must be resisted. In some instances, Islam became relatively more resistant to changed women's roles than other Eastern religions.

Despite this litany of patriarchy, less patriarchal traditions can be found in South and East Asia as well. Even the oldest of today's religions have existed for only a few thousand years. Behind them we can detect an older substrata of religious beliefs and practices in South and East Asia that date to earlier times when the role of women was very different from what it is today. Traces of matrilineal society, which can be found throughout the region, have left legacies of varying strengths. In ancient times, Sri Lanka had queens such as Anula Devi and Sugala "who led the armies of her kingdom into battle" (Jayawardena, 1986: 109). In Indonesia, women queens ruled the Kingdom of Arjeh as late as 1699 (Jayawardena, 1986), and it was not alone in having female sovereigns. In China, Mulan was a popular sixth-century woman general who led troops for twelve years. A significant number of the Taiping Rebellion (mid-nineteenth–century) generals and soldiers were women. Queen Sima and Princess Urduja commanded armies in the precolonial Philippines. Sisters Trung Trac and Trung Nhi in 45 B.C. drove the Chinese out of Vietnam with an army that included women generals (Jayawardena, 1986). The Vietnamese woman general Trieu Thi Trinh wrote in A.D. 245 (quoted in Jayawardena, 1986: 196):

> I only want to ride the wind and walk the waves,
> Slay the big whale of the Eastern Sea,
> Clean up the frontiers and save the people from drowning.
> Why should I imitate others,
> Bow my head, stoop over and be a slave?
> Why resign myself to menial housework?

In Korea, the first dynasty to unite the country, Silla, had three ruling queens. Important roles from ancient societies that continued through to modern times were shaman, healer, and *kisaeng*. About 70 percent of the shamans today are women, as their powers are considered stronger than those of men. Kisaeng are entertainers similar to the Japanese geisha (Kim, 1976). Even in ancient Japan, women played important social roles. Empress Pimiko, for example, restored order after the anarchy of A.D. 147–190. Before the eighth-century ruling, empresses were common, a practice ending only with Empress Koken. Lady Murasaki (A.D. 970–1049), author of *The Tale of Genji*, is an example of a woman who achieved prominence despite the heightened restrictions of the eighth-century Confucian Taiho Code.

The lessons of ancient matrilineal societies and periods when men and women were more equal were not lost on reformers. Takamure Itsue (1894–1964) published *Research on the Matriarchal System, Research on the Adoption of Sons-in-Law, History of Marriage in Japan,* and *The History of Women,* all showing that early Japanese society treated women in a more egalitarian way than at present. Because the condition of women in Japan was not "natural," but rather a product of historical circumstances, she argued the situation could be changed (Jayawardena, 1986).

Nineteenth- and Early-Twentieth-Century Reform Movements

In South and East Asia, calls for governmental reforms took place at the same time, or even earlier, than movements in the West. In India, Raja Rammohan Roy (1772–1833) was among those who published criticisms of sati and polygamy. He advocated women's property rights and education for women (Jayawardena, 1986). Sati was outlawed in 1829, but other women's issues continued on the agenda for the next century and a half, including child marriage, widow remarriage, polygamy, dowries, and prostitution (Ramusack, 1981). Raden Ajeng Kartini (1879–1904), an Indonesian woman, wrote against polygamy, restrictions women faced in education and entering professions, child marriage, and the absence of civil and political rights for women. Women in Malolos in the Philippines, supported by Philippine nationalists, petitioned the Spanish authorities for equal educational opportunities in 1887 (Jayawardena, 1986).

In China, Cantonese antimarriage associations started in the early 1800s and lasted for about a century. These consisted of large groups of women workers who lived together, thereby providing for themselves alternatives to subservience in the traditional family (Jayawardena, 1986). Calls against foot-binding, the painful and crippling practice of bandaging a girl's feet to make them smaller and supposedly more attractive, commenced in the 1890s. In 1911, for example, the Chinese Suffragette Society campaigned for an end to the by-then illegal but still practiced foot-binding, concubinage, child marriage, and prostitution and asked for women to have equal educational and political rights with men (Jayawardena, 1986; Siu, 1981). In Vietnam, Tran Thi Nhu Man, female editor of *Phu Nu Tung San* (Women's Review) in 1920, criticized the traditional social and family structure, one-sided chastity, arranged marriages, and female occupational and educational restrictions (Jayawardena, 1986). In 1892, Korean Yu Kil-chun published *Soyu Kyonmun* (An Account of Travel in the West) in which he compared the advantaged situation of American women to that of Korean women. Agitation resulted in the Kabo reform of 1894 abolishing child marriage, permitting widows to remarry, and allowing women to have short hair and to dress in the Western manner (Kim, 1976).

In Japan, the question of female suffrage was raised in the Hamamatsu prefectural assembly in 1876. The Japanese minister of education, Mori Arinori (1847–1889), attacked concubinage and the double standard of morality and advocated egalitarian contractual marriage and women's education (Jayawardena, 1986). Kishida Toshiko, a woman, was jailed in 1883 for a speech she gave entitled "Daughters Confined in Boxes." Kanno Suga in 1906 criticized the double standard (quoted in Jayawardena, 1986: 242):

> Among the many annoying things in the world, I think men are the most annoying . . . when I hear them carrying on interminably about female chastity I burst out laughing. . . . I greet with utmost cynicism and unbridled hatred the debauched male of today who rattles on about good wives and wise mothers. Where do all these depraved men get the right to emphasize chastity? Before they begin stressing women's chastity they ought to perfect their own male chastity, and concentrate on becoming wise fathers and good husbands!

Advocacy of women's issues began to enter the South and East Asian political agendas during the nineteenth century, if not earlier, and continued into the twentieth century. Women have formed organizations in South and East Asia as they have elsewhere. Jayawardena (1986) lists the following: the All-India Muslim Women's Conference (1916); the All-India Women's Conference (1927); the Women's Franchise Union in Sri Lanka (1927); the Indonesian Independent Woman Organization (1912); the Association of Philippine Women (1905); various Chinese suffragette associations (turn of the century); the Vietnamese Women's Labor Study Association (1926); and the Tokyo Women's Reform Society (1886). In the same year (1886) Ewha Haktang, the first girl's school in

Korea, was founded (Kim, 1976). Women's issues in Asia have thus varied from society to society. Concubinage and the sale of child brides, for example, have been concerns in China. In India, sati, polygamy, and child marriage were early concerns.

South and East Asians have hence not lagged behind Europeans and North Americans in challenging restrictions on women. Moreover, just as in Europe and North America, their success has been mixed. Comparing the Asian situations with nineteenth-century North America and the Seneca Falls Declaration, for instance, indicates that the nature of women's issues varied substantially between the two continents but that women's issues were being placed on the Asian political agenda at the very time of the Seneca Falls gathering. Women's issues, therefore, are indigenous to a society, and their shape and resolution have been determined by local conditions. Yet, even as early as the eighteenth century there were international influences in Asia at work as well. European missionaries and colonial administrators from England, France, Spain, the United States, and the Netherlands were vehicles for change. The suffrage movement created ripples that reached Asia, and the effects of Marxism's gender equality priorities went far beyond ripples. South and East Asians traveled and read and were not isolated from women's rights developments elsewhere. By the second half of this century communication among women's groups had been systematized; and the United Nations has supplied venues bringing together women from all parts of the globe (Nelson and Chowdhury, 1994).

THE EXTENT OF WOMEN'S LEGISLATION IN ASIA

At this point, a practical and strategic question emerges. Is each nation's situation so unique that the evolution of women's concerns and women's policies will be different, making cross-national measures of progress arbitrary? Or, despite real differences, are the nations of South and East Asia traveling down the same road of progress, some nations being further along than others? If there is one "road" of progress on women's issues, then this suggests there are stages along the road, stages marked by addressing "easier" issues, followed by progress on more "difficult" issues once progress on the easier issues has been achieved. Issues will still have to be addressed within the political, cultural, and economic situation of a particular nation. But if some issues are easier and others more difficult, then strategic priority should probably be placed on the easier ones.

Scaling Women's Issues in East and South Asia

Using a number of sources, especially United States government and United Nations documents, we were able to document eight areas of legislation relevant to women's rights for which uniform and recent information could be obtained for nineteen South and East Asian nations. These include the political rights of whether or not a woman was permitted to vote and whether or not she was permitted election to the national assembly. Economic rights included the right to own property and the right to equal pay for equal work. Legislation concerning rights to her person as a woman included the right to an abortion, the criminalization of spousal rape, legislation against domestic violence, and legislation prohibiting sexual harassment. A legal right, of course, does not necessarily mean that the relevant law is always or even usually observed. Still, the passage of the laws catalogued here give women in these societies a recourse against the abuses condoned by patriarchal cultures that they did not have previously. Thus, we believe that their very existence represents a positive step toward women's emancipation.

Our concern is to establish the relationship among these issues and to determine if they can be fitted into a single "women's issues" dimension. The simplest scale is the Guttman unidimensional scalogram (Darcy and Rohrs, 1995). A scale score is computed for each issue and each nation. For some of our items, nations are simply scored as to whether the legislation or right is present or not. For other items there is an intermediate category, present under some conditions, absent under others. In the case of India, for example, women governed by Muslim law do not have the same property rights enjoyed by other women. Thus, there are three possible states for legislation on any issue: present, indicated as X; intermediate, or in certain instances missing, indicated as O; and absent, indicated by a blank. A scale score for an issue or a nation consists of the number of Xs, followed by the number of Os, followed by the number of blanks.

The initial scale consists of the issues arranged from the lowest scale score to the highest and nations from the highest to the lowest. For convenience, the nations are arranged vertically and the issues horizontally. The initial scale is presented in Table 7.1. China and Singapore are at the top with scores of 6-0-2. That is, each has fully adopted six of the eight policies, but the other two are totally absent. Next come Malaysia and South Korea, each of which has adopted five of the policies, followed by Sri Lanka and Bangladesh, the only other Asian nations that have no legislation at all in two or fewer areas. Conversely, Burma, North Korea, Pakistan, and Laos are at the bot-

Table 7.1 Initial Guttman Scale

Nation	Spousal Rape	Domestic Violence	Abortion	Sexual Harassment	Equal Pay	Can Own Property	Can Be Elected	Can Vote	Score	Errors
China		X	X		X	X	X	X	6-0-2	2
Singapore			X	X	X	X	X	X	6-0-2	0
Malaysia	X	X	O		O	X	X	X	5-2-1	4
South Korea			O	X	X	X	X	X	5-1-2	0
Sri Lanka			O	X	O	X	X	X	4-2-2	2
Bangladesh		X	O		O	X	X	X	4-2-2	3
Japan			O		X	X	X	X	4-1-3	2
Indonesia			O		X	X	X	X	4-1-3	2
Vietnam			X		O	X	X	X	4-1-3	3
Philippines			O	X		X	X	X	4-1-3	2
Cambodia			O		X	X	O	X	3-2-3	4
Nepal			O		O	X	X	X	3-2-3	2
Thailand			O		O	X	X	X	3-2-3	2
India			O		X	O	X	X	3-2-3	4
Taiwan			O			X	X	X	3-1-4	2
Burma			O		O	X	O	X	2-3-3	4
North Korea			O		O	O	X	X	2-3-3	2
Pakistan			O		O	O	X	X	2-3-3	2
Laos					O	O	O	X	1-3-4	2
Total (X)	1	3	3	4	7	15	16	19	68	
Total (O)	0	0	15	0	10	4	3	0	32	
Total (blank)	18	16	1	15	2	0	0	0	52	
Errors	2	2	4	4	8	2	2	0		24

CR = .842   MMR = .447

Sources: Authors' calculations from Neft and Levine, 1997; UNICEF, 1997; U.S. Department of State, 1995–1997; United Nations, 1989, 1992–1995.

tom with only one or two fully adopted policies; and Taiwan joins Laos in not having any legislation in four of the eight areas.

A Guttman scale is evaluated by comparing it to a pattern of pure unidimensionality. For example, China has the highest initial scale score, 6-0-2. For that country we reproduce its codes from its scale score by starting at the right. We assign six X codes followed by no O codes followed by two "blank" codes. We make two errors. China is correctly categorized on six issues but incorrectly categorized on sexual harassment and domestic violence. When we do the same for Singapore, however, we get no errors. Overall, from the point of view of the nations there are 44 errors, making the coefficient of reproducibility CR = $[(152 - 44)/(8 \times 19)]$ = .710. We have 24 errors in reproducing the scale from the issue (or column) scale scores. This gives a CR = $[(152 - 24)/(8 \times 19)]$ = .842. The initial scale is an improvement over the minimal marginal reproducibility, which is the extent to which the scale could be reproduced by assigning each cell the modal score, here X, of which there are 68. The minimum marginal reproducibility, MMR = $68/(8 \times 19)$ = .447. The initial scale is not acceptable as a unidimensional scale, however, since a CR = .90 is required to be considered unidimensional. Malaysia, for example, has spousal rape and domestic violence legislation but not the "easier" sexual harassment statutes and the full right to an abortion.

The next step is to move issues and nations, changing their scale score in the process, so as to minimize the errors and make the errors uniform for columns and rows. There is an arbitrary element in creating the final scale. Taiwan, for example, would have one error with the scale score 3-2-3; the error would be the absence of equal pay legislation, which would be considered as partially present. But the equal pay legislation error could be considered as present, giving Taiwan the scale score 4-1-3, also one error. We selected the latter, grouping Taiwan with the industrialized or semi-industrialized nations. We were more arbitrary with Malaysia. We gave it a scale score of 8-0-0 with three errors rather than a scale score of 3-2-3 with two errors. This was done to better reflect the difficulty of the spousal rape and domestic violence issues.

The final Guttman scale is shown in Table 7.2. The reproducibility of the scale is now .901 from either the nations' or issues' scores. This meets the requirement for a unidimensional scale. Nations that have legislation on more "difficult" issues are higher than nations that do not have such legislation. Issues that are more difficult are more to the left on the scale than issues that are easier, although there are still some errors.

The issues group themselves into three areas of increasing diffi-

Table 7.2   Final Guttman Scale

Nation	Spousal Rape	Domestic Violence	Abortion	Sexual Harassment	Equal Pay	Can Own Property	Can Be Elected	Can Vote	Score	Errors
Malaysia	X	X	*	O*	O*	X	X	X	8-0-0	3
China		X	*	X	X	X	X	X	7-0-1	1
Singapore			X	X	X	X	X	X	6-0-2	0
South Korea			X	O*	X	X	X	X	6-0-2	1
Vietnam				X	O*	X	X	X	5-0-3	1
India				O	X	O*	X	X	4-1-3	1
Japan				O	X	X	X	X	4-1-3	0
Indonesia				O	X	X	X	X	4-1-3	0
Taiwan				O	*	X	O*	X	4-1-3	1
Cambodia				O	X	X	X	X	4-1-3	1
Sri Lanka			X*	O	O	X	X	X	3-2-3	1
Philippines			X*	*	O	X	X	X	3-2-3	2
Bangladesh		X*		O	O	X	X	X	3-2-3	1
Nepal				O	O	X	X	X	3-2-3	0
Thailand				O	O	X	X	X	3-2-3	0
Burma				O	O	X	O*	X	3-2-3	1
North Korea				O	O	O	X	X	2-3-3	0
Pakistan				O	O	O	X	X	2-3-3	0
Laos				O	*	O	O	X	1-4-3	1
Score:										
Total (X)	1	2	4	5	10	16	18	19	75	15
Total (O)	0	0	0	14	9	3	1	0	27	
Total (blank)	18	17	15	0	0	0	0	0	50	
Errors	0	1	4	3	4	1	2	0	15	15

CR = .901   MMR = .447

Sources: Authors' calculations from Neft and Levine, 1997; UNICEF, 1997; U.S. Department of State, 1995–1997; United Nations 1989, 1992–1995.

Note: An asterisk indicates error.

culty. The "easiest" area for these Asian nations today is political rights for women. All have extended the franchise and all permit women to serve, at least under certain conditions, in elected bodies. The next most difficult area is economic. India, Pakistan, and Laos still limit property rights for at least some women; and North Korea, the last Stalinist regime, restricts property rights generally. Equal pay legislation is absent in Taiwan and Laos but on the books in industrialized Singapore, South Korea, and Japan, as well as in China and Cambodia. Yet, even where it is the law, income equalization is treated cautiously for fear of "restricting the inflow of transnational capital, alarming indigenous capitalists, and burdening the public sector" (Salaff, 1981: 60). Equal pay legislation is a potential next step for industrialized Taiwan. Strengthening equal pay legislation is also a logical next step for Thailand, the Philippines, Bangladesh, and Sri Lanka with fast-growing industrial sectors employing large numbers of women.

Abortion policy comes next on our scale. Of course, abortion everywhere is an economic issue in that the "right" to an abortion is realistic for many poor in Europe and North America only if provided or supported by government health services. Likewise, it is an economic issue for poor women everywhere seeking to control their access to employment opportunities. But in North America and certain European nations, abortion is seen by many middle-class women as a freedom issue. For them, it is a question of who makes the decision concerning their bodies—doctors, legislators, or themselves. In North America and much of Europe, the economic aspects of abortion, while important, are peripheral to the central question of a woman's freedom to choose for herself.

In much of Asia, abortion is defined differently. Governments view overpopulation as a major impediment to economic development, growth, and the improvement of living standards. The "right" to an abortion in China, India, or Singapore, for example, is less a right and more a threat and obligation. For many Asian nations with strong population policies, the right *not* to have an abortion for a woman would be more comparable to the right to an abortion advocated by Western feminists. Many Asian women do not have this choice, especially after the birth of a first boy. For these reasons, abortion policy in the nineteen Asian nations examined is intermediary between the economic issue area and the abuse issue area.

The most "difficult" issue area for these Asian nations, as it is with European and North American nations, is in the area of rape, violence, and harassment. Each issue has its own difficulty. Domestic violence requires three steps for it to be addressed. First, the exclusion long enjoyed by domestic violence from statutes generally prohibiting violence of one person upon another needs change. Second, police forces and courts need to see domestic violence as something individuals, women in particular, need to be protected from. Third, the victims themselves need to have an environment in which they feel secure enough to press for their right to be free from domestic violence, should it occur. The last stage is particularly difficult, because many women have few alternatives to returning to a threatening home. Putting a provider and a father in prison, even for a short time, can increase family tensions and can appear to be an impossible alternative for the abused wife. Certainly, removing legal exceptions in the criminal code permitting domestic violence is essential. But it is only a first step. Few of the Asian nations in this study have taken this step.

Sexual harassment, likewise, is a new area of the law, even in North America and Europe. It is the unwanted attentions of a threatening supervisor or a work environment made demeaning by offensive sexual references. Until recently, women were "protected" from sexual harassment by being excluded from the work environment or by being segregated within the work environment. Women admitted to the male work environment were admitted only provisionally and were expected to "be one of the boys." In some sense the problem of sexual harassment is deceptively simple. Employers should provide a professional environment for all their employees. Employees should not be routinely humiliated or forced to submit to sexual demands as a condition of employment and advancement. But there is also a new sexual freedom, and it should be no one's business what two consenting adults do on their own time. At what point does a tasteless joke become sexual harassment? These questions are only now being asked, and answers are proving difficult to find.

Finally, the most difficult question for the Asian nations is spousal rape. In most Asian nations, like in most Western nations, marriage has been defined as sexual, at least in part. Women and men in marriage have been expected to have sexual relationships, and the marriage itself is seen to create an obligation for each partner to participate in sex. In the last century, Western nations and Asian nations began to recognize that some marriages were simply not working and some couples chose to live apart, either within the same house or in different locations. These situations, recognized to varying degrees by society as legitimate arrangements, raised the possibility of rape within a marriage. Once the possibility of rape within a marriage exists, the question of protection from such violence raises questions about the conditions under which protection should be available. Again, these questions are difficult to legislate. Among our Asian nations, only Malaysia has so far done so.

Spousal rape, domestic violence, and sexual harassment are newer issues in that governments are just beginning to address them with statutes and programs. At the moment, they provide a poor fit with the other issue areas among the South and East Asian nations examined. Bangladesh, for example, has domestic violence legislation but not sexual harassment laws and is only partially providing for equal pay and abortion, all "easier" or "prior" to domestic violence on the scale. From a strategic perspective, two things are suggested. First, local opportunities to address problems should be taken without regard to the "stage" of development of a nation. Second, our results suggest that there may be an opportunity for progress in some easier areas in nations where some more difficult areas have been successfully addressed.

ASIAN WOMEN IN A CHANGING WORLD

There is great diversity in problems women face in the South and East Asian nations. There is also diversity in the capacity of these societies to address such problems. Certainly, women's issues are not new to the area's political agenda, and local incidents continue to raise people's consciousness. Miss Chao's 1919 wedding-day suicide in China, for example, provoked criticism of forced marriages (Jayawardena, 1986). The 1872 *Maria Luz* incident in which Japanese women being shipped to Peru as prostitutes escaped also provoked outrage. The result was that prostitution in Japan was reformed. But the Japanese did not abolish prostitution until 1958 (Jayawardena, 1986; Koyama, 1961). Such episodes continue to occur and result in local consciousness-raising. But women's issues are no longer confined to the circumstances of a particular place or time. They are part of a worldwide process.

Today the easiest women's issues for South and East Asian nations to address have been those of political access, the vote, and the right to be elected. Perhaps these have been easy because they are rights only. Performance is something else, and women continue to lag in South and East Asia in getting elected to national assemblies and to other offices. The next most difficult set of issues is economic. Women have gained the right to own property in most nations, but equal pay for the same work remains rare. Because women still do not even have equal access to the same professions and positions as men in many societies, such legislation would have limited immediate impact. Currently, the most difficult areas are those dealing with violence and abuse from those with whom women should be the most secure—the family and fellow workers. These South and East Asian patterns mirror the development of these issue areas in the West.

8

Democratic Consolidation and Gender Politics in South Korea

ROSE J. LEE

The third wave of democratization led comparativists to focus on democratic transition and consolidation. Unlike the two preceding waves of democratization, the new wave raised a profound scholarly concern for the uncertainty of the road to democracy. No longer was democratization considered inevitable in societies where socioeconomic preconditions had been met. Instead, democratic transitions are explained primarily by the strategies of and negotiations between regime officials and opposition leaders. Moreover, as analytic attention shifted to conditions under which democratic consolidation is likely to occur, the focus continued to be on political elites (Diamond, Linz, and Lipset, 1989; Huntington, 1991; O'Donnell and Schmitter, 1991; O'Donnell, Schmitter, and Whitehead, 1986; Share, 1987).

This elitist approach, however, tends to overlook social forces working from below to bring authoritarian regimes to an end, in contrast to more participatory democratic theorists. Therefore, the recent literature on democratization that has been dominated by this elitist approach ignores the role of social forces at large and, more specifically, women's groups in the democratization process. Latin American feminist scholars in particular called attention to this theoretical negligence, chiding elitist democratic theorists for their narrow definition of democracy, which they blamed for ignoring significant social factors in their explanation of democratization.

The Latin American feminists' work, after establishing the linkage between the women's movement and democratic transition in Latin America, especially in Brazil, also critically examines the implications of democratization for the women's movement and its policy goals. According to their findings, as democratic consolidation leads to the institutionalization of political processes and the strengthening

123

of political parties, the women's movement and women's groups lose their autonomy. Coopted by political parties or integrated into the political system, women's groups no longer command special attention from party leaders, although some women's groups may benefit from the new political situation created by increased political participation. In general, political processes then return to politics as usual, in the sense that politics is male dominated, with a leading example seen in low levels of women's political representation (Alvarez, 1989, 1990; Carroll, 1983; Jaquette, 1994; Waylen, 1994).

The Latin American feminist scholars' findings, while serving to alert other feminist scholars to watch out for a potential danger that democratization may disappoint aspiring women's groups, seem to contradict some basic assumptions of democracy. One such assumption is that democratization fosters political and social equality, including that in gender relations. A democracy by definition means a responsive government that seeks to meet the demands made by various groups in society. Hence, the political opening that results from a democratic transition provides increased opportunities for voluntary groups, stimulating phenomenal numbers of active organizations. Women's groups are no exception. After decades of participation in the democratic movement—during which the focus of their activities alternated between the democratic struggle and women's issues—these women's groups are likely to emerge as a leading participant in the democratic political process (for the Korean example, see Lee 1995a, 1995b). Their strength derives from their earned legitimacy as a contributor to democratization and from their coming of age as an organization. Women's groups, hence, are likely to be effective in promoting their agenda through the political process; and their political effectiveness is likely to parallel the degree of the democratic consolidation. Consequently, the consolidation of democracy is likely to enhance the advancement of gender policy and gender equality.

This study explores the influence of democratization on gender politics in South Korea by examining the relationship between democratization and gender policy for the first two democratic governments that came to power following the democratic transition. Although gender policy generally results from the interaction between the regime and women's groups, this study focuses on the government as decisionmaker in democratic reforms and gender policy. First, I examine the degree of democratization of each government, mainly from the viewpoint of democratic reforms undertaken. Second, I describe the development of women's groups and the women's movement in Korea. Third, I examine the advancement of gender equality under each administration by focusing on the new gender policies—and the structural reform for such gender policies—that were implemented. Although the inputs and influence of women's groups are largely assumed, they are specified where their decisive roles became highly salient (see Chapter 6 for another discussion of women's groups in Korea). The discussion concludes with an assessment of whether the relative democratic standings of the two governments bear directly on gender equality—specifically, whether greater democratic reform led to a parallel advancement in gender policy. The conclusion relates these findings to the concerns expressed by Latin American feminist scholars over the negative consequences of democratic consolidation for women's political advancement.

DEMOCRATIZATION IN KOREA: TRANSITION AND CONSOLIDATION

The ruling elite's announcement on June 29, 1987, of a return to democracy marked the beginning of a transition to democracy in South Korea. Although the shift in the regime's fundamental political posture appeared to happen suddenly, the announcement resulted from an extended dialectical process between the elite, on the one hand, and opposition politicians and social movement groups, on the other. The proposal for constitutional revision that was presented by the opposition party and supported by democratic movement groups served as the beginning of a long negotiation process regarding the transition. Buoyed by the turning point of the 1985 election, which drew unexpectedly high popular support for the opposition party, the opposition party and democratic movement groups forged an alliance that the ruling party could no longer ignore. The ruling party's split, between hard-liners and moderates, bolstered the opposition's demand for a democratic constitutional revision. After a long struggle between the ruling elite and the opposition, as well as between hard-liners and moderates in each camp, negotiations finally resulted in the triumph of the moderates over hard-liners in both parties, ending in what is known as a conservative, centrist compromise (Im, 1990).

The pattern of Korea's democratic transition that emerged from the transition negotiations resembles Share's (1987) transaction and Huntington's (1991) transplacement types. Although this type of democratic transition is bent toward conservatism and therefore inherently limits the degree of reform, its success, according to Share

(1987), depends to a large degree on the ruling elite's willingness and ability to implement the announced reforms. The regime's willingness to fulfill its promises was first tested in the politics of making a constitution. When detailed negotiations began in August, some basic differences emerged regarding the military's status and labor rights, but both sides embraced the leading principles of the democratic transition that had been announced on June 29. The overriding importance of the basic principles, however, enabled both parties to reach a compromise on their earlier differences to produce a new constitution (Im, 1989).

The real test of the regime's willingness to carry out its promises centered on the transition elections. The presidential election held in December 1987 had special significance as the first popular presidential election since 1971. With a split in the leading opposition party, this election turned into a four-way contest between the ruling party and three other party candidates. This split, in fact, gave away the earlier opposition party's popular advantage to the ruling party, leading to the latter's electoral victory (Hyun, 1989; Kim, 1989). The legislative election was held in 1988 under the revised election law. The new law, which aimed at fair elections, resulted from a compromise allowing the ruling party's apportionment scheme as well as the opposition party's single-district system (Brady and Mo, 1992). With election laws that leveled their electoral chances, the political parties conducted a campaign to distinguish themselves from each other in the public's mind. The ruling party emphasized economic growth with political stability, and the opposition parties charged the ruling party with complicity in the previous regime's corruption. The ruling party's efforts to ward off the opposition charges apparently did not succeed; it won the election but not a majority of legislative seats. The resulting "*yoso-yadae* phenomenon," an unprecedented case of a ruling party's minority of legislative seats counterposed to the opposition parties' majority in the National Assembly, would haunt the ruling party in the ensuing legislative process until it found a remedy through a merger with other political parties.

From the transition elections emerged a few new campaign and election patterns. First, the Korean electorate's dogged determination to conduct fair elections was demonstrated through electoral supervision and monitoring by the Fair Election Committee as well as by citizens' volunteer groups. In fact, some critics contend that the candidates' campaigns were conducted according to standards that were too strict to ensure them an opportunity for an open and vigorous election campaign. Second, the electoral outcome of the transition elections had a high degree of unpredictability (Han, 1989;

O'Donnell and Schmitter, 1991), resulting from the demographic shift, voter realignment, and the disappearance of the ruling party's unqualified advantages in command of resources (Yoon, 1990). Such uncertainty was translated into a low rate of popular support for the winning presidential candidate, as well as for the ruling party in the legislative election. In short, the presence of the popular will to conduct fair elections and the uncertainty over the electoral outcomes boded well for Korean democracy.

The product of a centrist conservative compromise, the Roh government's political power was inherently limited. The new government moved to woo the key players of the preceding regime, the military and business, which resulted in vested interests left intact, the leftist forces politically excluded, and the opposition parties pushed rightward. Under such prevailing conservatism, reforms could not exceed some rudimentary changes (Lee et al., 1995; *Path to Democracy*, 1991). The priorities of reform that emerged from the Roh government's assumption of power related to labor rights, freedom of press and assembly, and the power of the national security agency. The national security agency was democratized through personnel change at the top and through refocusing the agency's function to external affairs. The government's censorship of the press through "voluntary restraint" was removed. However, the government resisted the restoration of labor's basic rights: although collective bargaining was permitted, third-party intervention in collective bargaining remained prohibited, and labor's political participation rights were unresolved. Judicial reform was perceived as equally pressing, leading to the appointment of nonpartisan judges to the supreme court and to the establishment of an independent constitutional court. The purpose of the reform was to establish the political neutrality of the judiciary and to delineate limits for executive and legislative power. Newly appointed judges, in fact, were disposed to adhere to political neutrality in judicial decisions, and the constitutional court handed down rulings on constitutional issues. The constitutional court, however, has yet to demonstrate its ultimate commitment to the constitution by ruling on cases significantly affecting the power of the other two branches of the government.

Although the Roh government's ambivalence toward reform did not result entirely from its party's legislative minority status, the government was in a political quandary because it needed the opposition parties' cooperation on legislative matters. To overcome its political vulnerability, the ruling party successfully negotiated a merger with two opposition parties. The merger, however, ended the opposition coalition's legislative majority, pushing the conservative alliance further in a reactionary direction to bring about *gongan-jungchi,* the "public security first" policy that resulted in a massive crackdown on student-labor unrest.

The fluid political situation generated by the democratic transition presented a wide range of political possibilities, creating political anomalies in Korea. As previously observed, unprecedented political events occurred: the governing party was relegated to a legislative minority status, and the ruling party merged with two opposition parties to form a legislative majority. The list of political anomalies expanded in the second legislative election, which was held in April 1992, creating the "Kookmindang phenomenon" (Park, 1992), a new party's success in the legislative election. The new entrant won enough legislative seats to qualify as an official political party in the National Assembly (meeting the minimum requirement of twenty seats).

The second presidential election presented the ruling party with unusual intraparty difficulties. The internal disarray revealed basic ideological differences between the mainstream faction and the non-mainstream faction, which held up the presidential nomination until the last moment. Y. S. Kim finally emerged as the party nominee and waged a presidential campaign successfully to be the next president. Kim's election to the presidency foreshadowed an ideological shift within the ruling party, as discussed later.

Heralding a new era of truly civilian government, the new administration initiated an open government with a wide range of reforms on its agenda. These reforms included the investigation of military corruption and the elimination of any private and secretive clubs within the military, the revitalization of the public service, banking law reform, and political and administrative reform. The investigation of the military brought to an end the modus vivendi that had hitherto been maintained between the government and the military through the earlier compromise reached during negotiations for the democratic transition. The investigation exposed irregularities in military acquisitions of fighter jets, known as the *yolgok-biri;* it also outlawed the secret elite organization within the military called the Hanahoe, which had long been regarded as the pool for the future military leadership. The resulting dismissals and prosecution of high-ranking officers led to the restructuring of the military. And ultimately, the reform left no doubt about the constitutional supremacy of the civilian authority over the military.

Another government priority was the revitalization of the public service. The government promoted fair and competitive elections through the revision of election laws, basically by consolidating a series of existing laws into one. The new law eliminated certain restrictions on campaign activities and increased government financial assistance to party candidates. Furthermore, in order to eliminate corruption and bribery in government, the government passed legislation mandating registration of high-ranking public officials' financial holdings and establishing ethical standards for public officials. The most radical of all reforms was banking legislation prohibiting bank accounts under false names, a reform that was a guarded secret until it was announced by an executive order. Because Korea had a sizable underground economy into which unidentified monies had been poured for decades under the authoritarian regimes, the banking reform was viewed as critical to dismantling the authoritarian legacy. These reforms signaled the Kim government's determination to break away from the authoritarian era (Chung, 1997; Im, 1997; Lee, 1997).

Although these reforms were well received by the general public, they faced resistance from vested interests, a situation that decelerated the initial momentum for the reforms. For instance, although legislative oversight was intended to be a control mechanism over the military and the national security agency, the exercise of this legislative control remained superficial and ineffective. The consolidated election law similarly revealed loopholes in regulating the uses and amounts of campaign funds, and campaign expenditures continued to escalate. The upholding of fairness standards in elections, however, emerged as the law's unmistakable success (Cho, 1994). Banking reform was credited with the reestablishment of standards for future banking, but its short-term results were less than satisfactory: some of the targeted monies were actually channeled into the national economy. In short, the first half of the Kim administration could not fully implement its reforms, as the administration vacillated between change and the status quo, which signaled the need for the ruling faction to rid itself of the dead weight from the conservative Roh faction (Chung, 1994).

The second half of the Kim administration instituted another round of reforms targeting corrupt politicians, bureaucrats, and business leaders, mostly associated with the preceding government. Such purges and prosecutions eventually led to the trial of the Fifth Republic revolving around two infamous historical incidents known as the 12.12 Incident and the Kwangjoo Incident, which implicated former presidents Chun and Roh. Preceded by investigations into illegal political funding and misappropriation of political funds, the trial established the illegitimacy of the Fifth Republic by establishing the 12.12 Incident as a military coup d'état and the Kwangjoo Incident as an illegal use of force against citizens protesting the military takeover. The historic verdict against the Fifth Republic, in effect, rewrote the history of the dark period of 1979–1980 by shedding light on and redefining the true heroes and true villains of that period. In this act, the Kim government firmly established its own identity.

How far then has Korea advanced in its democratic consolidation? The preceding discussion on the Roh and Kim governments sheds some light on the democratic consolidation. The succession of governments since the democratic transition reveals the strengthening of democratic processes and institutions, because reforms undertaken by these governments tended to be cumulative and reforms implemented by the succeeding government tended to be more profound, redressing the structural distortions created by the authoritarian regime. The Roh government, born of the centrist conservative compromise, was accountable to vested interests from the past as well as to reform pledges made during negotiations regarding the democratic transition and during the presidential election. Subject to inherent constraints arising from the pattern of democratic transition it adopted, the first democratic government implemented reforms that inevitably tended to be modest compared to those of the succeeding government. Reforms focused on removing the trappings of authoritarianism, mainly relating to civil liberties, and they had immediate impact. The national security agency shifted its focus from the surveillance of individual citizens to external affairs. The press was empowered by its liberation from government censorship. The full-blown freedom accorded to the press contrasted with the limited changes in labor's basic rights. An obvious difference between the two issues is that though the former did not affect vested interests, the latter affected business interests, in particular. Therefore, on labor matters, the first democratic government could not or would not go so far as to guarantee labor's three basic rights.

In contrast, one step removed from the transition compromise, the Kim government was not subject to the same constraints and therefore undertook bold reforms, such as the banking reforms, which had not previously been widely discussed because they had been regarded as unachievable. In spite of loopholes, the law reestablished banking standards, which had long been missing from Korean economic life. The fundamental restructuring of the military through a purge of political generals and corrupt officers proved to be also a major task, leading to the constitutional reestablishment of the civilian supremacy over the military. The government's alternation between radicalism and conservatism, however, suggested that the government was subject to constraints largely generated by discord with conservative partners in the ruling party. President Kim was able to dispel such conservative influence when he waged a frontal assault on the authoritarian past and the illegitimacy and corruption of the Fifth Republic, which also implicated core conservative leaders in the government party. Viewed from the reform perspective, the Kim government consolidated Korean democracy by securing a solid structural foundation for the military, banking, and public service and, moreover, by establishing the truth about the authoritarian past. Democratic consolidation in Korea was also studied from other perspectives, with similar findings for progress (Lee, 1995a; Shin, 1989; Shin and Chae, 1993).

A HISTORICAL PERSPECTIVE ON WOMEN'S ORGANIZATIONS AND THE WOMEN'S MOVEMENT

A brief historical background of the women's movement and its relationship to the state may help the reader to understand the evolving relationship between women's groups and the state since the democratic transition (Lee, 1995b). As is true in many Third World countries, the women's movement dates back to the national independence movement at the turn of the century. Women's groups, consisting mainly of students, participated in the historic anticolonial movement against Japan in 1919 and remained organized for the unfinished task of national independence. As the colonial power's repression intensified, women's groups retreated to their usual work of teaching the illiterate how to read and housewives how to improve family life. Whereas women's groups based in the south limited their activities to feminine tasks, women's groups in the north called for women's liberation. During this historic epoch, women's groups contributed substantially to national liberation.

Under the Rhee government, which was formed as Korea regained its independence at the end of World War II, women's groups were typically organized as middle-class wives' clubs volunteering to educate women in the countryside or to teach housewives how to become "a wise mother and a good wife." Elite women's groups, on the other hand, began engaging in what appeared to be a dramatic deviation from the past. Women's groups staged a battle against the traditional antiwomen practices of concubinage and prostitution as early as during the military occupation. Moreover, defying political convention, Y. S. Yim, a woman who earlier served as a cabinet member, founded a women's political party and ran for the vice-presidency under the party. A professional politician of even greater political stature—S. C. Park, who started as a rank-and-file legislative member of the leading opposition party and who had a long distinguished legislative career—was nominated as the party's presidential candidate. Although these women aspiring for top political positions did not win the elections, their sudden surge of activity was a defining element of the era. In fact, the number of women legislators elected from districts under the Rhee government turned out to be the largest in Korean legislative history (see Chapter 3). Women's political success during this period was largely due to the openness and good feelings generated by the national liberation and the incoming democratic government, which was led by Western-educated political leaders epitomized by President Rhee.

The national economic development effort under the ensuing authoritarian regime changed the role of women's groups and the women's movement vis-à-vis the state. Initially mobilized by the state, the women's movement played an enormous role in Korea's economic development. As the only women's national umbrella organization endorsed by the government, the Council of Korean Women's Organizations (CKWO) cooperated with the government and participated in its population control policy, as part of the economic development plan. Not consulted during the decisionmaking process, it was brought in to help execute the policy by disseminating birth control information in the countryside as well as in the cities. In this process of delivering the centrally planned program to the peripheries, CKWO established a linkage between the national women's organization and local women's groups, which were until then organizationally in their infancy. Such ties strengthened both central and local women's organizations through a mutual push and pull. This enhanced the self-confidence of these women's groups, which were now ready to negotiate with the government. At its widely attended national convention in 1978, to which member organizations and local chapters sent their delegates, CKWO called for a greater representation of women in the legislature. The government party responded favorably to this call at the next election, with more women being chosen for at-large legislative seats. By no means independent from the state, the women's groups, however, did not hesitate to demand rewards for their contributions to the national economic development when the opportunity arose.

In the early 1980s, under the new Chun government, which did not share the previous regime's singular national focus on economic development, women's groups were free to navigate in their own directions. Some returned to their traditional feminine pursuits centering on hobbies and voluntary services. The national leadership, however, had a different vision of the role of women and the women's movement in society. They sought the changes that became the structural foundation of gender policy. The World Women's Conference in Copenhagen provided the occasion for their action. The women leaders who returned from this meeting presented the governing party leadership with a United Nations mandate based on the conference resolutions that each government should establish a women's agency. The women's groups were able to exploit the government's political vulnerability to international pressures relating to the UN mandate and its need for domestic support. After quiet but persistent lobbying relying on the access developed under the previous government, the women leaders' two-pronged proposal for the establishment of a women's research institute and a women's policy agency won the ruling party leadership's support and passed the legislature. These two government organs were established in 1983 to become the Korean Women's Development Institute and the Council of Women's Policy (Kim, 1990). These accomplishments support Alvarez's observation that even an authoritarian regime affords political opening (Alvarez, 1989, 1990).

Initially, the women's groups involved in the women's movement and national economic development were middle-class feminine groups working closely with the establishment. In contrast, women's groups affiliated with the opposition did not emerge until the democratic movement got under way in the mid-1980s. These women's groups were composed primarily of highly educated, radical feminists, who had significant experience in the university protest movement. Initially, feminist groups sprouted from women's universities, notably the women's studies program at Ewha Women's University. Bred with an ideology that women's liberation cannot be complete without national liberation from authoritarianism as well as from imperialism, they alternated between working for the feminist cause and for the national cause. These groups, alongside women workers, protested against dismal working conditions in factories, organized against inhumane treatment of women prisoners (including sex torture), and demanded reform in the male dominated church hierarchy. In the critical days of the democratic movement, they redirected their energy toward the national cause.

In what is known as the Korean Broadcasting Service (KBS) Incident in 1986, feminist groups aligned with other social groups to boycott KBS subscriptions in protest against its gross mistreatment of a female employee. The incident, which started with a limited objective, escalated into a massive democratic movement, as the occasion provided the opportunity to voice popular grievances toward the repressive regime whose proprietorship of the broadcasting channel enabled it freely to distort information. The escalation was also partly due to the synchronization of the incident with the opposition's recent proposals for constitutional reform. It was in this context that the Korean Women's Associations United (KWAU), a national umbrella organization for feminist groups, emerged to unite all radical women's groups. National leadership for the feminist women's groups was critically needed to coordinate efforts with the leaderships of other social groups. At the forefront of the democratic movement, KWAU worked closely with the opposition party. The bond that formed continued with the opposition party supporting gender issues after the democratic transition. Feminist groups played a critical role in galvanizing the democratic movement, which succeeded in bringing the authoritarian leadership to the negotiating table.

Following the democratic transition in 1987, women's groups, along with other social groups, proliferated (Korean Women's Development Institute, 1995; Palley and Gelb, 1992). Women's groups remained divided into two general categories: the mainstream groups under the CKWO leadership, and the radical feminist groups under the KWAU leadership. Each coalition had more than twenty member organizations. Of the mainstream women's organizations, the YWCA, with the longest history and the largest memberships, has long been active in traditional feminine matters, engaging in education, relief service, and family law reform. The Korean Center for Family Law, the Business and Professional Women's Organization, the Korea University Women's Association, and the National Association of Nurses are other member organizations. Most occupational associations, including the hairdressers' organization, belong to CKWO. The leadership, consisting largely of educated middle-class women and representing a generally conservative approach to women's issues, derives its strengths from its nonthreatening gradualist style. After the democratic transition, CKWO's links with the ruling party remained intact, but the organization nevertheless regained its autonomy.

Feminist groups under KWAU, having the distinction of having been leading participants in the democratic movement, began to play an essential role in gender politics, ranging from the public arena to women's private lives. Although it had fewer individual members than CKWO, KWAU greatly expanded its activities to reach out to the unfortunate women in factories and homes. The Women's Society for Democracy, Women Workers Association, and Women's Hotline are some of the organizations in this category. Their earlier uncompromising position yielded to a more cooperative approach in dealing with the conservative women's groups. As described in the next section, gender-related policies under both the Roh and Kim governments largely owe their success to the cooperation between women's groups on both sides.

DEMOCRATIZATION AND GENDER POLICY

When the democratic transition brought the Roh government into power, there was in place a basic structure to address women's policy, including a mammoth research institute and a policymaking organ in the government. The Korean Women's Development Institute (KWDI) was established in 1983 as the culmination of women leaders' quiet lobbying. The establishment of the Council on Women's Policy followed, as these same women leaders sought a policy mechanism to convert research results into a policy agenda. Once these two critical vehicles of gender policy were established under the authoritarian Chun government, the new government's priority, as defined by women's groups, centered on converting outstanding women's issues into gender policy.

As the democratic transition activated civil society, women's organizations not only proliferated but also sought to be actively involved in gender policymaking. The recruitment of a woman to head the Ministry of Political Affairs II under the new government was one of their more visible achievements. The ministry, without portfolio, served as the coordinating office for women's policy, worked closely with bureaus in the Ministry of Labor and the Ministry of Health and Social Welfare, and functioned as the secretariat of the Council on Women's Policy. Successive appointments of women as head of the ministry turned it into the de facto ministry of women's affairs. Furthermore, the transfer of jurisdiction over the KWDI from the ministry of Health and Social Welfare made the Ministry's advocacy of women's policy more effective.

Under the Roh government, gender policy was formally inaugurated, and women's issues found institutional solutions through legislation for the first time. Gender-related legislation comprised three areas: family law revision, equal employment, and child care (Korean Women's Development Institute, 1995; *Women's Policy*, 1991). These three gender issues were the top priorities of women's groups who succeeded in politicizing them during the presidential election. This enabled them to extract campaign pledges from presidential candidates. Promising his support for the legislation as a candidate, President Roh soon faced an obligation to fulfill his campaign promise. Persistent reminders from women's groups served as an impetus for President Roh to direct the National Assembly to work on the legislation. Family law reform, having been the target of the women's movement for three decades, posed a greater challenge for the administration, given the opposition from traditional Confucianists who considered it to be destructive to the Confucian family structure. The revision finally passed, through a cooperative effort between the leading opposition party (PPD) and the ruling party (W. J. Lee, 1991). The revised law strengthened women' rights within the family, entitling women to community property, inheritance, and parental rights.

The equal employment revision was intended to change the existing Equal Employment Law, which had been hurriedly passed in 1987 before the adjournment of the National Assembly, from a mere declaration of intention to a realizable target of action by providing implementation mechanisms. Introduced into the national legislature under the sponsorship of opposition parties (Ministry of Political Affairs II, 1995; *Women's Policy*, 1993b), the revision left no room for ambiguity about equal treatment of workers in the workplace and equal pay for equal work. Once enacted, the revision permitted multiple routes to implement equal employment. For example, executive orders authorized monitoring gender discrimination in government and other public employment. The new law also dealt with the protection of working women and mothers and the creation of related services and facilities, including child care facilities, paid maternal leave for working mothers, and housing for single working women. Additional laws were passed, such as the Mother and Child Welfare Law and the Child Care Law, that expanded the scope of provisions relating to working mothers and child care in the Equal Employment Law. These legislative initiatives were not uncontroversial among women, however.

The succeeding Kim government manifested its willingness to abide by campaign promises to women's groups quite early, through the appointment of an unprecedented number of women (three) in the new cabinet. The government equally demonstrated its determination to support the rights of women when it presented a systematic and pervasive program for gender equality in the workplace as well as in the home. Behind such government efforts were the concentrated pressures of women's groups that finally converged on gender policy priorities after taking different paths under the authoritarian regime, when some acted as coopted groups and efficient lobbyists and others worked as outspoken feminist groups on the side of the democratic movement. Political space created for women by the democratic government enabled them to join forces in the vigorous pursuit of common objectives. The results included a more responsive government and substantially increased initiatives in the area of gender policy.

The Kim government's major accomplishments in gender policy came in two areas: family law and equal employment. These two broad policy areas, which had been initiated by the previous government, left room for constant improvement and the expansion of implementation and enforcement mechanisms. The family law revision aimed at strengthening the position of women in the family in several ways: by legally recognizing women as heads of household; by entitling women to the equal exercise of property ownership; and by increasing exemptions of gift and inheritance taxes, which tend to benefit mostly women. Extensive efforts were made to implement the equal employment law in the workplace as well. Child care services and child care leave were expanded to make more facilities available and to include paternity leave for child care.

The government also began to oversee employment rules and to police other potential sources of gender discrimination in the workplace, starting with large enterprises and moving to smaller companies of 100 employees in 1997. The government also eliminated existing restrictions on women's entry into technical training and specialized colleges. These efforts were combined with the enhancement of women's civil service opportunities by reducing bonus points given male applicants for military service and by eliminating upper limits on the percentage of women recruited for certain levels of the civil service. The results were highly visible, with greater numbers of women entering the civil service at the low to middle levels (*Women's Policy*, 1993a).

The reorganization of women's issue-related agencies/sections in the national as well as in local governments contributed greatly to the centralization of the gender policymaking structure and the empowerment of the Council on Women's Policy. The reorganization established a women's section in each ministry, bureau, and agency (a total of forty), which would present an annual report on plans and accomplishments to the council. Similarly, a women's section headed by a woman was established at the *kwangyok* and *kicho* administrative units. Following suit, the national legislature also created a special committee on gender issues to centralize all efforts relating to women's issues. Through such structural reform the government attempted to gain greater efficiency in implementing gender policy (*Women's Policy*, 1993b).

The Kim administration pioneered the frontiers of gender legislation in several areas: sex violence and the establishment of basic principles and broad guidelines on gender policy and the advancement of women's status. Early in the new administration, legislation on sex violence emerged as the top priority of women's groups. From the outset, the issue proved to be divisive among the various groups; and four versions of the legislation were presented at public hearings, ranging from moderate to radical (Kim, 1991). A weak version with a conservative slant finally passed to become the Special Law on Sex Violence. Although the legislation was defended as focusing on the rehabilitation of victims and the prevention of sex violence, it did not address many sex violence issues, including sex violence carried out by family members or relatives. Consequently, women's groups under feminist leadership continued their efforts to legislate against domestic violence. Toward the end of the Kim administration, domestic violence legislation was finally passed, but it too failed to address the critical issue of sex violence. Still, Korea's legislation on sex violence and domestic violence is unrivaled in any other Asian country.

Laying the legal foundation for the advancement of women's status and for gender policy, the passage of the Basic Law for Women's Development constitutes an equally crowning accomplishment in the struggle for gender equality. All gender laws and policies are subsumed under the Basic Law's guidelines. Included in ten programs for women's social participation recommended by the Presidential Committee on Globalization, the proposed legislation enjoyed the support of both the ruling and opposition parties from the outset. The law holds both the national and the local governments responsible for creating implementation mechanisms for gender policy under guidelines provided therein (*Women's Policy*, 1993b, 1995).

DEMOCRATIZATION AND WOMEN'S POLICIES IN KOREA

Democratic consolidation in Korea gradually took place while political power was transferred from one government to another. For the Roh government, conservative with roots in the outgoing authoritarian regime, changes were made to the extent necessary to render the government a semblance of democracy. On gender policy, the Roh government made modest progress. Faced with the politicization of gender issues by women's groups during the presidential election, candidate Roh made his pledge to the women's cause; President Roh translated it into gender policy. Under his administration, laws addressing basic gender issues were passed, such as family law revision, equal employment law with enforcement mechanisms, and child care law. In addition, a virtual women's policy department was established under the Roh administration. While such accomplishments indicate the government's receptivity to gender issues, the major credit goes to women's groups, which took initiatives from politicizing to legislating gender issues.

The Kim administration, the first civilian government since the Rhee regime, eventually broke away from the earlier constraints on reforms, carrying out radical reforms such as the restructuring of the military, banking reform, and the trial of the Fifth Republic and its leaders. The Kim government moved aggressively on gender policy, seeking broader opportunity for women on issues such as child care, education, and employment. Gender-related agencies were unified under a more efficient leadership structure. Similarly, the legal foundation was laid by the Basic Law for Women's Development, which provided guidelines for the existing gender policy and future initiatives. A strong presidential leadership in the absence of a strong party system, as Kim characterized his own leadership, facilitated the translation of women's issues into gender policy. More important, women's groups' mature organization and persistence formed a key factor in translating presidential campaign promises into policies. The two umbrella organizations for women's groups, the Council of Korean Women's Organizations and the Korean Women's Associations United, worked in concert with both the ruling party and the leading opposition party for legislation on major women's issues. These women's organizations (one moderate, the other progressive), founded under past authoritarian regimes, grew and became empowered with democratization. Activated under the Roh administration, they matured under the Kim administration, claiming the foremost position among interest groups.

The foregoing examination of the two administrations suggests that democratic consolidation enhances women's status through the introduction and implementation of gender policies. Although the politicization and legislation of women's issues commenced under the Roh administration, it was not fully effectuated until the democratic consolidation under the Kim administration. In fact, the strong reform posture of the new administration created a favorable political climate for women's groups to present various reform measures on gender issues, including the further revision of family law. Far surpassing what an incremental approach could produce, reform measures on gender issues led to the creation of a special committee on women in the National Assembly and produced legislation on sex violence and domestic violence. Moreover, the passage of the Basic Law for Women's Development, an equivalent of the ill-fated Equal Rights Amendment in the United States, crowned the Kim administration's accomplishments on gender issues. The social and political reforms carried out by the Kim administration to establish a firm institutional basis for democracy laid a solid institutional foundation for gender equality.

The successful performance of the two governments regarding women's policy is at least partly due to the cooperation, or in some cases the initiatives, of the major opposition party (the Kookmindang), which to some extent not only democratized the intraparty structure but also took a more progressive stand on gender equality. The speed at which gender-related legislation has proceeded and the degree to which it has been expanding are impressive. The legislative accomplishments have gone beyond the written laws and have begun to affect women's lives and their social and familial status. Decisions handed down by regular or family courts have led to the acceptance of an equitable distribution of community property, women's initiatives in divorce, and fair rules regarding child custody. Similarly, on equal employment, the government has been implementing a higher quota for women in government and other public sectors. The government's supervision has extended to the private sector as well, starting with large enterprises. Under the Kim administration, the Samsung conglomerate announced the special recruitment of hundreds of women; and the Hanjun corporation recently declared an employment policy to increase the percentage of women in its work force to 20 percent from the current 2 percent. To be sure, gender equality has a long way to go in Korea, but giant steps have been taken at an accelerating pace.

The Korean experience, therefore, does not bear out the predictions of Latin American feminist scholars regarding the consequences of democratic consolidation for gender politics. If gender policy and legislative outcomes are viewed as being determined by the interaction between the government and women's groups, the differences in such outcomes in each country must be explained by the different pattern of interaction between the government and women's groups. In Korea, after the democratic transition, the dominant opposition party, which had led the democratic movement, remained as the opposition. Feminist women's groups, which had joined the opposition in the democratic struggle and forged a close working relationship with the opposition, continued collaborating with the opposition on gender issues, remaining autonomous from the government. These autonomous women's groups invariably provided the leadership for gender legislation, although their proposals on gender issues were often compromised by the gradualist approach of the conservative mainstream women's groups. The continued autonomy of the feminist women's groups enabled them to pursue controversial women's issues vigorously (e.g., their successful initiatives for revisions of the Equal Employment Law and the Special Law on Sex Violence). Reinforced by the opposition party and the competing women's groups, the voices of these feminist groups could not go unheeded by the government. If, as Sonia Alvarez (1990) observed, women's groups' cooptation into the regime led to the loss of their autonomy and the weakening of their voice in the Brazilian political arena, the autonomy of women's groups' in Korea prevented such a result.

On the other hand, parallels to the Latin American experience may be found in Korea with respect to women's political representation. In fact, women's representation in both the national and local legislatures has not progressed as expected (see Chapters 3 and 6). Earlier, women's legislative representation declined; more recently, it recovered its losses through party appointments to at-large seats. Women's groups have advocated electoral reform as a means of enhancing women's legislative representation. The proposal has yet to capture the legislature's attention, and women's groups have to continue striving for gender equality. The recent transfer of power to the leading opposition party under D. J. Kim's leadership raises great expectations for women's issues, including legislative representation for women, since Kim and his party are known as being women's advocates. However, if representation politics indeed constitutes an island unto itself, as cross-national studies suggest (Norris, 1985; Rule, 1987), there is a high probability that upon assuming power, a progressive opposition party may become as conservative on women's representation as the preceding governments were.

9

Contradictory Implications of Socialism and Capitalism Under "East Asian Modernity" in China and Taiwan

CATHERINE S. P. FARRIS

The history of Chinese women's struggles for liberation since the nineteenth century holds a special place in the mythology of Western feminism. Socialist feminism begins with Frederick Engels's (1972) classic work, *The Origin of the Family, Private Property, and the State,* in which he argues that the rise of private property relations, monopolized by men, reduced women's status to one of dependency within the conjugal family. M. K. Whyte and W. Parish (1984) note that for Engels, women's liberation from the patriarchal family depended on participation in wage labor and the socialization of housework and child care under a socialist system of ownership. Socialist feminists looked in particular to communist China as the model society in which women had achieved true liberation.

As Emma Teng (1996: 139) points out, this argument was based on a simplistic periodization of "traditional" and postrevolutionary China, as socialist feminists "attempted to use the status of women in China as a test case of the viability of socialism for women's liberation." For example, Karen Sacks (1975) argues that women's housework and child care are devalued under capitalism, which regards women as less than social adults. Full social equality for women and men can come about only when family and society are no longer separate economic spheres of society: "Production, consumption, child-rearing, and economic decision-making all need to take place in a single social sphere—something analogous to the Iroquois *gens* as described by Engels, or to the production brigades of China during the Great Leap Forward" (Sacks, 1975: 234). However, we shall see that Chinese women did not necessarily experience the Great Leap Forward as liberating (Stacey, 1983; Wolf, 1985).

In a critique of women's position in socialist societies, Maxine Molyneux (1981: 167) argues that "while actually existing socialist states have not eradicated sexual inequality, they have promoted substantial improvements in the position of women." Further improvements are hindered in part by material constraints of underdevelopment and the rural nature of most of these societies, but more profoundly, attempts to change women's status are severely constrained by "the prevalence in official thinking of conservative ideologies which underlie policy on the family and women's position in it" (Molyneux, 1981: 198). For women, new roles in the labor force are simply grafted on to older roles of housewife and mother, and the burden of domestic labor falls almost completely on women's shoulders.

Nonetheless, many argue for real progress for women within a socialist framework. It is particularly instructive, therefore, to compare progress toward Chinese women's liberation in the People's Republic of China (PRC) with transformations in Chinese women's status in capitalist Taiwan. In Taiwan, the modernization processes have had a generally salutary effect on women's status, such as increases in educational levels, labor force participation, control over fertility, and greater power within marriage. However, cultural values about the nature of women and their proper place in society endure.

These contradictory trends suggest the need to reexamine the prevailing Western stereotypes of both women's liberation and modernization, be it socialist or capitalist. The emancipation of women is usually considered as part of the larger historical process of "modernization." I follow Stevan Harrell (1994: 166) in taking "modernity to be a set of characteristics shared to some extent by all industrial societies," and which include two levels of transformation: the material and the ideational. The "material factors are perhaps determinative, or at least necessary, conditions for the emergence of the ideational changes. But in practice, they interact" (Harrell, 1994: 167). Although modernization is a global trend, it is not to be equated with "Westernization." Harrell points to the example of Japan as a modernized society that has maintained significant cultural distinctiveness. Likewise, Tu (1991) argues that a distinctively East Asian modernity is emerging.

Moreover, Chinese and Western concepts of what constitutes "women's liberation" are far from identical. The Chinese cultural value of *nan zhu wai, nu zhu nei* (man rules the outside, woman, the inside) highlights a worldview of *gender complementary*, rather than equivalence, and is one that defines a fundamental difference in feminist movements in the United States and in Chinese societies. The mainstream feminist movement in the United States, previously dominated by educated, white, middle-class women, has focused on *gender equality*, with the goal of a gender-blind society in which ability, talent, and interest, not gender, are the basis for social roles—including occupation and leadership positions—as well as familial roles. Women of color in the United States have long criticized mainstream feminism not only for lack of attention to factors—such as class, ethnicity, and sexual orientation—that may divide women, but also for the selfish individualism they perceive is behind feminist demands for women's "rights." Where is the connection to family and community, they ask, in this vision of gender equality (Cole, 1986)? I have no doubt that many Chinese women in Taiwan and in the PRC would echo these sentiments.

In the sections below, I begin with a contrast between the radical Maoist period (1949–1976) in the PRC and the takeoff stage of industrial development in Taiwan (1949–1975). Next, I describe the changing lives of women in the PRC during the ongoing reform era, begun by Deng Xiaoping, and in Taiwan as a newly industrializing country (NIC) and newly emerging democracy. I hope to show that there are many enduring cultural values about the nature of women and their proper places in society that the PRC and Taiwan regimes share. But there are also important differences, which are contingent on their separate lines of historical and social development. Finally, I consider this question: Is there a "Chinese woman" whose liberation we in the West can once again attempt to measure?

WOMEN'S STATUS AND ECONOMIC
DEVELOPMENT IN THE EARLY POSTWAR YEARS

After the establishment of the PRC in 1949, China enacted dramatic reforms concerning women's roles, but actual social change was less than originally intended. In Taiwan, rapid industrialization significantly altered women's roles without necessarily "liberating" them from the Confucian patriarchal family; and the terms of Taiwan's incorporation into the world capitalist economy unevenly exploited women, depending on their economic and social positions. I first discuss women's lives in the countryside and cities of Mao Zedong's China, then contrast this with Taiwan during the early stages of industrialization.

The PRC During the Mao Years (1949–1976)

After the communist victory in 1949, the Chinese Communist Party (CCP) promulgated the Marriage Reform Law, which outlawed arranged marriages and concubinage and allowed women to initiate divorce. The continuing power of the patriarchal family was evident as attempts were made to educate the population concerning the new marriage law and the rights of women. At the time, the new divorce law most threatened the labor that peasant farmers depended on— their wives—for both productive and reproductive labor. Mothers-in-law were also against the new divorce laws, which would remove from them a source of household labor. After an initial surge in divorces, the party backed away from implementing this portion of the Marriage Reform Law (Andors, 1983).

During the 1950s, the party concentrated on economic development and socialist transformation. Few distinctions were made with regard to gender when ascribing positions for labor, and all women were encouraged to leave the home and participate in production. However, the government was confronted with contradictory goals of women's liberation versus the political loyalty of male peasants who had supported the revolution. Norma Diamond (1975a) notes that when women in the rural areas began to criticize male oppression within the family during "speak bitterness" campaigns, the women were persuaded to desist. Other campaigns urged the rural population to understand that women were as good workers as men. In the West we heard of "iron girl brigades," composed of young women who could work a field just as well as could a man (Davin, 1975). Croll (1995) argues that women's liberation was defined solely in terms of labor force participation; women were to embrace identities as workers first, women second. She also points out that the Maoist phrase "women hold up half of heaven" (commonly translated as "half the sky") rhetorically placed women in an untenable position symbolically, because in the Taoist cosmological system of *Yinyang* dualism, woman was associated with earth and man with heaven. During the Mao years, Croll argues, the disparity between government rhetoric about the liberation of women and their lived experiences of continuing patriarchy created an intellectual and emotional rupture for women that rendered them mute.

During the Great Leap Forward (1958–1961), giant communes in the countryside organized the lives of the rural residents completely, and communal kitchens and nurseries were established so that all adult women could take part in labor full-time. Diamond (1975a) notes that the lowest level of the commune —the production team— coincided with all or part of a village, and males related through patrilineal ties administered these new "work units." Consequently, in important ways patrilineal lineages continued to organize the lives of rural people. Patrilineal descent reckoning and patrilocal residence continued to be the norm in the countryside. However, Diamond (1975a) offers several examples from her fieldwork of women who married matrilocally and who were much more active in local politics than most women. This supports the assertion that matrilocal residence is beneficial for women (Pasternak, Ember, and Ember, 1997).

After the debacle of the Great Leap Forward's agricultural policies, pragmatists such as Deng Xiaoping gained control and decollectivization began. Rural women once again faced the double burden of housework and agricultural production (Gao, 1994). For many young married women, household help came from the mother-in-law, who might be too old or infirm to take part in farmwork. Diamond (1975a: 374) asserts that this changed the balance of power between these generations of women, but not between men and women. She concludes that the authority of patrilineal lineages during collectivization allowed the reproduction of "the feudal-patriarchal ideology."

During the Great Proletarian Cultural Revolution (1965–1975), most distinctions between the sexes were deliberately suppressed. Both men and women dressed in dull "Mao suits"; romance, fashion, and personal adornment were all looked down upon as "bourgeois"; and one was supposed to choose a mate based on good socialist ideological principles. Despite the continuation of a covert masculine standard for both sexes, women workers became pervasive throughout the labor force and even moved into some positions of authority in management or, less often, in politics (Andors, 1983). In the post-Mao era, major policy shifts beginning in 1978 accompanied the rise of Deng Xiaoping as paramount leader; and these new economic policies are having both positive and negative consequences for women's lives.

Women in the "Economic Miracle" of Taiwan

I turn now to a comparative look at women's statuses and roles during the first three decades of Kuomintang or Nationalist rule in Taiwan. Taiwan's gender system operates within the context of many of the same cultural values and beliefs about women's place as does the PRC's system. However, the historical context and political realities of Taiwan have resulted in sometimes very different strategies for emancipation.

The Chinese in Taiwan are justifiably proud of their "economic miracle" (Gold, 1986). Rubinstein (1994) points out that Taiwan's government had considerable economic and military aid from the United States, with which it was allied during the Cold War. However, in fairness to the Kuomintang, he goes on, many in the leadership were determined not to make the same disastrous economic policy mistakes that they had on the mainland. After firmly establishing authoritarian control, the Kuomintang stimulated industrial development through a policy of primary import substitution and also promoted domestic savings. Taiwan was able to build up its industrial sector, primarily in manufacturing, to a self-sustaining level by the 1960s. Industry then began to disperse to the countryside to gain access to cheap labor and raw materials. In addition, special export processing zones were established for foreign investors attracted by Taiwan's political stability and cheap and elastic labor supply, many of whom were young, unmarried women (Gallin, 1984). In the decade 1965–1975, Taiwan pursued a successful policy of export-oriented manufacturing, and the transformation from a primarily agriculturally based economy to an industrially based one was accomplished (Galenson, 1979). Women's status rose as they began to achieve levels of education nearly equal with men, as well as greater access to the job market. However, many women, particularly unmarried daughters and young wives, found themselves still subordinated to the patriarchal family and exploited by capital as workers in the new global assembly line.

Nora Chiang and Yenlin Ku (1985) point out that, in a continuation of Kuomintang policy on the mainland, women's status was declared to be equal to that of men, but their roles were portrayed as complementary. Urban middle- and upper-class women were expected to contribute to the stability and prosperity of Taiwanese society in their capacities as wives, mothers, and volunteer workers. For rural women during the early stages of industrialization, according to Margery Wolf's (1972) account, most traditional practices such as arranged marriages and patrilocal residence remained. Changes in the form of factory employment opportunities and "free-choice" marriage were just beginning in the rural communities studied by the Wolfs in the 1960s. By 1965, girl graduates of elementary and junior high schools were encouraged by government rhetoric to enter the workforce, helping to fuel economic expansion (Galenson, 1979). By this time, few farm families depended primarily on agriculture for income; and many families strategically deployed unmarried children, particularly their daughters, to work in the new factories. These girls either commuted from the family farm or lived in dormitories provided by the factory. They remitted their wages to the family head who gave them an allowance, usually spent on consumer goods. The remainder was used for other expenses, including the further education of a son. Such education was not thought necessary for a daughter who would marry out of the family (Arrigo, 1984; Kung, 1994).

Although these rural daughters were exploited by their natal families and by capital, they slowly gained increased independence and self-esteem through participation in the wider society. Their economic contribution encouraged their families to value them more, and delayed marriage meant they were more mature and had more influence over marriage arrangements than did their mothers' generation. For example, Ming-zheng Zhang (1980) examined the family backgrounds and changing lifestyles of women born between 1940 and 1959 and found that from the oldest to the youngest age cohort, women's educational level, work outside the home, self-arranged marriage, and premarital sex had all risen steadily. Women who lived away from home before marriage were most likely to control their own money, exercise free choice in marriage, and engage in premarital sex. Obviously, the complete subordination of the younger generation to the older was changing dramatically.

The modernization of Taiwan's society is also evident in rising educational levels and falling fertility rates. In 1968, universal public education was expanded from six to nine years. In 1965, 26 percent of the labor force was illiterate, Paul Liu (1983: 3) reports; in 1984, this figure was 5.8 percent for men and 13.4 percent for women. Of those born after World War II, educational levels are similar for women and men; in urban areas, this rate is about ten years. Beginning in 1966, family planning was actively promoted by the government, and the total fertility rate declined from 7.0 in 1951 to 2.5 in 1980.

By the 1970s, Taiwan's society had become quite urbanized, and nuclear family residence was more common than previously. With the rise of free-choice marriages, the conjugal bond is more important than before, but important emotional and often financial ties to the husband's family remain. Working women often depend on their mothers-in-law for child care, but care by the elder generation tends to reproduce traditional gender roles in the next generation. Gallin (1986) and Diamond (1975b) assert that a generational power shift from the mother-in-law to the daughter-in-law has not upset the subordinate relation of women vis-à-vis men. Hu Taili (1985) disagrees, arguing that women have enhanced their status through participation in the labor market and that increased dowries and closer ties to their natal families is a reflection of this. In her view, the power of the male head of family has decreased also.

By the 1970s, economic prosperity had contributed to the growth of a new urban middle class, and government rhetoric valorized *xian-qi liang-mu* (virtuous wife and good mother) roles as the proper sphere of women. Diamond (1973, 1975b) has characterized this era as a "variation on feminine mystique" for middle-class urban women in Taiwan, aptly invoking Betty Friedan's (1963) critique of the position of middle-class women in the United States during the 1950s. Indeed, I argue below that one of the effects of modernization on women's roles and status in all societies is obligatory passage through the "feminine mystique" era. Linda Arrigo (1991), using a Marxist framework, analyzes this decade of the 1970s in Taiwan as a period in which, for middle-class women, sex role differences—the woman as homemaker and the man as breadwinner—were mystified. Whereas working class women may aspire to the dependent status of homemaker, they also contributed much-needed labor to the family.

The newly bourgeois culture of urban Taiwan in the 1970s also witnessed the beginning of a women's movement, led by a Harvard-trained scholar, Annette Hsiu-lien Lu. She wrote the first feminist book in Taiwan, *Xin Nuxingzhuyi* (New Feminism), which criticized gender inequalities in educational levels, the feminization of low-status, low-paying jobs, a sexual double standard, and the continued denigration of women within a Confucian value system (Lu, 1986). Lu Hsiu-lien also felt it necessary to address the objection to feminism as a Western import. She does not deny that Taiwanese feminists were influenced by Western feminists, as many of them studied in the United States or read Simone de Beauvoir's *Second Sex* (1961) and Betty Friedan's *Feminine Mystique* (1963), which had been translated by an overseas Taiwanese feminist, Yang Mei-huei, in the early 1970s. But Lu also drew on the thought of Sun Yat-sen to argue for the universal necessity of a movement for women's liberation. Lu had to be very cautious about advocating women's liberation during the years of martial law in Taiwan, especially since she was also involved in the activities of the Dangwai, or the outside-the-party party, the unofficial opposition to Kuomintang rule.

Lu Hsiu-lien was one of the leaders of the Meilidao (beautiful island, a.k.a. Isle Formosa) group, which organized protests over the cancellation of local elections in 1979, after the government panicked in the wake of its "derecognition" by the Carter administration. She and her comrades were arrested after riots broke out in the wake of police oppression; they were tried and convicted in a military court for sedition, and all received long prison terms. Lu was released in 1986 on medical grounds and was allowed to go to the United States for treatment. Thus, at the end of the 1970s, Taiwan had emerged on the world stage with a distinctive Asian modernity, similar to that of

South Korea and Singapore, combining impressive economic growth within a strict authoritarian regime. In the next section, I turn to a comparison of women's liberation in the PRC under the Dengist economic reforms and in Taiwan under the democratization process.

RECENT CHANGES: TRENDS AND COUNTERTRENDS IN THE PRC AND TAIWAN

Recent economic and social change in the PRC and Taiwan suggest an ironic countertrend in women's liberation. Under the leadership of Deng Xiaoping and his successors, the PRC has "opened the door" to Western science and technology (while trying vainly to keep out "spiritual pollution") and has begun market reforms that are integrating the PRC into the global economy. The results of these sweeping reforms for the status of women have been mixed. In many ways, the economic reforms have brought regression for women; in the countryside, patriarchal norms and treatment of women are resurgent, and in the urban areas, job discrimination against women is blatant. Women (and men) do have more economic opportunities; rising prosperity has benefited many regions of the country; and there is far less government interference in people's daily lives. In Taiwan, agitation for democratic change in the 1970s and 1980s resulted in the lifting of martial law in 1987, and a raucous multiparty democracy has emerged in the 1990s. Taiwan's women have benefited from broader and more equal education and employment opportunities. In this section, I discuss changes in the countryside and in the cities of the PRC, then turn to recent changes in Taiwan.

Economic Reforms in the PRC and the Status of Women in the Countryside

Under the rural reforms, known as the "agricultural production responsibility system," individual farm families now contract with the commune to work a particular piece of land or to manage a rural enterprise. Anything produced over quota may be consumed by the farm household or sold on the free market (Spence, 1990). This resurgent household-based economy once again has reinforced the traditional value of child labor and, in particular, the value of sons. Daughters contribute to the household economy by helping their mothers with domestic chores or sideline production or by engaging in wage labor in rural enterprises; others migrate to urban areas to engage in seasonal labor, to work in factories, or to serve as "nannies" for a growing middle class of two-career couples. Gao Xiaoxian (1994) argues that the rural reforms have opened up many new opportunities for women and that social modernization is leading to individual modernization. She notes that many more peasant families today are accepting women's working outside the home; most young people believe in free-choice marriage (with the parents' consent!); and many believe that couples should have only two children (ideally, one boy and one girl). In her view, "The awakening of women's self-consciousness has been an intrinsic driving force in the changes in women's status. Its effects should not be underestimated" (Gao, 1994: 89).

Other scholars paint a more mixed picture of women's status in the countryside. Croll (1995: 127–128) notes that more than 75 percent of rural women are still engaged in agriculture, fisheries, or forestry. For many women this is an added burden to their domestic work. Many rural men have migrated to the cities for work, leaving millions of women as heads of household in "half-side families," who are often poorer than their neighbors. Increased demands for child labor has also resulted in daughters being pulled out of school, in earlier marriage age, in increased bride-price, and in reports of the selling and abduction of young women. Other forms of violence against women that have begun to receive public attention in the last decade include rape and wife battering (Honig and Hershatter, 1988). Gao (1994) points to continuing problems for rural women, such as lower labor force participation than men, poor working conditions, low wages and low-skilled work in rural enterprises, and exploitation in the special economic zones. She also mentions the continued practice of patrilineal inheritance and patrilocal residence.

With the breakdown of the commune system and increase in school fees, girls are more likely to be kept out of school than boys. Gao (1994: 94–95) reports that in 1988, 83 percent of school-age children who were not enrolled in school were girls, and 70 percent of the 3 million who left were girls. Yet, the modernization of agriculture requires literate farmers who can read about new technologies, and education is a prime force in individual modernization. Gao urges that the government and the Women's Federation concentrate on improving rural women's levels of education in order to aid in women's liberation.

In terms of marriage practices, Wolf's (1985) research in the first years of the post-Mao era shows that marriage arrangements are conducted by mothers and go-betweens, but the couple has "veto" power, itself a significant compromise with tradition but certainly not in keeping with the marriage laws, which grant free choice to children. The age at marriage has been set by law to regulate birthrates. The trend to later marriages than in the pre-1949 period (i.e., in one's twenties) has benefited daughters' status in the family as they contribute to their natal family's income through work in factories and the like (Wolf, 1985). Despite the retrogressive emphasis on sons as carriers of the patriline and parents' support in old age, Greenhalgh and Li (1995: 616) note in their study of demographic trends in Shaanxi province that cultural attitudes toward daughters are shifting. Many people desire to have a daughter (in addition to at least one son) for emotional support in old age. This has coincided with "the growing emotional distance between older parents and the culturally preferred caregivers, their sons and daughters-in-law."

Because of the implementation of the one child per family policy, fertility rates have fallen all over the country. However, the rate has decreased much more slowly in rural than in urban areas, as rural women are pressured by the husband and his family to bear at least one son. In the 1980s, reports in the Western press mentioned coercive family planning, including forced abortions, female infanticide, selective neglect (e.g., a shorter period of nursing for girls), out-adoption of daughters, underreported births, and falsified birth control records. Most distressing is the rise of sex-selective abortions among people who have access to this technology (Greenhalgh and Li, 1995). Incredibly, this seems to be occurring in Taiwan as well, with enough frequency to skew the sex ratio (Selya, 1994; cited in Gold, 1996). Despite these problems, most women in the countryside of China, both young and old, agree that women are infinitely better off now than in preliberation times.

Status of Women in Urban Areas

In the cities of China, the one child per family policy has been largely successful because of such factors as crowded living conditions, old age pensions, access to better jobs, the higher education of women, and more exposure to the party line on gender equality. Although marriage practices in urban areas still follow the patrilineal descent rule, in contrast to the rural pattern, mate selection is more likely to be by the couple. However, parents still have a say in children's marriages; and if they strongly disapprove of a proposed match, it is usually broken off. Arranged marriages still happen, however; elite urban families have been known to forge alliances through their children's marriage (Wolf, 1985). The majority of urban households are nuclear families. In Whyte and Parish's (1984) sample, based on data collected from 1972 to 1978, 68 percent of families were nuclear. Elite groups, especially government officials, are more likely to reside in extended families.

Educational levels for men and women clearly are more equal than in the countryside. Whyte and Parish (1984) note that the gender gap in education has been closing, a trend that began under the Nationalists, with men on average having about eight and a half years of education and women eight years. Croll (1995) reports that, as of 1990, females made up 45 percent of primary school enrollment, 44 percent of junior middle school, 39 percent of senior middle school, and 34 percent of college and university enrollment (technical schools are not included in these data). As is true in Taiwan today, an urban man in the PRC does not want to marry a woman more educated than himself, and women are perhaps responding to the marriage market here. It is also true that college-educated women have been experiencing much more difficulty than their male peers in finding employment, and this factor may also influence their striving for educational opportunities.

Looking now at participation in the labor force, the new economic reforms have been a mixed blessing for urban women. Many work units are often hesitant to hire women, as they must by law provide pregnancy leave and child care facilities, which are costly. And, with the government's move to shut down unprofitable state enterprises, women are often the first ones laid off, or they find it more difficult to get a job in the first place (Rai, 1994). Many state enterprises openly discriminate against hiring women or strongly encourage those already employed to take years of maternity leave. Whyte and Parish (1984) note that although the percentage of women in the workforce is extraordinarily high, even by the standards of developed countries (in their sample, more than 90 percent of women ages 20–39 were employed), sex segregation in the workplace—with women occupying mostly low-wage, dead-end jobs—is quite common. Urban women must also contend with the "second shift," that is, responsibility for child care and housekeeping on top of full-time employment. This limits overtime work and career advancement, and women's salary levels rise more slowly than men's. Nonetheless, urban women derive self-esteem from working for wages and agree with their rural counterparts that women in the PRC today have come a long way since preliberation times (Wolf, 1985).

Return of the Feminine Mystique?

In the reform era, the idea of women's liberation has clearly taken a backseat to the four modernizations that the PRC has made a goal. A biologically based model of sex differences that includes a perceived "natural" division of labor has reasserted itself. If the workforce must be reduced because of growing unemployment, it seems more appropriate for women to be the ones to return home. Or, if skilled women remain in the workforce, they occupy support positions and are encouraged to see the homefront as their most important duty. To me, this sounds a lot like the feminine mystique "with Chinese characteristics."

Lisa Rofel (1994: 244) notes:

> Ideas about biology have become central. Biology is inescapable and determines capabilities. This has replaced the emphasis on social explanations for women's oppression prevalent in the Maoist era . . . [thus] women are becoming more strongly tied to domesticity and motherhood. Women's activities in the home are no longer condemned as feudal social arrangements. Rather, they are said to be a natural expression of the female self.

Rofel (1994: 245) argues that rather than looking at Chinese women's choices through the lens of Western feminist standards, "these women who embrace motherhood and reject productivity are voicing their resistance to the state and attempting to wrest from it some measure of control over the definition of their bodies." Rather than view their choice as uninformed or simply a product of mystification, we—Western feminists—must learn to respect the autonomy and integrity of those choices. However, not all native observers are as sanguine about such choices. Gao (1994: 92) mentions the phenomenon of Dajiu Village in Tianjin, an area of heavy industry, where all women were sent home "to do full-time housework to compensate for the lack of service industries." She argues that this is not in women's best interests as it simply "repeats the historical pattern of women sacrificing individual development in exchange for men's realization of their greater social value."

In the past ten years, a vigorous women's studies movement has flourished, led by the Women's Federation, or Fulian. This also features semiautonomous NGO women's organizations active in scholarship and popular writing (Gilmartin et al., 1994; Li and Zhang, 1994). Tani Barlow (1997) has explored the debates on the question of women's subjectivity that have emerged in post-Mao China. In the late 1970s, Fulian began documenting Chinese women's gains under communism, thereby reviving *funu*, or woman, the Maoist revolutionary woman subject. This discourse provided a critical opening for historians of women's history, especially the influential Li Xiaojiang, to set into circulation a counteridentity, which they referred to as *nuxing*, or essential woman.

Li was the first to argue that Maoist policies denaturalized women's bodies during the Cultural Revolution. Her solution was to create an essentialized Woman who is the deficient other of Man. These theorists argued that women must recapture their femininity from state control, which obliterated it. Thus, in rejecting the state definition of them as workers first, women second, many women appear to be responding to this call for an essentialized woman. For women working in low-paying, dead-end jobs and coming home to the second shift, it is not difficult to see how "essential woman" might exert a powerful pull. Wang Zheng (1997) notes that the power to define women has shifted from the state to market forces, as commercial interests have found in femininity a lucrative commodity. In this light, Li Xiaojiang's writings may turn out to be, as Barlow (1997: 536) remarks, "nothing less than the ideological justification for a form of national womanhood that is handmaiden to economic boom and frontier capitalism."

Since 1990, the women's movement in China has become much more transnational in outlook but has retained an insistence on the indigenous historical and cultural background of Chinese women. This growth of indigenous Chinese feminism appears to be a response to the growing problems facing women as a result of the Deng reforms and industrialization. In particular, the cutback in social welfare protection has led both to the formation of new women's organizations and to the state-sponsored Fulian's greater response to women's grassroots pressures. As Zheng (1997) notes, this transnational Chinese feminism was accelerated by the UN's Fourth International Women's Conference held in Beijing in 1995. The government signed the Platform for Action and the Beijing Declaration, and the media declared that these two documents voice the aspirations of women all over the world. These documents have created the legitimacy of expanding Chinese women's activism and for "connecting the rails" or merging with international women's movements. Increasingly, women activists in the PRC and Taiwan see women's liberation as a global struggle, in which, however, local issues and interpretations play a crucial role.

Women, Democracy, and Liberation Under Capitalism in Taiwan?

The modern movement for women's liberation is part of the development of a civil society in Taiwan, which contributed to the more open political atmosphere since the twilight of President Chiang Ching-kuo's rule (Gold, 1996). In the 1980s, a plurality of public discourses began to flourish; and the social activism of women's groups, religious groups, environmental groups, and others began to agitate for reform (Gold, 1996; Tu, 1996; Winckler, 1994). Taiwan began a slow transformation from one-party authoritarian rule to a more democratic one. Martial law was lifted in 1987, opposition political parties were legalized, and multiparty elections were held. Unlike their mothers, young women in Taiwan today are staying in the workforce after marriage or the birth of children. For the generation that came of age in the 1980s, education levels are often much higher than when their parents were growing up. Fertility levels are lower, and women are increasingly seeking meaningful social roles in addition to the traditional familial ones. The women's movement in Taiwan is now in its third decade, and the roles and statuses of women have clearly been transformed in the modernization process (Ku, 1989). However, as we shall see, many patriarchal values remain.

Marriage and Family

In Taiwan, a successful family planning program reduced population growth, and today women have an average of 1.86 children. In fact, since 1984, the birth rate has fallen below the replacement level, prompting the government to urge people to marry earlier and to have two children (Gold, 1996; Li, 1984). The population of Taiwan is also aging, which has the potential to create a crisis in elder care. Traditionally, adult sons took responsibility for the care of elderly parents as part of the obligations of *xiao,* or filial piety. As the age structure of the population changes, however, there is an increasing burden on the younger working population. This can have a significant impact on women's roles in particular, for it is usually the daughter-in-law who is responsible for the day-to-day care of an aged parent-in-law who lives with the son. This increases the double burden on the woman, who is now being encouraged by government rhetoric to have more children and at the same time to participate in the workforce part- or full-time. Many women of child-bearing age are very interested in maintaining a lowered fertility rate. However, for those in the generations that came of age in the prewar period or shortly thereafter, sons still are more valued than daughters; and in-laws often pressure their daughters-in-law to keep trying until they give birth to a son.

Although there has been much change in relations among family members in the postwar years, there is also a continuity of Chinese values regarding masculinity and femininity—notably, the ideal of a "virtuous wife and good mother." Even for working women, social mores still dictate that they take primary responsibility for housework and child care. For unmarried children, "although the role of parents in controlling mate choice has decreased, they still exercise considerable influence over marriage and even dating, although in consultation with children" (Gold, 1996: 1096). Nuclear family residence in urban areas is now quite common; but this is not the nuclear family as Westerners know it. Rather, it is the "new nuclear family" or *xin hexin jiating*, which is still dominated by patrilineal principles. Daughters are still viewed as "marrying out" of their natal families; sons are still seen as being responsible for parents in old age; and only sons expect to inherit (Y. B. Chen, 1994). However, some women are beginning to assert the right to maintain strong ties with their natal families or *niangjia*. Tsui Yi-lan (1987) has shown that highly educated urban women after marriage use their greater economic independence to help their natal families financially. Thus, various tensions within the family are evident as women assume new roles in the larger society. Many men resent challenges to their traditional prerogatives of domination in the public domain and also resent challenges to a sexual double standard. This contributes to domestic discord and a slowly rising divorce rate.

Education and the Law

The social and juridical status of women in Taiwan has also improved. In 1968, compulsory education was extended from six to nine years, and today educational levels in the cities are comparable for men and women. Island-wide, almost all elementary graduates go on to junior high school, and the illiteracy rate is only 6 percent (Gold, 1996: 1097). In senior high school, however, for which students must take joint entrance exams, there are fewer girls than boys. A sex-based quota system is used, and girls are disadvantaged here. Other sex-discriminatory issues in education include such practices as gender bias in curriculum materials and the tracking of students into sex-stereotypic fields. For example, girls are encouraged to study humanities and fine arts and boys to study natural sciences and computers (Hsieh, 1997).

Women now have nearly equal rights under the law, although these rights are not always realized in practice. For example, the legal code stipulates equal inheritance for sons and daughters, but many people are either unaware of this law or choose to ignore it. In 1994, the Council of Grand Justice ruled that the article of the civil code that granted the husband the right to the couple's property and to custody of children (in cases of divorce) was unconstitutional. In

1996, the code was amended so that "married couples can now own their assets separately . . . [and] upon divorce, the father is no longer guaranteed the right to custody" (Huang, 1997: 5–6). Indeed, as I pointed out in an analysis of the "social discourse on women's roles" (Farris, 1994), the fact that husbands still controlled the joint property and were automatically awarded custody of children discouraged many women from seeking a divorce despite an unhappy marriage. Although the legal code is now changed, it will be interesting to see to what extent women are still pressured by their husband's family, or even their own, to let him take custody of the children (especially a son), who many people still believe "belong" to the husband's lineage.

A segment of the women's movement, led by The Awakening Group (Funu Xinzhi), has been active in promoting changes in public policy and legislation to give women equal rights. Ku Yenlin (1997) has analyzed the processes by which the feminist movement effected changes in two areas: the legalization of abortion and equal employment opportunity. She argues that the language of the Eugenic Healthcare Act of 1984 that legalized abortion "continued to reflect the concerns of a patriarchal state to reproduce the labor market and to reduce population growth as a threat to national security and development." Feminist concerns, such as control over one's own body, were absent from the document and thus "could not act as a catalyst to raise women's collective awareness of their subordination" (Farris and Johnson, 1997: 4). Although abortion is now legal, patriarchal constraints remain; a woman must obtain consent of her husband or legal guardian to have an abortion. However, the fight for equal opportunity in employment—especially the outlawing of the de facto rule that women must quit their jobs after marriage or the birth of their first child—because it came after the lifting of martial law, "was more successful in touting the feminist agenda and in rallying women to the cause" (Farris and Johnson, 1997: 4). Other areas in which Taiwan's feminists urge legal change include sexual harassment on the job and spousal abuse.

The Workforce Participation of Women

In 1990s Taiwan, women's domain is not only in the home; women, including married women with small children, are in the workforce in large numbers (44 percent of all women). The division of labor in the workplace mirrors traditional roles (e.g., women are preschool and elementary schoolteachers, nurses, secretaries, clerks, unskilled or semiskilled factory workers, farmers, or unpaid employees in family businesses). Chou Bih-er (1994) has analyzed the changing patterns of women's employment in Taiwan from 1966 to 1986. She finds that women workers are well integrated horizontally into all areas of the economy, including manufacturing, commerce, and service industries. However, in terms of vertical integration, "although women workers have made significant gains in commerce and service industries at all levels, including employer class in commerce, the majority of women are still located in the lower end of the production relationship. . . . Sex segregation at the level of ownership of the means of production remains the biggest obstacle in the way of gender equality" (Chou, 1994: 352).

Rural Women's Lives

In the rural areas of Taiwan, although traditional values and customs regarding women remain strong in many ways, here too modernization has had a significant impact. Young women typically have a junior high school education and often work in rural industries. Because they contribute to the family purse, they usually have more say in family decisionmaking than their mother's generation did. Although parents still have an important role in marriage decisions, rural couples may certainly veto any choice with which they do not agree. According to Gallin (1991: 14), many married women work in family businesses, often without wages, and are resentful of this: "They felt their husbands were withholding a resource which, they believed, gave a woman a degree of control over her life and a measure of self-respect."

Anru Lee (1996) has also documented some of the gendered contradictions of industrial development in Taiwan for women in small towns. She shows how young women who work in a family-owned textile factory are exploited by capital and by patriarchy. Because these daughters are needed for the survival of a textile industry that is on the decline, they are often discouraged from going on to higher education. Instead, they are encouraged to work long hours for the family firm, while all the family pride is placed in brothers. Nonetheless, the woman Lee interviewed eventually returned to school, hoping to find a job that she really liked. In addition to the familial exploitation of young women, this example shows intergenerational tensions in the family, as parents' authority is increasingly challenged. Indeed, Gallin (1986) argues that it is the older generation of women, those who are now mothers-in-law, who have seen their status in the family decline relative to their mothers'. These older women usually have little or no education. They are primarily responsible for house and farmwork and also for the care of their grandchildren, while their daughters-in-law work for wages. Social mores no longer sanction the complete subjugation of daughters-in-law, and the traditional closeness of mothers with their adult sons is often lost as husbands establish closer and more equal relations with their wives. In short, an increase in status and power within the family for young women has to some extent been at the expense of the older generation of women. This is undoubtedly true in the PRC as well.

The Women's Movement

Some leaders of the Taiwanese women's movement espouse values of gender equality in the sense in which mainstream white feminists in the United States argue (for example, liberation from a sexual double standard). Other women's leaders perceive this as a misguided attempt by Western-educated Chinese women to impose a foreign value system on Taiwan's society. Some women's studies scholars in Taiwan are concerned with locating indigenous sources for a "women's consciousness," such as nineteenth-century anti–foot-binding societies or the May 4th Movement. Other scholars focus on modern women's organizations, such as the Warm Life Association (Wan Qing Funu Xiehui), an advocacy group for widows and divorcees, which may not directly promote gender equality but nonetheless acts to empower women (Lu, 1991). Nonetheless, the women's movement and its sympathizers have introduced into Taiwan concepts and values originating in Western feminist movements, including equal opportunity in education and work, and freedom from abuse and harassment.

The women's movement in Taiwan is now in its third decade and is by no means a unified institution. Advocates range from conservative "work within the status quo" people to those considered radical in Taiwan society, such as He Chun Rui (Josephine Ho), whose recent articles in Taiwan on "sexual liberation" (*xing jiefang*) have, as the cliché goes, ignited a storm of controversy. In her book, *Haoshuang Noren* (The Unruly Woman: Women's Liberation and Sexual Emancipation), He (1995) advocates sexual liberation for Chinese women; an end to the cult of virginity for unmarried women; and, for married women, an end to a lifetime of sometimes frigid love given to one, probably unfaithful, man followed by enforced celibacy in widowhood or divorce. Needless to say, He's advocacy has been met with a strong conservative reaction. Men, of course, are threatened by this challenge to their traditional sexual license. But He's advocacy of sexual liberation also threatens women, especially the woman who has devoted herself to being a "virtuous wife and good mother." For her, the "new woman" (*xin nuxing*) in Taiwan's society—that is, the educated career woman—is a real threat to her marriage and to her self-image. Calls for sexual liberation only reinforce the fear that many women felt toward the "new woman." However, He's writings have opened up new spaces for public discourse on sexuality, including (in her words) "sexual minorities," by which I believe she means anyone whose sexual practices do not conform to the heterosexual norm.

WOMEN'S LIBERATION IN
CONTEMPORARY CHINESE SOCIETIES

Mainstream Western feminists have pointed to women's labor force participation and familial roles as particularly important sites for the struggle over gender equality. Socialist feminists draw on Engels's work to argue that economic independence through paid work, along with public child care and an end to kinship structures that subordinate females to male descent groups, are necessary prerequisites for the true liberation of women. In the context of the Chinese societies in the PRC and Taiwan, these assertions generate a number of questions. First, how have the modernization processes of socialism versus capitalism affected progress toward women's liberation? Are there distinct types of modernization based on different modes of production or different cultural contexts? Specifically, is there an East Asian model of modernity; and, if so, can women be liberated within it? Do Chinese women themselves see "liberation" in the same light as Western feminists?

Women in the PRC clearly participate in the labor force in higher numbers than do women in Taiwan, and there is some evidence that this contributes to greater equality in terms of marital role attitudes, if not behavior. Hsieh and Burgess (1994) found that college students in the PRC expressed more egalitarian attitudes toward the importance of the wife's career and role alterations between husband and wife (e.g, the woman having a higher education level), whereas college students in Taiwan had more egalitarian attitudes toward institutionalized equality, such as legal rights to family property or responsibility for family finances. But does participation in paid labor necessarily allow women more independence and autonomy? In Taiwan and in the PRC, women are often relegated to low-paying, often menial jobs and have the second shift to do when they return home. Because of the relative lack of consumer goods and services in the PRC, housework is considerably more onerous there than in more economically advanced Taiwan. If it is true that women who make an economic contribution to the family, either as unmarried daughters or wives and mothers, have more power within the family, then women in the PRC with their higher labor force participation are better situated to achieve equality within the family than are their counterparts in Taiwan.

Contradictory trends for women in the current reform era in the PRC make generalizations difficult. We have seen that urban women are increasingly becoming marginalized within the reform policies, while rural women have more employment opportunities than before but also more responsibilities in farmwork and domestic labor. In the cities of Taiwan, many women and men still feel that women's most important job is household work and child care; if they work outside the home, these earnings are viewed as supplemental. Career women are frustrated by discrimination in the workplace and by the familiar demands of the second shift. Comparing groups of college students in the PRC and Taiwan, Hsieh and Burgess (1994: 417) hypothesized that marital attitudes would be more egalitarian in the PRC and were surprised to find that this was not so for all measures. They speculate that a "regressive trend in gender equality in post-Mao China may have occurred," whereas in Taiwan, due to "increasing contacts with Western societies and their egalitarian ideology during the past decade, the people in Taiwan may have advanced further in their views."

I agree that Western feminist ideas have influenced the women's movement in Taiwan, but this may also be seen as the expected outcome of modernization processes that open up space in which to challenge traditional values and practices. And the regression that Hsieh and Burgess (1994) and many other scholars (e.g., Rofel, 1994) have noted regarding women's liberation in the PRC seems to me to be largely an effect of changing economic circumstances, as the PRC is pulled inexorably into the world capitalist system. In that process, women become surplus labor, pulled into or pushed out of the workforce as the needs of capital dictate. Recent economic changes in the PRC as they affect women's status resemble those in Taiwan in its early stages of industrialization and support the claim that modernization has similar effects in diverse societies. We would also expect the PRC to resemble East European socialist countries that are also attempting to integrate into the global economy. These countries have a similar history of official rhetoric concerning the necessity of liberating women; thus, their current trajectories will be somewhat different from a society like Taiwan's, which has evolved from a state capitalist system under authoritarian rule.

In the PRC, the Maoist state discourse that denied femaleness to women has been followed predictably in the reform era by a reactionary emphasis on the "essential woman." This fits neatly with the "frontier capitalism" brought about by the state's new economic policies. This suggests to me that the feminine mystique is just around the corner for increasingly prosperous urban families. Faced with increasing discrimination in the workplace (or the difficulty of finding employment in the first place), we should not be surprised to learn that many women prefer to make home and family life their first priority. For those who do wish to have a career, I predict an uphill battle. Insomuch as Taiwan's economy is more advanced, women should have more success in the workplace, although, as we have seen, they also face such issues as discrimination and harassment.

In her book on the "unfinished liberation" of Chinese women, Phyllis Andors (1983) points out that many scholars argue that the family is the historical root of women's oppression. Thus, without changes in family dynamics, the beneficial effects on women's status of economic changes will be limited. Gayle Rubin (1975) utilizes Engels's thesis, which emphasized relations of sexuality, to argue that a focus on kinship systems should be seen as the key to women's secondary status. Rubin draws on the anthropologist Claude Levi-Strauss (1969), who posited that human cultural complexes emerged in prehistory with the universal incest taboo, necessitating that men "exchange" women in marriage. If this is so, then true liberation for women, Rubin concludes, will come about only with a revolution in kinship. In Chinese society, women's subordination was supported structurally and ideologically by a patrilineal system of descent, which forced women to "marry out" of their natal family, serving as the means through which their husband's family reproduced its descent line, and by the principle of patrilocal postmarital residence, in which the woman went to reside with her new husband and his family (Baker, 1979; Pasternak, Ember, and Ember, 1997).

In the PRC, despite the radical transformations of collectivization in the countryside that occurred in the 1950s, the rural agricultural economy continued to support a patriarchal social structure. Aspects of the economic reforms, begun in 1978, have actually allowed traditional practices—such as large dowries and bride-price, and also female infanticide and neglect—to reemerge. In Taiwan, large extended families wherein the young were subordinated to the old and women to men have largely disappeared, yet important elements of the patrilineal principle remain. Consequently, while socialist and capitalist modernization processes both in the PRC and in Taiwan have indisputably improved the status of women, the circle of logic returns again to the family as the final refuge of patriarchy. Looking at the Confucian patriarchal family in the PRC and in Taiwan, I see enduring cultural values about men and women and their places in society. Although there are clearly differences between rural and urban populations in both societies, the patrilineal principle, hierarchical relations between the generations, and the duties of filial piety still have a strong, although diminished, hold on individuals' imagination.

There is some evidence, however, that the hegemonic model of patrilineal and patrilocal family structure in the countryside of the PRC is now being challenged. Judd (1989, 1994) has described the continuing ties between a married woman and her natal family (*niangjia*), which include "dual residence" (especially during the first year of marriage), frequent visiting, and emotional and financial help when possible. It is clear from the ethnographic record that the patrilineal-patrilocal family structure is disadvantageous to women. Judd (1989, 1994) argues that the solution the government has previously encouraged, uxorilocal (i.e., matrilocal) residence, is simply not viable. In smaller families, sometimes with only one son, parents are unwilling to allow their sons to marry into the wife's family. However, informally, many rural families have found other solutions to the patrilocal trap, such as intravillage marriage or marriage between people from neighboring villages. Judd (1989) also notes that the revised marriage law of 1981 makes daughters as well as sons responsible for the care of elderly parents. Together these trends suggest that Chinese rural women as agents creatively manipulate a system that is structurally biased against them.

In Taiwan, the modernization processes have resulted in urbanization, smaller families, more nuclear family patterns, an end to the complete domination of the younger generation by the older, and a strengthening of the spousal tie at the expense of the parent-child one. Yet here also, enduring family ties and patrilineal principles remain. Women in Taiwan have been more successful than those in the PRC in realizing equality in a legal sense within the family, but these legal victories have not always been realized in practice. Yet, despite evidence of their continued subordination within the family, most women in Taiwan do not see it as a source of oppression. Skoggard (1998:4) ponders an issue that many First World feminists have trouble accepting: "Why do Third World women remain loyal to the family and endure such hardship?" He argues that because of the corporate nature of family property in Taiwan's society, both women and men have a stake in it; in addition, "under capitalism, the family becomes a site of resistance to the alienation of capitalist social relations." The family as a refuge for women is also a point made by many women of color in the United States, as Cole (1986) points out. These women argue that the classism and racism of American society represent a more fundamental problem for them than does patriarchy. Feminism for Chinese women does not necessarily mean liberation from the family, as it does for many second-wave feminists in the West. Anthropologist Aihwa Ong (1994: 397) agrees:

> By giving up our accustomed ways of looking at non-western women, we may begin to understand better. We may come to accept their living according to their own cultural interpretations of a changing world, and not simply acted upon by inherited traditions and modernization projects. They may not seek our goal of secularized autonomy, nor renounce the bonds of family and community.

Although both men and women seek some autonomy from the Confucian patriarchal family of the past, they probably do not seek independence in the Western sense. Chinese on both sides of the Taiwan Strait are still deeply attached to family, and both these Chinese societies continue to be sociocentric rather than egocentric; they emphasize the interconnectedness among people and the rights and obligations that adhere to specific social roles (Hsu, 1985). The Western, and in some ways peculiarly American, focus on individual rights and personal autonomy remains largely outside the value system of Chinese societies.

And what of a distinctive "East Asian modernity" and women's liberation within it? The Chinese Communist Party and the Nationalist Party envisioned dramatically different paths to women's liberation. For both parties, the emancipation of women was not the central concern; rather, it was to be an index of modern nationhood. Both the bourgeois and the communist visions of gender equality were, of course, imported from the West. Does this mean they are largely irrelevant for Chinese women? I think not. Problems of female infanticide and neglect, wife beating, forced prostitution, and denial of equal educational and employment opportunities are truly global women's issues. At the same time, recognition of these problems and solutions to them must come largely from women and men within their own communities. Other issues dear to the hearts of Western feminists, such as sexual liberation and freedom from family constraints, may not be relevant to most Chinese women. I will leave the question of an East Asian modernity to more qualified scholars. However, I agree with Gao (1994: 90) that "the immediate goal of modernization is to develop the economy, not to improve women's status" and that modernization has both positive and negative effects for women. We have seen this to be true for both socialist and capitalist modernization in these Chinese societies.

Although the progress of women's liberation in Taiwan may seem much more familiar to an American audience than the process on mainland China, there are significant differences. We should not assume that just because Taiwan is a newly industrialized society its quest for modernity has the same goals or outcomes of that in Western societies. In conclusion, I believe that we—Western scholars—must be sensitive to the need to be self-reflexive about our formulations of "women's liberation" and to try to not make the intellectual error that Ong (1994) warns against of participating in the neocolonial enterprise of constructing a "nonfeminist other" as a foil for our own yearnings. The process of women's liberation from Chinese patriarchy is taking different forms in the PRC and in Taiwan and cannot be expected to have the same outcomes in both places. To the extent that the battle is waged against a similar set of values, beliefs, and customs, we can expect the solutions to look similar. To the extent that these Chinese societies have distinct modern histories, we might see divergent outcomes. In either case, we should not make the assumption that the evolution of women's liberation in either Chinese society will resemble that of our own.

NOTE

This chapter originated as an invited lecture in spring 1997 which was delivered to the University of Northern Iowa History Department's *Phi Alpha Theta* colloquium series and was co-sponsored by the UNI Women's Studies Program. Revised versions of the paper were presented at the Second Annual Conference on the History and Culture of Taiwan, sponsored by Columbia University's Department of East Asian Studies, 28–31 August 1997 in New York; at the symposium "Social Change in Postwar Taiwan," sponsored by the Joint Center for East Asian Studies, Washington University and the University of Missouri–St. Louis, 16–18 October 1997; and at Tsing Hua University, Institute of Sociology, May 1999 in Taiwan. I am very grateful for participant comments at these fora. In particular I wish to thank Anru Lee, Cal Clark, Murray Rubinstein, Charles Jones, and Douglas Fix, while reserving responsibility for all errors.

10

The Limits of Democratization
for Women in East Asia

L. H. M. LING

A recent essay by Gerald L. Curtis (1998) exemplifies conventional liberal wisdom for democratization in East Asia (see Ling, 1996, for a analysis of the larger body of such literature). One of three "concluding remarks" to a volume devoted to this subject, Curtis's essay outlines six developmental "lessons": the importance of (1) local political leadership committed to democratization, (2) liberal institutions in both public and private sectors, (3) growth through capitalist economic development, (4) equitable distribution of wealth, (5) the leadership role of the United States, and (6) the ability to transcend cultural constraints.

These guidelines, however, encapsulate precisely what is wrong with current thinking about democratization in East Asia. Though sound in principle, they lack a serious reflection on the cultural/ideological origins of (Western) liberal theory and, consequently, on their applicability to postcolonial East Asia. What results is Western, liberal complicity in fostering antidemocratic processes that are intentionally, self-interestedly protected by local patriarchal elites. Feminist interventions and a newfound model of "illiberal democracy" aim to redress these gaps in liberal theory, but both still fall short. The former focuses on male-female relations only when gender in East Asia involves domestic family and imported colonial relations as well. Conversely, illiberal democracy presumes greater social and political cohesion in the region than actually exists.

This chapter places culture at democratization's analytical, not substantive, center. A substantive cultural approach usually takes culture as given and contained within a specific location. Though rich in content, it tends to overlook the larger context to cultural formations—that is, the power relations between one set of cultural signifiers (e.g., "international," "liberal") and another (e.g., "national,"

"Confucian"). An analytical cultural approach, in contrast, treats culture in terms of organic, open, ever unstable multiple traditions of thinking and doing that are, moreover, multilayered, interactive, and full of resistance as well as transformation. Put differently, culture-as-analytic appropriates and rephrases Harold Lasswell's (1958) classical political question into "Who *signifies* what, when, how" and adds, "so what"?

This approach pertains especially to postcolonial societies. They echo still with the dislocating effects of colonialism and imperialism where the colonizer's culture is systematically imposed on that of the colonized, thereby producing unanticipated hybridities, simulacra, and mimicries (Ashcroft, Griffiths, and Tiffin, 1995). Economic development in this context conveys more than just a neutral process of production, consumption, and accumulation. It becomes also part of a public discourse that casts national reconstruction as a patriarchal assertion of long-suppressed grievances or rights. Likewise, postcolonial politics operates within, under, across, and over various institutions of masculinity, both internally produced and externally imposed. For this reason, political leaders can play off one set of masculine signs against another for personal gain even in the guise of promoting "democracy."

Throughout, gender rules. Not only does it serve as a resonant metaphor for the "national family" struggling/competing against former colonial masters, but gender also takes on concrete, bodily form as East Asia's hypermasculine economies rely on one group in particular for its surplus: women. Invariably, they are rationalized as invisible (housewives), cheap (factory girls), expendable (migrant workers), and/or available (sex workers)—all for the greater glory of family, state, and economy.

CURTIS'S "LESSONS" FOR DEMOCRATIZATION

For simplicity's sake, I reorder Curtis's six lessons into three primary principles:

1. *Democracy transcends culture.* Democratization, to Curtis, is not about culture. Here he draws a distinction between culture and history. Whereas the latter accounts for the evolution (sometimes revolution) of East Asian politics, Curtis dismisses the former as "at best . . . a broad and changing framework within which a great variety of political regimes and behaviors are possible." It is, Curtis suggests, too

hazy a concept to wield explanatory power. He offers Confucianism as an example:

> A hundred years ago, Confucianism was identified as a root cause of the Chinese failure to modernize; now it is popular to explain the economic development of China (as well as that of Korea and Taiwan and even Japan) in terms of the same Confucianism that previously was confidently identified as responsible for Asian economic backwardness. (Curtis, 1998: 222)

Curtis affirms democracy's universal appeal. Everyone, he declares, wants "respect for individual dignity and personal freedom and the desire for responsible government." (Curtis, 1998: 222)

2. *Growth with equity facilitates democracy.* "Economic growth," Curtis (1998: 219–220) writes, "undermines authoritarianism," especially when matched with a "relatively equitable distribution of income." By economic development, Curtis (1998: 219) means capitalism, given its ability to create an independent middle class, a rights-conscious working class, and "a business community that may have been spawned by the state [but] develops its own resources and demands autonomy." Here he cites Korea's conglomerates, the *chaebol*, as a case of successful "limited autonomy" after initial dependence on the state. Curtis adds, at this point, the salutary "association" with and "influence" of the United States in promoting democratization in East Asia, especially after World War II. The U.S. occupation of Japan, for example, ensured the growth and legitimacy of civil interest groups such as "labor unions, agricultural cooperatives, business associations, and other groups" to counter authoritarian tendencies in the state (Curtis, 1998: 219).

3. *Democratically committed institutions and leaders matter.* A civic infrastructure, Curtis emphasizes, is critical to democratization. In East Asia, civil society pales next to the power of the state. For this reason, the role of liberal political institutions and individual leaders is paramount. Where leaders are personally committed to democracy—such as in postwar Japan, Roh Dae Woo's South Korea, or Chiang Ching-kuo's Taiwan, in contrast to Lee Kuan Yew's Singapore—it has a higher probability of surviving and thriving.

A POSTCOLONIAL-FEMINIST CRITIQUE

These principles seem eminently reasonable. Who would object that democracy appeals "universally," that growth with equity wins, or that democratically committed institutions and leaders are important? But when these principles are placed within East Asia's postcolonial context, they bear quite different results. Let us examine how and why.

Democratization's Need for Culture and History

Acknowledging history's differential impact on East Asian politics may wiggle Curtis and other like-minded liberals from accusations of absolutism or Western neoimperialism. He notes, for example, that "each East Asian country . . . is bound to follow its own path of political development" and that "it is hubris that leads to the view that there is only one, or one best, form of democracy" (Curtis, 1998: 222). But devaluing the significance of culture in mediating democratic signifiers—say, substituting collective for personal dignity and freedom—effectively denies history to peoples with non-Western, nonliberal traditions. Culture and history cannot be separated, because each interprets the other. Just contrast, for instance, American Indian views on Columbus's "discovery" of the "New World" with those presented in Anglo-European history textbooks. Or, for an example closer to this chapter's focus, compare Chinese and British treatments of their imperial clashes in the last century. One small indication lies in each party's designation of their defining conflict: the Opium War versus the Anglo-Chinese War. Given that different cultures interpret the same history differently, we need to ask: Whose culture and whose history are recognized and why?

Curtis's own reference to Confucianism serves as an apt example. The fact that Max Weber and Karl Marx, among others, denounced Confucianism as a barrier to modernization says more about Orientalist strains in Western scholarship on Asia than anything particular about Chinese culture. That "miracle" theorists reverse this judgment further underscores the mercurial nature of knowledge and power. After all, Asian economies now constitute a significant portion of the world economy by working capitalism through local traditions rather than abandoning them. With the region's recent financial crisis, these same theorists are backtracking into the culture-as-impediment camp as they indict the affected economies with crony capitalism, incompetence, and other forms of corruption (Krugman, 1997; Sen, 1998). Meanwhile, what have we learned about Confucianism and capitalism from those who live, work, and play in that context? Little, indeed.

When local agents react with their own vision of democratization, they are castigated with "Asian exceptionalism." Those who gasp in horror (e.g., Fukuyama, 1998) neglect to note their own brand of

"Western exceptionalism" rationalized as liberal universalism or, more trendily, globalization (Ling, 1999). Samuel P. Huntington (1996) stretches this reasoning to its logical extreme. Given that liberal capitalism is Western in origin, he declares, countries must choose: to Westernize or not. If they do, they can join a harmonious compact of Western civilization. If not, they are implacable enemies of the West and responsible for the next century's great conflict.

Neither argument is convincing. Anything, including democracy, can be mined from Asia's ancient civilizations. Moreover, Asia and the West cross-fertilized long ago, leaving neither culture pristine or singular. Advocates of "Asian values" seek only to deflect attention away from or even justify local authoritarianism just as battle cries of "Western civilization or bust" mask racism of the deepest, most (self-) deceptive kind.

Nevertheless, culture retains an analytical relevance. It provides a starting point for understanding how the world is constructed and why. Culture orders for us that immense, swirling mass of chaos known as life and renders it into familiar, distinguishable narratives of reality that we can subsequently reject, accept, innovate upon, or transform. Culture, though, is by no means pristine, singular, or self-enclosed. Just the opposite, it is hybrid, multilayered, and unpredictably, defiantly, maddingly open. Even before the onset of colonialism and imperialism, cultures mixed, collided, and learned from one another (Abu-Lughod, 1989; Bozeman, 1994).

What distinguishes East Asia's cultures is their *particular* mix. Western civilization is but the latest addition to a region already enriched by older processes of cultural hybridity—Confucianism, Islam, Hinduism, Buddhism, Taoism, Shinto, and so on. Throughout, one strain persists: the patriarchal family. It accounts for the region's classic triad of family, state, and economy.

Family, State, and Economy: Hypermasculine Development

Patriarchal family relations predominate in East Asia. These extend beyond the nuclear family to include multiple generations within and across families, as well as social relations in general. The state in Confucian East Asia represents the patriarchal family writ large. Historically, representatives of the state act as father-mother officials (*fumu guan*) to the people, who in turn serve as their children-subjects. Accordingly, state-society relations correspond directly to those between Confucian parents and child: firm benevolence from parents/state in exchange for filial devotion from children/subjects.

Even Taoism, usually a source of laissez-faire heterodoxy to Confucian hegemony, instructs rulers to treat their subjects as "children" (Laozi quoted in Thomas, 1968: 163). Outside the Confucian world order, Islam also transfers to the state governance rules derived from family relations, especially where women are concerned (Fernea, 1985). Only Buddhism and Hinduism renounce any concern with earthly matters, although each strictly regulates relations between men and women as well (Nandy, 1988).

Modernization in East Asia begins as a national family enterprise. Western colonialism and imperialism mobilized patriarchy's preexisting hegemony to develop domestically for international purposes. Meiji Japan, East Asia's prototypical miracle economy, illustrates the case. It succeeded in coercing large-scale Westernization from a society primarily based on a virulent antiforeignism (Wakabayashi, 1991). Japan saw imperial China arrogantly refuse modernization/Westernization only to implode fatally under the awesome might of Western military-industrial power. "Can the Chinese still consider themselves men?" wailed Taiping rebels in a nineteenth-century China riddled with opium addicts and carved up "like a melon" by Western imperial powers (Spence, 1990: 173). Japan sought to withstand China's fate by imperializing like the West, but its claim to a Greater East Asia Co-Prosperity Sphere in the 1930s alienated neighbors and provoked atomic devastation. Japan's quest for empire ended with Allied victory in 1945, but its battle cry of national reconstruction as avenging manhood still resonates. Note, for example, Korea's Park Chung Hee in the 1960s and 1970s when he declared "trade as war!"

Capitalism, though, mutates local traditions to suit its competitive, masculinist edge. It does not, as Maria Mies (1986) suggests, simply rework the rest of the world in a universalized patriarchal image. In Confucian Asia, for instance, the state hypermasculinizes in reaction to its historical feminization/emasculation by the West. Previous parental relations between state and society now give way to a conjugal one as the hypermasculinized state compels society to take on all the characteristics of classical Confucian womanhood: deference, discipline, and self-sacrifice (Han and Ling, 1998). Relegated to the role of privileged first sons are corporations, which now serve as heirs apparent to the hypermasculinized state. Society, moreover, tacitly consents to state control over labor unions and other potentially "disruptive" organizations by accepting their reidentification as subordinate members of the national family. The Park regime, for example, reconfigured management-labor relations into "the father-son relation in the family [and] not so-called 'labour contracts'" (Kim, 1986:

42). Given frequent state-management collusion against labor, it is not difficult to imagine who commands as father and who obeys as son. Moreover, women workers are locked out of this Confucian father-son relationship altogether.

State-economy relations in East Asia, therefore, can never reproduce the kind of "separate but equal" status that liberals presuppose. Korea's chaebol, Curtis's exemplar of dependence-turned-autonomy-through-prosperity, offer another reason why. The chaebol may have gained greater leverage over governmental control in recent years, but a bastion of democracy they are not. Patriarchal, hierarchical, and conservative, the chaebol resist, rather than embrace, democratic reform from their father-figure founders to male managers to hyper-feminized workers (Fields, 1995; S. M. Lee, 1989). Increased economic power may, at most, allow the chaebol to transform their current son-father relationship with the state to one of younger to older brother. But to abolish this familial relationship as a governing principle would, in effect, destroy the chaebol themselves.

Hypermasculine development also uses family as an instrument of policy. It predicates national modernization on modernizing the household—which means regulating women. The Meiji government, again prototypically, sought to enhance industrialization and modernization by propagating a samurai ideal for all women—"good wife, wise mother" (*ryosai kembo*)—whose sole purpose in life was to bear and raise sons. Erased from public recognition, then, was the hardy peasant woman tilling fields or competent matron managing household goods and accounts (Bernstein, 1993). This good wife, wise mother model subsequently permeated the rest of Confucian Asia (*xianqi liangmu* in Chinese, *hyonmo yangcho* in Korean, *me hien vo thao* in Vietnamese) and reverberates presently even in Islamic Indonesia and Malaysia. Note this speech made in the 1980s by Tien Suharto, wife of the now deposed dictator of Indonesia:

> A harmonious and orderly household is a great contribution to the smooth running of development efforts. . . . It is the duty of the wife to see to it that her household is in order so that when her husband comes home from a busy day he will find peace and harmony at home. The children, too, will be happier and healthier. (Blackwood, 1995: 136)

Today, as economies in East Asia recuperate from financial crises, the state once again deploys the family as metaphor and policy. Malaysia's government, for instance, urges women to sell their jewelry in order to buy bonds to shore up the national treasury. At the same time, it portrays the crisis as a blessing in disguise. Men took to gambling and other nonfamily-oriented entertainments when the economy was good, the government clucks. Now that times are harder, men are returning to the family hearth. But women need to nurse their wayward husbands and sons from this (national) "depression" by pampering them.

Thus, "growth with equity" in East Asia overlooks a vital portion of the population: women. Last hired and first fired, women's wages, promotions, and opportunities consistently lag behind men's across sectors and type of firm despite women's lasting contribution to the region's capitalist accumulation (Truong, 1999). Indeed, the region's entrenched exploitation of women in the household as well as in the economy generally accounts for the rapid spread of another sector linked to modernization and power politics: prostitution (Barry, 1995; Enloe, 1989). The International Labour Organization (ILO) reports that "between 0.25 per cent and 1.5 per cent of the total female population in Indonesia, Malaysia, the Philippines and Thailand are prostitutes and that the sex sector accounts for between 2 per cent and 14 per cent of gross domestic product (GDP)" (Lim, 1998: 7). Prostitution, however, perfectly complements the social, political, and economic demands of hypermasculine development. From the brothels of Jakarta, Bangkok, Manila, Taipei, Seoul, and increasingly Shanghai and Hanoi, prostitutes repeatedly cite family obligations for selling their bodies. The hypermasculinized state, furthermore, explicitly links national development with foreign policy with female subjugation with sex. Note this "pep talk" from a government official to camptown prostitutes in South Korea:

> The Japanese prostitute, when she finished with the GI, did not get up to go get the next GI (for more money) but knelt before him and pleaded with him to help rebuild Japan. The spirit of the Japanese prostitute was concerned with the survival of her fatherland. The patriotism of the Japanese prostitute spread to the rest of the society to develop Japan. (Moon, 1997: 103)

Of course, this official did not mention that a camptown prostitute would not receive a medal, parade, compensation, or any other tribute heaped on war heroes. She would, if lucky, grow old as a pariah among her own or marry a foreigner and live out the rest of her days in a foreign land. Or, she could die of disease, drugs, alcohol, or abuse. Worse yet, she could die of disease, drugs, alcohol, or abuse in a foreign country. What he did recognize, however inadvertently, was the Asian woman's common exploitation under hypermasculine development.

Sage Man Politics

In politics as in economics, hypermasculinity protects the patriarchal elite. It allows individual (male) leaders to maneuver contending ideologies and institutions for personal gain, as long as they conform to a traditional moral rhetoric about public life. Politicians in Taiwan, for example, manipulate the island's legacy of Confucian hegemony, Japanese colonialism, U.S. liberalism, and local nativism/nationalism to simulate democratic politics, but they end up with "sage man" (*xian ren*) politics anyway (Ling and Shih, 1998). This refers to the implicit belief of politicians and the public alike that only a wise man with the proper moral credentials can lead the nation. Elections, accordingly, serve to confirm (or invalidate) the public's trust in a politician (usually male) to protect, rather than represent, its interests. Hence, the public may excuse personal power-mongering if it is cloaked in the rhetoric of Confucian selflessness. Note this mix of Confucian morals with liberal institutions in a speech by Lee Tenghui, Taiwan's president, to inaugurate an ad hoc committee in 1990 that would summarily replace several key functions of the democratically elected National Assembly:

> From a position filled with a sense of mission and open-mindedness, each of you should jettison all stereotyped partisan or personal perspectives and faithfully act upon a sincere devotion to the country so as to concentrate on the issues through an overall and thorough discussion. . . . I would see to it that all of your recommendations would later become reality through institutional and legal procedures. (*Records of the National Affairs Council*, 1990: 226)

Another example comes from Taiwan's charismatic governor, James C. Y. Soong. He resigned dramatically on New Year's Day 1997 to protest attempts by President Lee to "freeze" Taiwan's provincial status (*dongsheng*) under the rubric of eliminating "duplication" in government. A diversionary tactic clearly aimed to prepare for Taiwan's eventual declaration of sovereignty vis-à-vis China, freezing Taiwan's provincial status also pulled the political rug from under Soong's ambitious feet. Soong, a presidential hopeful, could not allow Lee to rob him of a political platform and an important constituency. In July 1999, Soong announced that he would run as an Independent in the March 2000 presidential election. Consequently, Soong challenged Lee with a moral play of his own: in resigning, Soong analogized himself to a historical figure, Jie Zhitui, who would rather burn to death than verbally rebuke his (abusive) prince. Jie's death, though, indicted his prince far more resoundingly through the ages than mere words could ever match. Recognizing the rhetorical power behind Soong's resignation—and the public's emotional support of it—President Lee inveighed upon his vice-president, Lien Chan, to convince Soong to take sick leave instead. This political sleight of hand transmuted Soong's resignation, with its full moral implications, into a mundane, legal matter—sick leave—over which the president and vice-president have complete and obligatory jurisdiction. But what of the public interest or common good? Not much. Lee, Lien, Soong, and other aspiring sage men continue to play out politics in Taiwan with little input or impact from "others," such as non–sage men as well as women. Non–sage men are all those who fail the Confucian criteria for "gentleman" (*junzi*) status: college-educated or higher, married with children, a filial son, and a patriotic servant of the nation.

For South Korea, Byung-Kook Kim (1998) attributes this phenomenon to a "crisis of success." Like in Taiwan, politics in South Korea exhibits the same kind of personal power-mongering abetted by liberal party politics couched in Confucian moral rhetoric. What results, Kim laments, is endless factionalism led by a few personalities (all men) who, at will, change party allegiances, memberships, and even the parties themselves—all the while intoning the sanctity of democracy. Ironically, Kim blames this political disarray on Korea's developmental success. Whereas economic necessities curbed power-mongering in the past, he claims, such constraints no longer apply in a newly prosperous Korea. Hence, personal ambitions are unleashed ferociously and flagrantly, rarely to the public good.

Kim's formulation of development versus democracy, however, overlooks their underlying mutuality. Hypermasculine development reinforces sage man politics, and vice versa, because each is grounded in the other materially, ideologically, and normatively. Consequently, a common pattern beguiles East Asia's miracle societies: they are economically wealthy but politically factionalized, ideologically competitive but normatively patriarchal, and institutionally liberal but substantively authoritarian.

FEMINIST INTERVENTIONS AND ILLIBERAL DEMOCRACY

Feminists have long critiqued liberal theory along similar lines. They unmask liberalism's own gendered and authoritarian history/culture by reexamining its concepts as well as practices (Ferguson, 1991; Jones, 1993; Pateman, 1989; Phillips, 1991, 1993; Young, 1990a, 1990b). Feminists also question liberalism's abiding faith in market mechanisms and political institutions as separate, unproblematic venues for democracy. How democratic, they ask, is it to glorify "one person, one vote" when women are consistently underpaid, underemployed, and overly vulnerable in the workplace? Similarly, how democratic are political institutions that continue to undermine women's democratic rights either through legislation (e.g., defeat of the Equal Rights Amendment) or the masculinist nature of party politics (e.g., abortion becoming a litmus test of "family values")?

Liberal feminism, however, is hardly monolithic. Debates on liberalism's public/private distinction, for example, range from those who uphold it to resist a personalization of public life (Elshtain, 1981) to others who demand democracy in "the kitchen, the nursery, and the bedroom" (Pateman quoted in Phillips, 1991: 115). Whatever their position, feminists shatter the liberal illusion that democratization is so universally appealing, economically empowering, and institutionally open that it is culture blind and gender mute.

Nevertheless, liberal feminism offers few options for women and other feminized subjects in postcolonial societies. Gender for the latter is not just about relations between men and women but involves, as demonstrated above, family and colonial relations as well. How do women enmeshed in Confucian family relations argue for equal work for equal pay when their employer may be their father/husband/brother? How does legislation or oppositional politics combat sage man politics when they are infused with patriarchal elites and with society's consent? Where patriarchal family relations model state-society relations, how does the public/private distinction apply? How can politics *not* be personalized? Conversely, how does installing democracy in the kitchen, nursery, and bedroom deal with relations between parents and children? Older and younger siblings? Mothers- and daughters-in-law?

Colonialism further blurs the correlation between masculinity or femininity and biology. In naturalizing power as masculine, colonizers feminize all Others. From these historical confrontations arises hypermasculinity's ugly head as colonized men seek to retrieve their manhood by out-masculinizing the colonizers. For this reason, notes Gayatri Spivak (1988), subaltern women "cannot speak," as they are squeezed between two masculinist discourses: Western imperialism and local patriarchy. Indeed, Chandra Mohanty (1991) and Linda Lim (1990) warn, unreflexive application of liberal feminism to postcolonial contexts risks reproducing the sort of masculinist, Western hegemony that liberal feminists themselves abhor.

Those who examine the intersection of race with gender in a multicultural democracy come closest to this issue. Patricia Hill Collins

(1991), for example, identifies an "outsider-within" status for black women, who often perform intimate tasks inside white majority households (e.g., cleaning, cooking, caregiving) but who are systematically peripheralized by white majority society nonetheless. Lisa Lowe (1991) probes into alternatives to the assimilationism versus nativism dilemma that prohibits Asian Americans from coalescing within as well as across communities. Gary Okihiro (1994) calls for a "re-centering" of women as one means of transforming "margins into mainstreams." But the challenges to racial minorities in a preestablished liberal context still differ significantly from a postcolonial legacy of multiple norms, practices, ideologies, and institutions.

Bell, Brown, Jayasuriya, and Jones (1995) coin the term "illiberal democracy" to describe this kind of politics in East Asia. The state mobilizes society, they explain, precisely due to the latter's immersion in this postcolonial mélange. Accordingly, the illiberal democratic state is more committed to developmental problem solving than "accomodat[ing] . . . a plurality of interests"; it allows a "technocratic and managerial approach to politics . . . in the guise of political liberalization" (Bell and Jayasuriya, 1995: 13). This comes in the form of (1) an interventionist state, (2) a rationalistic and legalistic technocracy, and (3) a government-managed public space and civil society.

Illiberal democracy begins to redraft the meaning of liberal politics in postcolonial East Asia. It does not force the square peg of Western liberalism into the round hole of East Asian postcoloniality. Nor does it pretend that local traditions like Confucianism are more liberal than they really are. But this notion of illiberal democracy seems overly resolved. It presumes that East Asian technocrats have little to contend with but the problems of economic development. Overlooked are the roiling dilemmas that preoccupy every postcolonial subject daily. These range from the personal (e.g., Should I, as a competent woman entrepreneur who is doing all the work, seek refuge in "good wife, wise mother" rhetoric by pretending that I am merely "helping out" my father/husband/brother? Or, should I simply claim all the credit? Which is more beneficial in the long run?) to the public and institutional (e.g., What is the *moral* basis of public dissent? Liberal rights and representation, or Confucian filial loyalty?).

(RE)TURN TO CULTURE?

Hypermasculine development, in sum, exerts a frightening dual efficiency. Not only does it reserve women for economic exploitation, but hypermasculinity also elevates men to high and comprehensive political power. Aspirants in the region, including postsocialist China and Vietnam, now take hypermasculinity as their developmental model of choice. After all, it salves traditional patriarchal family relations while pushing capitalist accumulation. Moreover, hypermasculine development gives an impression of democratizing politics without actually delivering it in content.

Liberal theory misfires in this context. It presumes that capitalist market mechanisms "even out" gender and other social biases. But East Asia's miracle economies were built precisely on those stratifications of gender, age, and rank that anchor traditional family relations but that also undermine political representation and voice for women, the younger generation, and institutional subordinates whether located in families, firms, or government. Similarly, conventional theories of democratization believe that liberal institutions (such as opposition parties, open elections, a free press, and so on) lay the foundation for a more democratic politics. These institutions in East Asia, however, often serve as a public cover for private power-mongering. The public accepts such grabs for power if leaders can wrap themselves with the sage man mantle of patriarchal lore. Accordingly, mere reliance on liberal institutions like capitalism and oppositional politics merely enhances a ritualistic, performative democratic politics primarily for public relations purposes. Put differently, liberal democratic theory not only fails to address the governance problems that East Asians face but also tends to compound them. Neither do feminist interventions nor a model of illiberal democracy help. Though more sensitive to issues of gender, race, and colonialism, they still offer little awareness of the multilayered, multicultural, and multigendered nature of hypermasculinized, postcolonial societies.

Let us (re)turn to culture. Contemporary art and literature in East Asia are less shackled by hypermasculine development, as in the economy, or sage man expectations, as in politics. They allow for expressions of self that are normally silenced, excluded, or exiled but that offer valuable insight into contemporary negotiations of identity within hypermasculine postcoloniality. "A. Taiwaner" (1996), for example, explores what homosexual love means in an economically liberal but normatively conservative Taiwan. Similarly, Shih Shu-mei (1998) traces the intricacies of China's relations with Taiwan and Hong Kong through the latter's media representations of femininity and masculinity for all three. Other examples abound, but restrictions on space here prohibit delving into them in detail. What summarizes these artistic expressions is that though they may seem highly personalized or commercialized for entertainment purposes only, they also help us overcome hackneyed notions of development versus democracy, individual versus family, patriarch versus subordinate, masculinity versus femininity. From this basis, we may cull a more accurate, comprehensive representation of not just interests but also identities in East Asia, thereby laying the foundation for a sustainable democratization in the region. By this, I mean the emergence of a generalized heuristic for managing democratic debate and dissent to inform public decisionmaking. In contrast to the current patchwork of institutions and ideologies contesting for normative supremacy within an essentially elitist, patriarchal cultural context, this heuristic for democratization would draw on culturally resonant means to allow space for and articulate identities/voices usually silenced by hypermasculine development and sage man politics.

PART 3

Conclusion

11

Democracy and "Softening" Society

CAL CLARK & ROSE J. LEE

In essence, as sketched in Chapter 1, the study of development was turned on its head during the postwar era in a cruel reversal concerning the emancipation of women in societies with strong patriarchal traditions. Initially, it was generally believed that women would be prime beneficiaries of industrialization and the concomitant social change that it unleashed. Unfortunately, this turned out to be overly optimistic; patriarchal relations were reproduced in industrial and urban societies with surprising ease. More insidiously perhaps, even the positive prescriptions for improving the status of women in developing societies were reversed. As Catherine Scott (1995) observes, underdevelopment in the Third World has increasingly come to be blamed on traditional societies that are viewed as the "feminized other" in contrast to advanced industrial societies. This leads to the argument that the imposition of either a hard (masculinized) state or a hard (masculinized) market is necessary to subdue the "economy of affection," which must be done if a developing country is to become competitive in the global capitalist economy. Consequently, women are implicitly (and sometimes even explicitly) transformed from victims to be liberated by development into underminers of development who must be resubjugated in the name of economic progress.

Although the preceding paragraph paints a dreary picture for women, the logic it describes should not necessarily be taken as the last word on the subject. After all, it was not so long ago that development was assumed to emancipate, rather than subjugate, women. Thus, the learned consensus could well change in a more positive direction in the future. In fact, the study of development seems to be moving toward an emphasis on meeting basic human needs and on viewing "human capital" as playing a key role in stimulating economic growth and transformation (Clark and Roy, 1997). Such a perspective

185

should almost inevitably bring women and the development of their talents and self-potential back to the center of the equation for attaining social and economic progress in both the developing and developed worlds. What is needed, consequently, is not a hard state or hard market to masculinize "soft, feminized" societies in the developing areas. Rather, the need would seem to be the reverse: to soften hard patriarchal societies in order to permit women to find self-fulfillment and to increase their potential contributions to society.

Democratization provides another venue that might promote women's emancipation and empowerment. If women are free to organize and to push for policies outlawing discriminatory practices, the power of the state can be used to end the worst abuses of patriarchy. The studies collected in this book hence explore whether democracy has had any discernible impact on softening highly patriarchal societies in East Asia. It is difficult to draw a precise balance sheet of the findings and arguments presented here. Clearly, some contributors are much more optimistic or pessimistic than others on whether democracy holds out much hope for improving the status of women in East Asia. Rather than creating a stable list of advantages and disadvantages, however, the various chapters suggest nuances and exceptions to each other's perspectives that are maddeningly difficult to sum up in any straightforward accounting system.

In terms of macroperspectives, Ling's conceptualization of East Asia's political economy seemingly implies that democratization will have little impact on the successful reproduction of patriarchy that has been produced by these nations' strategy of hypermasculine development, because the prevailing democratic style of governance there is dominated by a "sage man politics." Conversely, the pessimism of Ling's model is at least partially challenged by the two major conclusions of the Hipsher-Darcy study: (1) autonomous and indigenous women's movements can be found in the histories of most of Asia's highly patriarchal societies; and (2) contemporary constitutional and legal reforms in a surprisingly wide range of Asian countries guarantee many basic economic and political rights for women. This suggests that, even within patriarchal cultural traditions, women may be able to use such rights to evolve new and more fulfilling roles. Moreover, even if patriarchal relations have been recreated in industrialized East Asia, women now have much higher levels of education and participation in the formal workforce than in preindustrial Confucian society—two important resources that can be utilized for political organization.

Yet, one should not be too hasty in gainsaying the structural constraints on women's ability to use democratic institutions to further their interests that were suggested in Ling's analysis. Consider, for example, the four top-ranking nations on the Hipsher-Darcy scale of legislation promoting women's rights. Farris's essay shows that China's guarantee of women's rights in the early 1950s, though representing substantial progress, certainly did not revolutionize women's position in Chinese society; in fact, under Deng's marketization reforms during the 1980s and 1990s, their position has clearly deteriorated. South Korea, as Lee and Chin show, continues to have a pitifully low legislative representation of women at both the national and local levels. Finally, Singapore's Lee Kuan Yew and Malaysia's Mahathir Mohammed represent the epitome of what Ling calls sage man politics.

Any discussion of women's roles and potential liberation in East Asia must pay special attention to social relations, in particular women's roles in kinship systems and the family. Here, Farris's nuanced discussion of "women's liberation" in Chinese societies appears quite ambiguous in terms of whether its implications are positive or negative for women in East Asia today. She argues that Chinese women define gender roles much more in terms of complementarity than do middle-class Western feminists and that they still consider their relationships within the family and other social networks as the centerpiece of their power and identity. On the one hand, the idea that there are "many roads to emancipation" could be reassuring, because it implies that East Asian women themselves see progress in terms of their own self-definitions. On the other hand, Ling's persuasive linking of both hypermasculine development and sage man politics to the patriarchal model of the Confucian family indicates that any such progress might well be limited. Certainly, Chin's depiction of the Confucian family and broader sets of social relations in Korea indicates the prevalence of patriarchal norms in a largely industrialized nation. Moreover, Hipsher and Darcy found that it was precisely the area of domestic and family relations that had proved most resistant to women's attempts to establish legal protection in East Asian societies (as it has in the industrialized West).

A similar conundrum exists over how to interpret Atienza's conclusion that although some (but certainly not all) of the women's groups that she studied in the Philippines have made significant progress in promoting beneficial social reform, they remain self-limited by their lack of "conscientization." Women in the Philippines have done a remarkable job of creating dense networks of organizations that work for the social reforms that women advocate. Yet, success will remain limited as long as women and their groups consider themselves only to be trying to influence male-dominated governmental institutions, even at the local level. Rather, major progress will almost certainly have to wait until women, with their distinct interests, share equally in decisionmaking for their societies.

Another somewhat confusing set of pluses and minuses is raised by the comparative assessment of South Korea, Taiwan, and China in the chapters by Lee, Chin, Farris, and the Clarks. These essays examine women's political representation, the activities of women's groups, policies affecting women, and women's place in social hierarchies in three seemingly comparable countries, in conjunction with the Hipsher-Darcy ratings of women's legislation in them. At the abstract level, these four dimensions—group activism, political representation, public policy, and social outcomes—should be linked. Greater group activity and enhanced political representation, for instance, would be expected to be highly correlated. When women gain greater representation, they should be able to use their enhanced political power to enact policies furthering their agenda, which in turn should produce more favorable social outcomes by using the power of the state to control the grosser manifestations of patriarchy.

But the picture that emerges from the various comparisons drawn from these chapters is far more confusing. Taiwan has made impressive strides toward increasing women's representation (now in the 15 to 20 percent range) in all its legislative bodies; yet, it scores quite badly on legislation to protect and enforce women's rights. South Korea, in direct contrast, is one of the most advanced Asian nations in terms of women's legislation, despite women's extremely low representation in elected decisionmaking bodies (generally about 2 to 3 percent). Furthermore, Lee's case study directly links growing democratic competition in Korean politics to a series of policy changes that were quite favorable to women. An equally puzzling picture emerges when Taiwan is juxtaposed to China. The PRC is far more advanced in terms of the legal protection of women (the idea suggested by this finding that socialism is favorable to women's emancipation is belied, however, by the shoddy records of the other Asian communist nations). Yet, Farris concludes that women in Taiwan have made considerable progress due to the positive social changes accompanying its advanced level of industrialization (note that China, where rapid industrialization has seemingly stimulated a resurgence of patriarchy, is at a significantly earlier stage of industrial transformation than is Taiwan).

These inconsistencies do not appear to be random, though. Rather, they can be explained by the activity and autonomy of women's groups in the various nations. In particular, having strong

women's advocacy groups seems far more effective than having a fairly high level of women's legislative representation, as does having a
permanent voice in the executive. Feminist groups in South Korea
have much more political influence than their counterparts in
Taiwan. Even the fact that they are split along class lines is evidently
not the hindrance that splitting the women's movement would normally be since it means that women can appeal to and gain policy
support from both ends of the ideological spectrum. Korea's feminist
groups have also been shrewd in creating formalized organizations,
such as the Council on Women's Policy, to push for women's empowerment within the executive continuously and cumulatively, rather
than relying upon the vagaries of legislative action. Turning to another country, Atienza's field research did find significant cases where
women's groups in the Philippines have been able to promote their
agendas by influencing local governments and officials, but she
points out that they remain limited by women's nearly total exclusion
from directly participating in local government decisionmaking.

Conversely, some surprisingly bad outcomes for women stem
from the absence of influential women's groups. The lower level of
political influence that women's groups have in Taiwan probably
accounts for the country's fairly low score on the scale of women's
rights, despite the country's good record in increasing women's legislative representation. Likewise, the relative weakness of independent women's groups in China, where strict limits are still in place over
political participation, provides the most plausible explanation for
the serious gap that exists there between formal guarantees of
women's rights and a rising level of patriarchy in actual social relations.

These findings from East Asia are consistent with recent research
that demonstrates the efficacy of activities by grassroots women's
groups in a wide range of contexts in both the developing and developed worlds (Bystydzienski and Sekhon, 1999). Democratization,
hence, may be less important for its ability to increase the formal representation of women among political decisionmakers than for its
contribution to the expansion of "civil society," or organizations and
institutions in a society that are independent of state control (Barber,
1998; Cohen and Arato, 1992; Ehrenberg, 1999; Seligman, 1992).
Obviously, the growth of civil society in East Asia has somewhat mixed
implications for women. On the one hand, it can facilitate the resurgence of patriarchal interests and norms (e.g., the upswing of patriarchy accompanying the recent economic reforms in China). Yet,
autonomous women's groups can also be empowered, not just to
lobby for favorable policies but also to work together to improve their

own lives and status in society. Many of the essays in this book (see Chapters 3–6, 8, and 9) indicate that the second positive trend more than counterbalances the first negative one (e.g., as Farris notes, the "return to patriarchy" in China helped stimulate the rise of independent feminist groups).

Although the evidence on women's empowerment is certainly mixed, these studies do point toward a conclusion that culture (which most Western theories tend to overlook) *is* important, although its implications for the status of women in East Asia are somewhat cross-cutting. This is most evident in Farris's argument that what constitutes women's emancipation should be defined by specific groups of women themselves, rather than be assumed a priori to represent one universal pattern. She then shows how political and economic change in both China and Taiwan has had quite different impacts on women situated in different social and economic conditions. Thus, women's empowerment and emancipation are contextually conditioned in two important senses. First, women from different cultures and subcultures define emancipation in their own personal and group terms; second, the same policy or socioeconomic process may have very different impacts on women within the same society.

How these cultural dynamics play out in East Asia varies widely, however. In many instances, patriarchal cultures present formidable barriers to women's advancement. Ling constructs a complex model of how culturally conditioned political styles in East Asia limit the potential of women to use democratic political institutions; Chin emphasizes the harsh consequences of patriarchal conditions in Korea, including feminist groups' acquiescence to patriarchal stereotypes in their recent electoral strategy of focusing on local governments; and Atienza shows the limits imposed on women's groups by both uncooperative male government leaders in some situations and by their own lack of conscientization in others. Yet, East Asian cultures do not inevitably doom women's efforts either. Hipsher and Darcy remind us of a series of important women's movements that have occurred even in traditional East Asian society, and the Clarks argue that local factionalism in Taiwan's traditionally male-dominated politics actually helped make the reserved seats system more effective in creating autonomous women politicians (although these cultural influences also limit how high women's representation can probably go).

In addition, the implications of broad culture factors appear to be filtered through specific institutions. In terms of using electoral reform to increase women's political representation, the studies by Lee and the Clarks indicate that a quota system can be effective, not just in electing token women but in ultimately changing the political game in ways that allow broader entrance for independent women politicians. In contrast, the findings of Christensen and Lee indicate that the favorable effects for women of proportional representation systems and multimember districts are probably much more muted in East Asia than in the advanced industrial democracies. Moreover, women's subordinate position in East Asian cultures makes them vulnerable not only to purposeful barriers but also to the unintended side effects of policy decisions. For example, Christensen offers an intriguing explanation for women's extremely low representation in Japan's House of Representatives by linking Japan's strict laws about campaigning to the overriding importance of personal support organizations, which are very hard for women to develop independently.

The importance of culture also raises the question of the relative impact of internal and external forces on the status of women in East Asia. The Farris essay is the most explicit in distinguishing the feminist goals of specific groups of Asian women from Western stereotypes of feminism. Although Western feminism contributed important ideas and ideals to women's movements in East Asia, these were refracted through Asian cultures. Thus, what Farris terms "women's liberation" in East Asia has its unique components and objectives. Ling's postcolonial theory, in contrast, views the interaction of East and West much more darkly. She argues that patriarchal elites in Asia have used popular anti-imperialist ideology to justify intensifying patriarchy through hypermasculine development and sage man politics. These differing perspectives are consistent, though, in that they again indicate the vital importance for women of creating autonomous organizations and pushing for the expansion of a "civil society" in which such women's groups can flourish.

The foregoing evidence has brought us to a positive but ambivalent conclusion. Legal reforms have only slightly softened old (and, unfortunately, new or "reproduced") patriarchal practices. Women's groups have become quite active in most of the democracies from the Philippines to South Korea; yet, their success has varied considerably and become dependent on political factors outside their control. Moreover, women's representation and access to the political elites remain quite circumscribed. More broadly, as Ling argues, the overarching culture and political economy of East Asia have many hidden (and not so hidden) biases against women. These are no small obstacles, given the importance of culture and institutional arrangements that many of the essays found.

The status of women in Asia is clearly in flux. Democracy seems to have helped by creating an environment or "civil society" in which autonomous women's groups can form, network, and develop some political influence. Progress in terms of the formal political representation of women has been much more gradual in most Asian nations, though. The practice of reserving parliamentary quotas for women seems to be spreading, although this obviously will be a lengthy process. Women in Asia, therefore, face substantial political challenges with significant but definitely limited resources at their disposal. Overall, we argue, democratization has given women new tools to improve their position. How effective these tools can be and how well they are used differ radically among the individual East Asian nations. Still, we believe that a long journey toward women's emancipation in East Asia has begun.

References

Abu-Lughod, J.L. 1989. *Before European Hegemony: The World System A.D. 1250–1350.* Oxford: Oxford University Press.

Agbayani, R.V.R. 1996. "'Waiting for Godot': The GO-NGO Cooperation in the Province of Bukidnon." Manila: Institute for Strategic and Development Studies.

Aguilar, C.T. 1997. "Challenges to Women Politicians in a Democratized Asian Society." Paper presented at the 17th World Congress of the International Political Science Association, Seoul.

Alvarez, S.E. 1989. "Politicizing Gender and Engendering Democracy." In A. Stepan, ed., *Democratizing Brazil: Problems of Transition and Consolidation.* New York: Oxford University Press.

———. 1990. *Engineering Democracy in Brazil: Women's Movements in Transition Politics.* Princeton: Princeton University Press.

Amsden, A.H. 1989. *Asia's Next Giant: South Korea and Late Industrialization.* New York: Oxford University Press.

Andors, P. 1983. *The Unfinished Liberation of Chinese Women, 1949–1980.* Bloomington: Indiana University Press.

Arrigo, L. 1984. "Taiwan Electronics Workers." In M. Sheridan and J. Salaff, eds., *Lives: Chinese Working Women.* Bloomington: Indiana University Press.

———. 1991. "The Dimensions of Gender Ideology Among Young Working Women in Taiwan." Paper presented at "Conversations in the Disciplines: Gender and Industrialization in Asia," State University of New York at Purchase.

———. 1994. "From Democratic Movement to Bourgeois Democracy: The Internal Politics of the Taiwan Democratic Progressive Party in 1991." In M.A. Rubinstein, ed., *The Other Taiwan: 1945 to Present.* Armonk, NY: M.E. Sharpe.

Asahi Shimbun. 1992–1995.

Asahi Shimbun Senkyo Hombu (Asahi Newspaper, Election Central). 1990. *Asahi Senkyo Taikan: Dai 39 Kai Shūgiin Sōsenkyo, Dai 15 Kai Sangiin Tsūjō Senkyo* (Asahi Election Overview: The 39th House of Representatives General Election, the 15th House of Councillors Ordinary Election). Tokyo: *Asahi Shimbunsha.*

Ashcroft, B., G. Griffiths, and H. Tiffin, eds. 1995. *The Post-Colonial Studies Reader.* London: Routledge.

Atienza, M.E.L. 1995. "The Lipa City Women's Council: An Attempt Towards Women Empowerment at the Local Level." *GO-NGO Watch* 6/7: 48–59.

———. 1996. "Local Autonomy and Decentralization in Lipa City: Innovations and Challenges." *SalinLakas* 9: 7–12.

Baker. H. 1979. *Chinese Family and Kinship.* London: Macmillan.

Barber, B.R. 1998. *A Place for Us: How to Make Civil Society and Democracy Strong.* New York: Hill and Wang.

Barlow, T.S. 1997. "Women at the Close of the Maoist Era in the Polemics of Li Xiaojiang and Her Associates." In L. Lowe and D. Lloyd, eds., *The Politics of Culture in the Shadow of Capital.* Durham, NC: Duke University Press.

Barry, K. 1995. *The Prostitution of Sexuality.* New York: New York University Press.

Beauvoir, S. de. 1961. *The Second Sex.* New York: Bantam Books.

Bell, D.A., D. Brown, K. Jayasuriya, and D.M. Jones, eds. 1995. *Towards Illiberal Democracy in Pacific Asia.* New York: St. Martin's.

Bell, D.A., and K. Jayasuriya. 1995. "Understanding Illiberal Democracy: A Framework." In D.A. Bell, D. Brown, K. Jayasuriya, and D.M. Jones, eds., *Towards Illiberal Democracy in Pacific Asia.* New York: St. Martin's.

Bernstein, G.L., ed. 1993. *Recreating Japanese Women, 1600–1945.* Berkeley: University of California Press.

Black, C.E. 1966. *The Dynamics of Modernization: Essays in Comparative History.* New York: Harper and Row.

Blackwood, E. 1995. "Senior Women, Model Mothers, and Dutiful Wives: Managing Gender Contradictions in a Minangkabau Village." In A. Ong and M.G. Peletz, eds., *Bewitching Women, Pious Men: Gender and Body Politics in Southeast Asia.* Berkeley: University of California Press.

Bosco, J. 1994. "Taiwan Factions: *Guanxi,* Patronage, and the State in Local Politics." In M.A. Rubinstein, ed., *The Other Taiwan: 1945 to Present.* Armonk, NY: M.E. Sharpe.

Boserup, E. 1970. *Women's Role in Economic Development.* London: Allen and Unwin.

Bozeman, A. 1994. *Politics and Culture in International History: From the Ancient Near East to the Opening of the Modern Age.* New Brunswick, NJ: Transaction.

Brady, D., and J. Mo. 1992. "Electoral Systems and Institutional Choice." *Comparative Political Studies* 24: 405–429.

Brillantes, A.B., Jr. 1997. "Local Governments in a Democratizing Polity: Trends and Prospects." In F.B. Miranda, ed., *Democratization: Philippine Perspectives.* Quezon City: University of the Philippines Press.

Bystydzienski, J., and J. Sekhon, eds. 1999. *Democratization and Women's Grassroots Movements.* Bloomington: Indiana University Press.

Calder, K. 1988. *Crisis and Compensation: Public Policy and Political Stability in Japan, 1949–1986.* Princeton: Princeton University Press.

Carroll, S.J. 1983. *Women as Candidates in American Politics.* Bloomington: Indiana University Press.

Case, W. 1994. "Elites and Regimes in Comparative Perspective: Indonesia, Thailand and Malaysia." *Governance* 7: 431–460.

Center for Asia-Pacific Women. N.d. *Transformative Politics: A Paradigm for Change in the 21st Century.* Manila: Center for Asia-Pacific Women.

Chan, S. 1993. *East Asian Dynamism: Growth, Order, and Security in the Pacific Region*, 2d ed. Boulder, CO: Westview.

Charlton, S.E. 1984. *Women in Third World Development*. Boulder, CO: Westview.

Chen, D.W. 1994. "The Emergence of an Environmental Consciousness in Taiwan." In M.A. Rubinstein, ed., *The Other Taiwan: 1945 to Present*. Armonk, NY: M.E. Sharpe.

Chen, Y.B. 1994. "*Xin 'Hexin Jiating*" (The New "Nuclear Family"). *Bulletin of the Women's Research Program* (National Taiwan University, Population Studies Center) 32(6): 14–15.

Chiang, L.H.N., and Y.L. Ku. 1985. *Past and Current Status of Women in Taiwan*. Taipei: National Taiwan University, Population Studies Center.

Cho, C.H., and R. Rothlach, eds. 1988. *Local Self-Government: A Comparative Approach*. Seoul: Hanyang University.

Cho, J.B. 1994. "Democratization and Institutionalization of Electoral Process in Korea." Paper presented at the International Workshop of the Korean Political Science Association, Seoul.

Choi, M. 1979. "A Study on the Korean Feminist Movement." in H. Lee, ed., *Theory and Practice of Women's Liberation*. Seoul: Writing and Criticism.

Chosun Daily. 1991. "Local Elections and the Success Rate of Women Candidates," June 26, p. 5.

Chou, B.E. 1994. "Changing Patterns of Women's Employment in Taiwan, 1966–1986." In M. Rubinstein, ed., *The Other Taiwan, 1945 to the Present*. Armonk, NY: M.E. Sharpe.

Chou, B.E., C. Clark, and J. Clark. 1990. *Women in Taiwan Politics: Overcoming Barriers to Women's Participation in a Modernizing Society*. Boulder, CO: Lynne Rienner.

Chowdhury, N., and B.J. Nelson. 1994. "Redefining Politics: Patterns of Women's Political Engagement from a Global Perspective." In B.J. Nelson and N. Chowdhury, eds., *Women and Politics Worldwide*. New Haven: Yale University Press.

Chu, Y.H. 1992. *Crafting Democracy in Taiwan*. Taipei: Institute for International Policy Research.

Chung, Y. 1991. *A History of Korean Women's Movement*. Seoul: Iljo.

Chung, Y.T. 1994. "Political Reform and Party Politics Under the Kim Administration." Paper presented at the International Workshop of the Korean Political Science Association, Seoul.

———. 1997. "The Sixth Republic and the Characteristics of the Civilian Government." In *Proceedings, the Joint Conference of Korean Political Science Association and Korean Sociological Association*. Seoul: Korean Political Science Association.

Clark, C. 1989. *Taiwan's Development: Implications for Contending Political Economy Paradigms*. Westport, CT: Greenwood.

Clark, C., and K.C. Roy. 1997. *Comparing Development Patterns in Asia*. Boulder, CO: Lynne Rienner.

Clough, R.N. 1978. *Island China*. Cambridge: Harvard University Press.

Cohen, J.L., and A. Arato. 1992. *Civil Society and Political Theory*. Cambridge: MIT Press.

Cohen, M. 1988. *Taiwan at the Crossroads: Human Rights, Political Development, and Social Change on the Beautiful Island*. Washington, DC: Asia Resource Center.

Cole, J., ed. 1986. *All American Women: Lines That Divide, Ties That Bind.* New York: Free Press.

Collins, P.H. 1991. *Black Feminist Thought: Knowledge, Consciousness, and the Politics of Empowerment.* New York: Routledge.

Constitution of the Philippines, 1987. Manila: Government of the Philippines.

Copper, J.F. 1988. *A Quiet Revolution: Political Development in the Republic of China.* Washington, DC: Ethics and Public Policy Center.

Croll, E. 1995. *Changing Identities of Chinese Women: Rhetoric, Experience and Self-Perception in Twentieth-Century China.* London: Hong Kong University Press.

Curtis, G.L. 1971. *Election Campaigning Japanese Style.* New York: Columbia University Press.

———. 1998. "A 'Recipe' for Democratic Development." In L. Diamond and M.F. Plattner, eds., *Democracy in East Asia.* Baltimore: Johns Hopkins University Press.

Darcy, R., and D.L. Nixon. 1996. "Women in the 1946 and 1993 Japanese House of Representatives Elections: The Role of the Election System." *Journal of Northeast Asian Studies* 15: 3–19.

Darcy, R., and R. Rohrs. 1995. *A Guide to Quantitative History.* New York: Praeger.

Darcy, R., S. Welch, and J. Clark. 1994. *Women, Elections, and Representation,* 2d ed. Lincoln: University of Nebraska Press.

Davin, D. 1975. "The Women's Movement in the People's Republic of China: A Survey." In R. Rohrlic-Leavitt, ed., *Women Cross-Culturally.* The Hague: Mouton.

Diamond, L., J. Linz, and S.M. Lipset, eds. 1989. *Democracy in Developing Countries in Asia.* Boulder, CO: Lynne Rienner.

Diamond, N. 1973. "The Status of Women in Taiwan: One Step Forward, Two Steps Back." In M. Young, ed., *Women in China.* Ann Arbor: University of Michigan Press.

———. 1975a. "Collectivization, Kinship, and the Status of Rural Women in China." In R. Reiter, ed., *Toward an Anthropology of Women.* New York: Monthly Review Press.

———. 1975b. "Women Under Kuomintang Rule: Variations on the Feminine Mystique." *Modern China* 1: 3–45.

Donovan, J. 1985. *Feminist Theory: The Intellectual Traditions of American Feminism.* New York: Frederick Ungar.

Duverger, M. 1955. *The Political Role of Women.* Paris: UNESCO.

Ehrenberg, J. 1999. *Civil Society: The Critical History of an Ideal.* New York: New York University Press.

Eisenstadt, S.N. 1973. *Tradition, Change, and Modernity.* New York: John Wiley.

Elshtain, J.B. 1981. *Public Man, Private Woman: Women in Social and Political Thought.* Princeton: Princeton University Press.

Engels, F. 1972. *The Origin of the Family, Private Property, and the State.* New York: Pathfinder Press.

Enloe, C. 1989. *Bananas, Beaches, and Bases.* Berkeley: University of California Press.

Fallows, J.M. 1994. *Looking at the Sun: The Rise of the New East Asian Economic and Political System.* New York: Pantheon.

Farris, C.S. 1994. "The Social Discourse on Women's Roles in Taiwan: A Textual Analysis." In M.A. Rubinstein, ed., *The Other Taiwan: 1945 to Present.* Armonk, NY: M.E. Sharpe.

Farris, C. S. and M. Johnson, eds. 1997. *Gender in the Wai (Outside) World. Taiwan Studies, A Journal of Translations* 1(4).

Ferguson, A. 1991. *Sexual Democracy.* Boulder, CO: Westview.

Fernea, E.W., ed. 1985. *Women and the Family in the Middle East: New Voices of Change.* Austin: University of Texas Press.

Fields, K.J. 1995. *Enterprise and the State in Korea and Taiwan.* Ithaca: Cornell University Press.

Friedan, B. 1963. *The Feminine Mystique.* New York: Norton.

Fukuyama, F. 1998. "The Illusion of 'Asian Exceptionalism.'" In L. Diamond and M.F. Plattner, eds., *Democracy in East Asia.* Baltimore: Johns Hopkins University Press.

Galenson, W., ed. 1979. *Economic Growth and Structural Change in Taiwan: The Postwar Experience of the Republic of China.* Ithaca: Cornell University Press.

Gallin, R. 1984. "Women, the Family, and the Political Economy of Taiwan." *Journal of Peasant Studies* 12:76–92.

———. 1986. "Mothers-in-Law and Daughters-in-Law: Intergenerational Relations Within the Chinese Family in Taiwan." *Journal of Cross-cultural Gerontology* 1:31–49.

———. 1991. "State, Gender, and the Organization of Business in Rural Taiwan." In V. Moghadam, ed., *Trajectories of Patriarchy and Development.* Oxford: Clarendon.

Gao, X. 1994. "Chinese Modernization and Changes in the Social Status of Rural Women." In C. Gilmartin, G. Hershatter, L. Rofel, and T. White, eds., *Engendering China: Women, Culture, and the State.* Cambridge: Harvard University Press.

Gilmartin, C., G. Hershatter, L. Rofel, and T. White, eds. 1994. *Engendering China: Women, Culture, and the State.* Cambridge: Harvard University Press.

Gold, T.B. 1986. *State and Society in the Taiwan Miracle.* Armonk, NY: M.E. Sharpe.

———. 1996. "Taiwan Society at the *Fin de Siècle.*" *China Quarterly* 148: 1091–1114.

Goldberg, G.S., and E. Kremen, eds. 1990. *The Feminization of Poverty: Only in America?* New York: Greenwood.

Greenhalgh, S. 1988. "Families and Networks in Taiwan's Economic Development." In E.A. Winckler and S. Greenhalgh, eds., *Contending Approaches to the Political Economy of Taiwan.* Armonk, NY: M.E. Sharpe.

Greenhalgh, S., and J. Li. 1995. "Engendering Reproductive Policy and Practice in Peasant China: For a Feminist Demography of Reproduction." *Signs* 20: 601–641.

Grofman, B., and A. Lijphart. 1986. "Introduction." In B. Grofman and A. Lijphart, eds., *Electoral Laws and Their Political Consequences.* New York: Agathon Press.

Hahm, S.D., and L.C. Plein. 1997. *After Development: The Transformation of the Korean Presidency and Bureaucracy.* Washington, DC: Georgetown University Press.

Han, J., and L.H.M. Ling. 1998. "Authoritarianism in the Hypermasculinized State: Hybridity, Patriarchy, and Capitalism in Korea." *International Studies Quarterly* 42: 53–78.

Han, S.J. 1989 "South Korea: Politics in Transition." In L. Diamond, J. Linz, and S.M. Lipset, eds., *Democracy in Developing Countries in Asia.* Boulder, CO: Lynne Rienner.

Harrell, S. 1994. "Playing in the Valley: A Metonym of Modernization in Taiwan." In S. Harrell and C.C. Huang, eds., *Cultural Change in Postwar Taiwan*. Boulder, CO: Westview.

He, C.R. (J. Ho). 1995. *Haoshuang Nuren* (The Unruly Woman: Women's Liberation and Sexual Emancipation). In Chinese. Taipei: Crown.

Hofheinz, R., Jr., and K.E. Calder. 1982. *The Eastasia Edge*. New York: Basic Books.

Honig, E., and G. Hershatter. 1988. *Personal Voices: Chinese Women in the 1980s*. Stanford: Stanford University Press.

Hori, Y. 1985. "*Senkyo to shukyo dantai*" (Elections and Religious Groups). *Jurisuto Zokan Sogo Tokushu* 38: 120–125.

Hsiao, H.H.M. 1991. "The Changing State-Society Relations in the ROC: Economic Change, the Transformation of Class Structure, and the Rise of Social Movements." In R.H. Myers, ed., *Two Societies in Opposition: The Republic of China and the People's Republic of China After Forty Years*. Stanford: Hoover Institution Press.

Hsieh, H.C. 1997. "Gender Differences in Educational Opportunity in Taiwan: Two Taipei Junior High Schools." In C. Farris and M. Johnson, eds., *Gender in the Wai (Outside) World. Taiwan Studies, A Journal of Translations* 1(4).

Hsieh, K.H., and R. Burgess. 1994. "Marital Role Attitudes and Expected Role Behaviors of College Youth in Mainland China and Taiwan." *Journal of Family Issues* 15: 403–423.

Hsu, F. 1985. "The Self in Cross-Cultural Perspective." In A. Marsella, G. DeVos, and F. Hsu, eds., *Culture and Self: Asian and Western Perspectives*. New York: Tavistock.

Hu, T. 1985. "The Influence of Taiwan's Rural Industrialization on Women's Status." In *Proceedings of the Conference on the Role of Women in the National Development Process in Taiwan*, Vol. 2. Taipei: National Taiwan University, Population Studies Center.

Huang, A. 1997. "Women Wronged." *Free China Review* 47(2): 4–11.

Huntington, S.P. 1991. *The Third Wave: Democratization in the Late Twentieth Century*. Norman: University of Oklahoma Press.

———. 1996. *The Clash of Civilizations and the Remaking of World Order*. New York: Simon and Schuster.

Hyden, G. 1987. "Capital Accumulation, Resource Distribution, and Governance in Kenya: The Role of the Economy of Affection." In M.G. Schatzberg, ed., *The Political Economy of Kenya*. New York: Praeger.

Hyun, C.M. 1989. "Voter Realignment—A Voting Analysis of the 1987 Presidential Election in South Korea." *Korean Political Science Review* 23: 209–226.

Im, H.B. 1989. *Politics of Transition: Democratic Transition from Authoritarian Rule in South Korea*. Ph.D. diss., University of Chicago.

———. 1990. "An Analysis of Democratization in South Korea." *Korean Political Science Review* 24: 51–77.

———. 1997. "The Delayed Democratic Consolidation: Process of Political Democratization and Accompanying Problems." In *Proceedings, the Joint Conference of Korean Political Science Association and Korean Sociological Association*. Seoul: Korean Political Science Association.

Jaquette, J.S., ed. 1994. *The Women's Movement in Latin America: Feminism and the Transition to Democracy*, 2d ed. Boston: Unwin Hymen.

Jayawardena, K. 1986. *Feminism and Nationalism in the Third World*. London: Zed Books.

Jones, K. 1993. *Compassionate Authority*. New York: Routledge.

Judd, E. 1989. "*Niangjia:* Chinese Women and Their Natal Families." *Journal of Asian Studies* 48: 525–544.

———. 1994. *Gender and Power in Rural North China*. Stanford: Stanford University Press.

Kemp, A.A. 1994. *Women's Work: Degraded and Devalued*. Englewood Cliffs, NJ: Prentice Hall.

Kim, B.K. 1998. "Korea's Crisis of Success." In L. Diamond and M.F. Plattner, eds., *Democracy in East Asia*. Baltimore: Johns Hopkins University Press.

Kim, B.S. 1991. Personal interview.

Kim, H.J. 1990. Personal interview.

Kim, H.N. 1989. "The 1988 Parliamentary Election in South Korea." *Asian Survey* 29: 489–495.

Kim, Y. 1976. *Women of Korea: A History from Ancient Times to 1945*. Seoul: Ewha Women's University Press.

———. 1986. "The Position of Women Workers in Manufacturing Industries in South Korea: A Marxist-Feminist Analysis." Working Paper No. 6, Subseries on Women's History and Development. The Hague: Institute of Social Studies.

Kitagawa K., and Gogatsukai. 1995. *Dare Mo Shiranai Soka Gakkai No Senkyo* (Soka Gakkai and Elections: What Nobody Knows). Tokyo: Hamano Publishing.

Korean National Council of Women. 1998. Web page: http://www.kncw.or. kr/kncw/bal.html.

Korean Women and Politics Institute. 1995. *Local Elections and Women's Participation*. Seoul: Korean Women and Politics Institute.

Korean Women's Development Institute. 1995. *Women's White Paper 1995*. Seoul: Korean Women's Development Institute.

———. 1997. *Statistical Yearbook on Women, 1997*. Seoul: Korean Women's Development Institute.

Koyama, T. 1961. *The Changing Social Position of Women in Japan*. Paris: UNESCO.

Krugman, P. 1997. "Whatever Happened to the Asian Miracle?" *Fortune,* August 18, pp. 12–14.

Ku, Y.L. 1989. "The Women's Movement in Taiwan, 1972–1987." *Bulletin of Concerned Asian Scholars* 21(1): 12–22.

———. 1997. "Interaction Between the Women's Movement and Policy Formation." In C. Farris and M. Johnson, eds., *Gender in the Wai (Outside) World. Taiwan Studies, A Journal of Translations* 1(4).

———. 1998. "The Uneasy Marriage Between Women's Studies and Feminism in Taiwan." In G. Hershatter, E. Honig, S. Mann, and L. Rofel, eds., *Guide to Women's Studies in China*. Berkeley: Institute of East Asian Studies, University of California.

Kung, L. 1994. *Factory Women in Taiwan*. New York: Columbia University Press.

Kunihiro, M. (former Socialist member of the House of Councillors). 1996. Personal interview, Tokyo.

Kuo, C.T. 1995. *Global Competitiveness: Industrial Growth in Taiwan and the Philippines*. Pittsburgh: University of Pittsburgh Press.

Kyung Hyang Daily. 1991. "Local Elections and Their Outcomes," June 23, p. 6.

Lam, D.K.K., and C. Clark. 1994. "Beyond the Developmental State: The Cultural Roots of 'Guerrilla Capitalism' in Taiwan." *Governance* 7: 412–430.

Lam, D.K.K., and I. Lee. 1992. "Guerrilla Capitalism and the Limits of Statist Theory." In C. Clark and S. Chan, eds., *The Evolving Pacific Basin in the Global Political Economy: Domestic and International Linkages.* Boulder, CO: Lynne Rienner.

Lasswell, H.D. 1958. *Politics: Who Gets What, When, How?* New York: Meridian.

Lee, A. 1996. "A Tale of Two Sisters: Gender in Taiwan's Small-Scale Industry." In A. Marcus, ed., *Anthropology for a Small Planet: Culture and Community in Global Perspective.* St. James, NY: Brandywine Press.

Lee, B. 1998. "Politics and Women in the 21st Century." In B. Lee, ed., *Politics and Women in the 21st Century.* Seoul: Nanam.

Lee, C.G. et al. 1995. *The Economy of the Sixth Republic.* Seoul: Chungang Daily Publishing.

Lee, H. 1991. *Feminist Movement in Korea.* Seoul: Jungusa.

———. 1994. "Korean Feminism and Feminist Movement." *Korean Feminism* 10: 7–17.

Lee, M. 1989. "State's Policy on Family Planning." *Feminist Studies Review* 6: 49–78.

Lee, O. 1985. *The History of Modern Korean Women.* Seoul: Kyumoonkak.

Lee, R.J. 1995a. "Democratization and Gender Politics in South Korea." Paper presented at the annual meeting of the American Political Science Association, Chicago.

———. 1995b. "Women's Movement in South Korea: Reflections on the Path That It Took the Past Fifty Years." *Modern Society* 13: 48–65.

Lee, S.M. 1989. "Management Styles of Korean Chaebols." In K.H. Chung and H.C. Lee, eds., *Korean Managerial Dynamics.* New York: Praeger.

Lee, W.J. 1991. Personal interview.

Lee, Y.J. 1997. "Dilemma of the Kim Government's Reform Politics." In *Proceedings, the Joint Conference of Korean Political Science Association and Korean Sociological Association.* Seoul: Korean Political Science Association.

Lerner, D. 1958. *The Passing of Traditional Society: Modernizing the Middle East.* New York: Free Press.

Levi-Strauss, C. 1969. *The Elementary Structures of Kinship.* Boston: Beacon Press.

Li, D.M. 1984. "The Study of Newly Married Couples' Family Planning Knowledge, Attitudes, and Practices." In *Gonggong Weisheng* (Public Health). Taipei: Taiwan Provincial Public Health Institute. In Chinese.

Li, X., and X. Zhang. 1994. "Creating a Space for Women: Women's Studies in China in the 1980's." *Signs* 20:137–151.

Lijphart, A. 1994. *Electoral Systems and PAM Systems: A Study of Twenty-Seven Democracies, 1945–1990.* New York: Oxford University Press.

Lim, L.L. 1998. *The Sex Sector: The Economic and Social Bases of Prostitution in Southeast Asia.* Geneva: International Labour Office.

Lim, L.Y.C. 1990. "Women's Work in Export Factories: The Politics of a Cause." In I. Tinker, ed., *Persistent Inequalities: Women and World Development.* New York: Oxford University Press.

Ling, L.H.M. 1996. "Democratization Under Internationalization: Media Reconstructions of Gender Identity in Shanghai." *Democratization* 3: 140–157.

———. 1999. "Sex Machine: Global Hypermasculinity and Images of the Asian Woman in Modernity." *Positions: East Asia Cultures Critique* 72(2): 1–30.

Ling, L.H.M., and C.Y. Shih. 1998. "Confucianism with a Liberal Face: The Meaning of Democratic Politics in Postcolonial Taiwan." *Review of Politics* 60: 55–82.

Liu, P. 1983. "Trends in Female Labor Force Participation in Taiwan: The Transition Towards Higher Technological Activities." *Academia Economic Papers* (Academia Sinica, Institute of Economics) 11: 293–323.

Lowe, L. 1991. "Heterogeneity, Hybridity, Multiplicity: Marking American Differences." *Public Culture* 1: 24–44.

Lu, H.L.A. 1986. *Xin Nuxingzhuyi* (New Feminism). In Chinese. Taipei: Dunli.

———. "Women's Liberation: The Taiwanese Experience." In M.A. Rubinstein, ed., *The Other Taiwan: 1945 to Present.* Armonk, NY: M.E. Sharpe.

Lu, H.S. 1991. "Women's Self-Growth Groups and Empowerment of the 'Uterine Family' in Taiwan." *Bulletin of the Institute of Ethnology* (Academia Sinica) 71: 29–62.

Matland, R. 1994. "Women's Legislative Participation in National Legislatures: A Comparison of Democracies in Developed and Developing Countries." Paper presented at the annual meeting of the American Political Science Association, New York.

Mies, M. 1986. *Patriarchy and Accumulation on a World Scale.* London: Zed Books.

Mill, J.S. 1970. *The Subjection of Women.* Cambridge: MIT Press.

Ministry of Government. 1996. *Statistical Yearbook of Ministry of Government, 1996.* Seoul: Ministry of Government.

Ministry of Political Affairs II. 1995. *Advancement of Women's Status Under the New Administration.* Seoul: Ministry of Political Affairs II.

Ministry of Women. 1995. *Fifty Years of Korean Women's Development.* Seoul: Ministry of Women.

Mohanty, C. 1991. "Under Western Eyes: Feminist Scholarship and Colonial Discourses." In C.T. Mohanty, A. Russo, and L. Torres, eds., *Third World Women and the Politics of Feminism.* Bloomington: Indiana University Press.

Molyneux, M. 1981. "Women in Socialist Societies: Problems of Theory and Practice." In K. Young, C. Wolkowitz, and R. McCullagh, eds., *Of Marriage and the Market: Women's Subordination in International Perspectives.* London: CSE Books.

———.1985. "Mobilization Without Emancipation? Women's Interests, the State and Revolution in Nicaragua." *Feminist Studies* 11: 227–254.

———.1986. "Mobilization Without Emancipation? Women's Interests, State, and Revolution." In R.R. Fagen, C. Deere, and J.L. Coraggio, eds., *Transition and Development: Problems of Third World Socialism.* New York: Monthly Review Press.

Moody, P.R. 1992. *Political Change on Taiwan: A Study of Ruling Party Adaptability.* New York: Praeger.

Moon, K. 1997. *Sex Among Allies: Military Prostitution in U.S.-Korea Relations.* New York: Columbia University Press.

Nandy, A. 1988. *The Intimate Enemy: Loss and Recovery of Self Under Colonialism.* Delhi: Oxford University Press.

National Assembly. 1997. *The National Assembly.* Seoul: Information Service of the National Assembly.

National Statistics Office. 1990. *Statistical Handbook of the Philippines.* Manila: National Statistics Office.

Neft, N., and A.D. Levine. 1997. *Where Women Stand: An International Report on the Status of Women in 140 Countries 1997–1998.* New York: Random House.

Nelson, B.J., and N. Chowdhury, eds. 1994. *Women and Politics Worldwide.* New Haven: Yale University Press.

Nihon Keizai Shimbun. 1989. July 10, evening edition.

Norris, P. 1985. "Women's Legislative Participation in Western Europe." *Western European Politics* 8: 90–101.

Norris, P., and J. Lovenduski. 1990. *Gender and Party Politics.* London: Sage.

O'Donnell, G., and P.C. Schmitter. 1991. *Transitions from Authoritarian Rule: Tentative Conclusions About Uncertain Democracies.* Baltimore: Johns Hopkins University Press.

O'Donnell, G., P.C. Schmitter, and L. Whitehead, eds. 1986. *Transitions from Authoritarian Rule: Prospects for Democracy.* Baltimore: Johns Hopkins University Press.

Ogai T. 1995. "Nihon No Josei Kokkai Giin" (Women Members of the Diet). *Hogaku Kenkyu* 15: 1–45.

Okihiro, G. 1994. *Margins and Mainstreams: Asians in American History and Culture.* Seattle: University of Washington Press.

Ong, A. 1994. "Colonialism and Modernity: Feminist Representations of Women in Non-Western Societies." In A. Herrmann and A. Stewart, eds., *Theorizing Feminism: Parallel Trends in the Humanities and Social Sciences.* Boulder, CO: Westview.

Ostrogorski, M. 1893. *The Rights of Women: A Comparative Study in History and Legislation.* London: Swan Sonnenschein.

Palley M.L., and J. Gelb. 1992. "Women's Organizations in South Korea." Paper presented at the annual meeting of the American Political Science Association, San Francisco.

Park, C.W. 1992. "An Analysis of Voter Party Support in the 14th National Assembly Election." In *Elections and the Korean Politics.* Seoul: Korean Political Science Association.

Park, Y. 1984. *A Study on the Modern Feminist Movement.* Seoul: Korean Spirit and Culture Institute.

Pasternak, B., C. Ember, and M. Ember. 1997. *Sex, Gender, and Kinship: A Cross-Cultural Perspective.* Upper Saddle River, NJ: Prentice Hall.

Pateman, C. 1970. *Participation and Democratic Theory.* Cambridge: Cambridge University Press.

———. 1989. *The Disorder of Women.* Stanford: Stanford University Press.

The Path to Democracy: Reforms and Future Tasks Since the June 29 Announcement. 1991. Seoul: Dana Publishing Co.

Phillips, A. 1991. *Engendering Democracy.* University Park: Pennsylvania State University Press.

———. 1993. *Democracy and Difference.* University Park: Pennsylvania State University Press.

Przeworski, A. 1991. *Democracy and the Market: Political and Economic Reforms in Eastern Europe and Latin America.* Cambridge: Cambridge University Press.

Pye, L.W. 1985. *Asian Power and Politics: The Cultural Dimensions of Authority.* Cambridge: Harvard University Press.

Rai, S.M. 1994. "Modernization and Gender: Education and Employment in Post-Mao China." *Gender and Education* 6: 119–129.

Ramusack, B.N. 1981. "Women's Organizations and Social Change: The Age-of-Marriage Issue in India." In N. Black and A.B. Cottrell, eds., *Women and World Change: Equity Issues in Development*. Beverly Hills: Sage.

Records of the National Affairs Council. 1990. Taipei: National Affairs Council.

Richardson, L.E., Jr., and P.K. Freeman. 1995. "Gender Differences in Constituency Service Among State Legislators." *Political Research Quarterly* 48: 169–179.

Rikken, R., and M. Foy-os. 1996. "Democratically Empowering the People: The Cordillera Women's Experience." Paper presented at the National Conference of the Philippine Political Science Association, Lingayen, Pangasinan, Philippines.

Rofel, L. 1994. "Liberation Nostalgia and a Yearning for Modernity." In C. Gilmartin, G. Hershatter, L. Rofel, and T. White, eds., *Engendering China: Women, Culture, and the State*. Cambridge: Harvard University Press.

Roy, K.C. 1994. "Landless and Land-Poor Women in India Under Technological Change: A Case for Technology Transfer." In K.C. Roy and C. Clark, eds., *Technological Change and Rural Development in Poor Countries: Neglected Issues*. Delhi: Oxford University Press.

Rubin, G. 1975. "The Traffic in Women: Notes on the "Political Economy' of Sex." In R. Reiter, ed., *Toward an Anthropology of Women*. New York: Monthly Review Press.

Rubinstein, M.A., ed. 1994. *The Other Taiwan: 1945 to the Present*. Armonk, NY: M.E. Sharpe.

Rule, W. 1981. "Why Women Don't Run: The Critical Factors in Women's Legislative Recruitment." *Western Political Quarterly* 34: 60–77.

———. 1987. "Electoral Systems, Contextual Factors, and Women's Opportunity for Election to Parliament in Twenty-Three Democracies." *Western Political Quarterly* 40: 477–498.

———. 1994. "Parliaments of, by, and for the People: Except for Women?" In W. Rule and J. Zimmerman, eds., *Electoral Systems in Comparative Perspective: Their Impact on Women and Minorities*. Westport, CT: Greenwood.

Sacks, K. 1975. "Engels Revisited: Women, the Organization of Production, and Private Property." In R. Reiter, ed., *Toward an Anthropology of Women*. New York: Monthly Review Press.

Saint-Germain, M. 1997. "*Mujeres* '94: Democratic Transition and the Women's Movement in El Salvador." *Women and Politics* 18: 75–99.

Sakata, K. 1995. (office manager of Representative Tsukada Enjū). 1995. Personal interview, Mito.

Salaff, J. 1981. "Singapore Women: Women and the Family." In N. Black and A.B. Cottrell, eds., *Women and World Change: Equity Issues in Development*. Beverly Hills: Sage.

Sanshū Ryōin Meikan (A Directory of the National Diet). 1990. Tokyo: Nihon Kokusei Chōsakai.

Scott, C.V. 1995. *Gender and Development: Rethinking Modernization and Dependency Theory*. Boulder, CO: Lynne Rienner.

Seligman, A. 1992. *The Idea of Civil Society*. New York: Free Press.

Selya, R.M. 1994. "Abnormally Elevated Sex Ratios in the Republic of China on Taiwan: An Exploratory Review." *American Asian Review* 12(3): 15–36.

Sen, S. 1998. "Asia: Myth of a Miracle." *Economic and Political Weekly*, January 17, pp. 111–114.

"Seneca Falls Declaration of Sentiments." 1995. In N.E. McGlen and K.

O'Connor, *Women, Politics, and American Society.* Englewood Cliffs, NJ: Prentice Hall.

Senkyo. 1983–1995.

Share, D. 1987. "Transition to Democracy and Transition Through Transaction." *Comparative Political Studies* 19: 525–548.

Shih, S. 1998. "Gender and a New Geopolitics of Desire: The Seduction of Mainland Women in Taiwan and Hong Kong Media." *Signs* 23: 287–318.

Shin, D.C. 1989. "Political Democracy and the Quality of Citizens' Lives: A Cross-National Study." *Journal of Developing Societies* 5: 30–41.

Shin, D.C., and M. Chae. 1993. "A Survey Research on the Public Support of Democratization in South Korea." *Korean Political Science Review* 27: 137–160.

Shin, M.S. 1990. "Women's Participation in the National Assembly." In B.S. Sohn, ed., *Politicization of Women and Localization of Politics.* Seoul: Korean Women and Politics Institute.

Shrivastava, R. 1997. "Minority Representation of a Political Majority Group." Paper presented at the 17th World Congress of the International Political Science Association, Seoul.

Shugart, M.S. 1994. "Minorities Represented and Unrepresented." In W. Rule and J.F. Zimmerman, eds., *Electoral Systems in Comparative Perspective: Their Impact on Women and Minorities.* Westport, CT: Greenwood.

"Siew Cabinet Shuffle." 1999. *Free China Review* 49 (4): 4–9.

Siu, B. 1981. *Women of China: Imperialism and Women's Resistance 1900–1949.* London: Zed Books.

Sivard, R. 1985. *Women: A World Survey.* New York: Ford, Rockefeller, and Carnegie.

Skoggard, I.A. 1996. *The Indigenous Dynamic in Taiwan's Postwar Development: The Religious and Historical Roots of Entrepreneurship.* Armonk, NY: M.E. Sharpe.

———. 1998. "Women's Work and Family Property in Taiwan's Postwar Development." Manuscript.

Sohn, B. 1998. "Local Autonomy and Women's Political Participation." In B. Lee, ed., *Politics and Women in the 21st Century.* Seoul: Nanam.

Song, Y.H. 1986. "Women's Political Participation: A Comparative Study." *Women's Studies* (fall): 218–240.

Spence, J.D. 1990. *The Search for Modern China.* New York: Norton.

Spivak, G.C. 1988. "Can the Subaltern Speak?" In C. Nelson and L. Grossberg, eds., *Marxism and the Interpretation of Culture.* Chicago: University of Illinois Press.

Stacey, J. 1983. *Patriarchy and Socialist Revolution in China.* Berkeley: University of California Press.

Stokes, G. 1993. *The Walls Came Tumbling Down: The Collapse of Communism in Eastern Europe.* New York: Oxford University Press.

Sugai, Y. (official of Zensen Dōmei National Labor Federation). 1996. Personal interview, Tokyo.

Taagepera, R. 1994. "Beating the Law of Minority Attrition." In W. Rule and J.F. Zimmerman, eds., *Electoral Systems in Comparative Perspective: Their Impact on Women and Minorities.* Westport, CT: Greenwood.

Taagepera, R., and M.S. Shugart. 1989. *Seats and Votes: The Effects and Determinants of Electoral Systems.* New Haven: Yale University Press.

Taiwaner, A. 1996. "Pseudo-Taiwanese: Isle Margin Editorials." *Positions* 4: 145–171.

Teng, J.E. 1991. *Women Leaders in Taiwan's Opposition.* Cambridge: Unpublished M.A. thesis, Harvard University.

———. 1996. "The Construction of the 'Traditional Chinese Woman' in the Western Academy: A Critical Review." *Signs* 22: 115- 151.

Thomas, E.D. 1968. *Chinese Political Thought.* New York: Prentice Hall.

Thomas, S. 1994. *How Women Legislate.* New York: Oxford University Press.

Tien, H.M. 1989. *The Great Transformation: Political and Social Change in the Republic of China.* Stanford: Hoover Institution Press.

———, ed. 1996. *Taiwan's Electoral Politics and Democratic Transition: Riding the Third Wave.* Armonk, NY: M.E. Sharpe.

Tingsten, H. 1937. *Political Behaviour: Studies in Election Statistics.* London: King.

Tinker, I., ed. 1990. *Persistent Inequalities: Women and World Development.* New York: Oxford University Press.

Tong, R. 1989. *Feminist Thought: A Comprehensive Introduction.* Boulder, CO: Westview.

Truong, T.D. 1999. "The Underbelly of the Tiger: Gender and the Demystification of the Asian Miracle." *Review of International Political Economy* 6: 133–165.

Tsui, Y.L.E. 1987. *Are Married Daughters "Spilled Water?" A Study of Working Women in Urban Taiwan.* Monograph 4. Taipei: Women's Research Program, Population Studies Center, National Taiwan University.

Tu, W. 1991. "Cultural China: The Periphery as the Center." *Daedalus* 120: 1–32.

———. 1996. "Cultural Identity and the Politics of Recognition in Contemporary Taiwan." *China Quarterly* 148: 1115–1140.

UNICEF. 1993. "The Women's Empowerment Framework." *Women and Girls Advance* 1(1): 5.

———. 1997. www.unicef.org/pon97/ie4t048.htm.

United Nations. 1989. *Compendium of Statistics and Indicators on the Situation of Women, 1986.* New York: United Nations.

———. 1992–1995. *Abortion Policies: A Global Review,* 3 vols. New York: United Nations.

United States Department of State. 1995–1997. *Country Reports on Human Rights Practices for 1994–1996, Report Submitted to Committee on International Relations, U.S. House of Representatives and Committee on Foreign Relations U.S. Senate.* Washington, DC: Government Printing Office.

Wachman, A.M. 1994. *Taiwan: National Identity and Democratization.* Armonk, NY: M.E. Sharpe.

Wakabayashi, B.T. 1991. *Anti-Foreignism and Western Learning in Early-Modern Japan.* Cambridge: Harvard University Press.

Wang, F. 1994. "The Political Economy of Authoritarian Clientelism in Taiwan." In L. Roniger and A. Gunes-Ayata, eds., *Democracy, Clientelism, and Civil Society.* Boulder, CO: Lynne Rienner.

Watson, P. 1993. "The Rise of Masculinism in Eastern Europe." *New Left Review* 198: 71–82. March/April.

Waylen, G. 1994. "Women and Democratization: Conceptualizing Gender Relations in Transition Politics." *World Politics* 46: 327–354.

Wellesley Editorial Committee. 1977. *Women and National Development: The Complexities of Change.* Chicago: University of Chicago Press.

Whyte, M.K., and W. Parish. 1984. *Urban Life in Contemporary China.* Chicago: University of Chicago Press.

Winckler, E. 1994. "Cultural Policy on Postwar Taiwan." In S. Harrell and C.C. Huang, eds., *Cultural Change in Postwar Taiwan*. Boulder, CO: Westview Press.

Winn, J.K. 1994. "Not by Rule of Law: Mediating State-Society Relations in Taiwan Through the Underground Economy." In M.A. Rubinstein, ed., *The Other Taiwan: 1945 to Present*. Armonk, NY: M.E. Sharpe.

Wolf, M. 1972. *Women and the Family in Rural Taiwan*. Stanford: Stanford University Press.

———. 1985. *Revolution Postponed: Women in Contemporary China*. Stanford: Stanford University Press.

Women. 1991. April.

Women's Department. 1995. *Statistical Information on Women's Political and Social Participation in the Republic of China*. Taipei: Central Committee of the Kuomintang.

Women's Policy. 1991. April 11.

———. 1993a. May 22.

———. 1993b. December 30.

———. 1995. December 31.

Woo, J.E. 1991. *Race to Swift: State and Finance in Korean Industrialization*. New York: Columbia University Press.

Wu, J.J. 1995. *Taiwan's Democratization: Forces Behind the New Momentum*. Hong Kong: Oxford University Press.

Yoon, C.J. 1990. "Changing Voting Behavior and Political Development." In K.W. Kim, ed., *Electoral Politics in South Korea*. Seoul: Nanam Press.

Young, I.M. 1990a. *Justice and the Politics of Difference*. Princeton: Princeton University Press.

———. 1990b. *Throwing Like a Girl and Other Essays*. Bloomington: Indiana University Press.

Zhang, M.Z. 1980. "The Modernization of Taiwan and Behavioral Tendencies of Women in Young Adulthood." *Bulletin of the Institute of Economics* (Academia Sinica) 11(10): 209–226. In Chinese.

Zheng, W. 1997. "Maoism, Feminism, and the U.N. Conference on Women: Women's Studies Research in Contemporary China." *Journal of Women's History* 8: 126–152.

The Contributors

Maria Ela L. Atienza is assistant professor of political science at the University of the Philippines and a fellow of the Institute for Strategic and Development Studies. She received an M.A. from the University of the Philippines and a postgraduate degree at the University of Amsterdam. She has published articles in such journals as *GO-NGO Watch* and *SalinLakas*.

Mikyung Chin, associate professor of political science at Ajou University in Seoul, received her Ph.D. from the University of California, Berkeley. Her primary research interests include comparative politics, political theory, and women's studies. She is currently working on democracy in Korea. She has published articles in the *Korean Political Science Review* and *New Political Science*.

Ray Christensen, assistant professor of political science at Brigham Young University, received his Ph.D. from Harvard University. He is the author of *Ending the LDP Hegemony: Party Alliances in Japan,* and his articles have appeared in such journals as *American Journal of Political Science, Asian Survey,* and *Comparative Political Studies*.

Cal Clark, alumni professor of political science at Auburn University, received his Ph.D. from the University of Illinois at Urbana-Champaign. He is author of *Taiwan's Development,* coauthor of *Women in Taiwan Politics* and *Comparative Development Patterns in Asia,* and coeditor of *The Evolving Pacific Basin* and *Beyond the Developmental State*.

Janet Clark, professor and chair of political science at the State University of West Georgia, received her Ph.D. from the University of

Illinois at Urbana-Champaign. She is coauthor of *Women, Elections, and Representation* and *Women in Taiwan Politics.* She is now finishing a ten-year term as editor of *Women & Politics.*

R. Darcy, regents professor of political science and statistics at Oklahoma State University, is coauthor of *Guide to Quantitative History, Women, Elections, and Representation,* and *Yeo Sung, Seon guh, Ui hoe Jinchul.* He has also authored or coauthored articles on women and politics, statistics, and elections. He has held academic appointments in South Korea, India, Ireland, and the United Kingdom. He serves on Oklahoma's Commission on the Status of Women and the state Judicial Evaluation Commission. He has recently begun publishing works of fiction.

Catherine S. P. Farris is an independent scholar living in Austin, Texas. She was most recently a Fellow of the Institute of Anthropology of National Tsing Hua University in Taiwan (1998-99) where she conducted a Chiang Ching-Kuo Foundation funded research project on gender and classroom interaction in two elementary school classes. She has been coeditor of *Taiwan Studies, A Journal of Translations,* and her work has appeared in *Journal of Linguistic Anthropology, Modern China, Taiwan Unbound,* and *The Other Taiwan.*

Patty Hipsher, assistant professor of political science at Oklahoma State University, received her Ph.D. from Cornell University. Her publications include articles in *Comparative Politics* and *Politics and Society.*

Rose Jungja Lee, professor of political science at Kwandong University in Seoul, received her Ph.D. from Rutgers University. She is coauthor of *Challenges from the New International Order,* and her work has appeared in such journals as *Asiatic Studies, Journal of Modern Society,* and *Pacific Focus.*

L. H. M. Ling, senior lecturer at the Institute of Social Studies in the Hague, received her Ph.D. in political science from MIT. Author of *Conquest and Desire: Postcolonial Learning Between Asia and the West,* she has published articles in *Asian Survey, Democratization, International Studies Quarterly, Journal of Peace Research, Review of International Political Economy,* and *Women's Studies Quarterly.*

Index

209

About the Book

Though modernization and democratization have benefited many women in developing countries, capitalist development has often reproduced patriarchal roles and stereotypes. This collection examines how the processes of modernization and democratization have affected women in East Asia.

Rose J. Lee is professor of political science at Kwandong University in Korea. She is coauthor of *Challenges from the New International Order.* **Cal Clark** is professor of political science at Auburn University. His books include *Comparing Development Patterns in Asia* (with K.C. Roy) and *Women in Taiwan Politics* (with Chou Bih-er and Janet Clark).

213